Over a C

An Introduction to Chinese Life and Culture

Jing Luo

University Press of America,® Inc.
Dallas · Lanham · Boulder · New York · Oxford

Copyright © 2004 by
University Press of America,® Inc.
4501 Forbes Boulevard
Suite 200
Lanham, Maryland 20706
UPA Acquisitions Department (301) 459-3366

PO Box 317
Oxford
OX2 9RU, UK

Library of Congress Control Number: 2004108485
ISBN 0-7618-2937-7 (paperback : alk. ppr.)

Contents

List of Tables

Preface

The economic reforms launched by Deng Xiaoping in 1978 have transformed China from communism to quasi-capitalism. The rapid changes, however, are better understood from a historical/cultural perspective. This book is intended to connect the dots without being overly theoretical. While my own perception had much influence on the way the data is organized, I draw widely from the research and wisdom of other scholars.

Much like the Yangtze River meandering 3,915 miles across the land, the Chinese civilization has run a long course. Rooted in its agrarian way of life, locked into the dynastic cycles, delimited by the traditional family structure, and bounded by the Confucian-Legalist-Daoist value system, the Chinese civilization forged its own distinct pattern. There were times of glory where classical thoughts, artistic creativity, scientific ingenuity, territorial expansions, and sophisticated bureaucracy all contributed to a dazzling brilliance. There were also times of failure during which the Chinese empire was taken over by the "barbarians." However, the short sessions of foreign rule invariably ended with the conquerors culturally conquered and eventually assimilated. In general, the history had progressed as such until the 19th century.

The scenario changed with the coming of the West. Challenges from industrial civilizations were more than an eye-opener. The efficiency of machinery as evidenced both in warfare and productivity, the pursuit of truth from the perspective of science and technology, the rule of law that contrasts widely with the order of hierarchy. . . all combined with the possessing power of opium to derail the traditional Chinese system.

The most dramatic moments of history yet belong to the 20th century. The failure of Sun Zhongshan's Republican Revolution in 1912 was followed by the Communist victory of 1949. The Maoist regime, after having plunged the nation into economic disasters, was eventually reversed after Mao Zedong's passing in 1976. The economic and political reforms under Deng Xiaoping have led China onto the road of modernization, political decentralization, and a market-oriented economy. President Jiang Zemin's theory of the "Three Representations" opened the door of the Chinese Communist Party to capitalist entrepreneurs; meanwhile, his successor, President Hu Jintao, manages to maintain the balance by ramping up the rural economy. At any rate, westernization has been the theme throughout the past two centuries.

To illustrate these changes, I included excerpts from historical documents, some of which were translated by myself. The *close-ups* provide snapshots of various aspects of the culture. The book is structured in a way that common readers as well as classroom teachers will find it a rich and adaptable source of information.

As a final suggestion to the reader, it might be a good idea to read this book while sipping a cup of tea. As the traditional wisdom holds, the tea is not only a relaxant but also a soberant, hence, good stuff that readers of this book may enjoy. The author admittedly couldn't have enough of it while writing these pages. Cheers.

Jing Luo

1
Land and People

Geography

Located in East Asia, on the western shore of the Pacific Ocean, the People's Republic of China (PRC) has a total area of 9.6 million square kilometers (3.70 million square miles), which is comparable to the area of the United States (9.62 million square kilometers or about 3.72 million square miles).[1] China borders Korea in the east; Mongolia in the north; Russia in the northeast; Kazakhstan, Kyrgyzstan, and Tajikistan in the northwest; Afghanistan, Pakistan, India, Nepal, Sikkim, and Bhutan in the west and southwest; and Myanmar, Laos, and Vietnam in the south. Across the seas to the east and southeast are Japan, the Philippines, Brunei, Malaysia, and Indonesia.

China is primarily an inland country, with 11,184 miles of coastline which is about one fourth of its border line. China's territorial waters extend twelve nautical miles from the coast measuring about 1.8 million square miles. Over this vast territorial sea are 5,400 islands of which Taiwan is the biggest with a total area of 13,127 square miles.

The topography of China is one of a great variety. One of its features is known as the "four-step staircase configuration." The first step is the Qinghai-Tibetan Plateau with an average elevation of 13,120 feet above the sea level. The Himalayas rise up along the Sino-Nepalese border forming the "roof of the world." Mount Everest, measuring 29,140 feet above sea level, is the highest point in the world.

The second step is represented by lower mountain ranges measuring 3,000 to 6,000 feet above the sea level including the Kunlun, the Qilian, and the Hengduan mountains stretching along the north and the east of the Qinghai-Tibetan plateau. This vast stretch of formation includes Inner Mongolia, the Yellow-Dirt Plateau, and the Yunnan-Guizhou Plateau. The three geographical basins, Tarim, Junggar, and Sichuan, are also part of the same step.

The third step features lower mountains of approximately 1,500 to 3,000 feet in elevation including the Greater Hinggan, the Taihang ranges and the three plains — the Northern Plain, the Northeastern Plain, and the Middle-Lower Yangtze Plain. The fourth step includes the shallow waters of less than 656 feet in depth, formed by silt and sand gushed out by inland rivers along the coast of the South Sea, the East Sea, and the Yellow Sea.

Out of the many rivers that irrigate the vast land, two are known to be cradles of the Chinese civilization: The Yellow River in the north and the Yangtze River in the south. The Yellow River originates from the Mount Yaladaze in the Bayanhar Mountains and runs into the Bohai Sea. The 3,395-mile course cuts across ten provinces including Qinghai, Sichuan, Gansu, Ningxia, Inner Mongolia, Shanxi, Shaanxi, Henan, and Shandong. From the Yellow Dirt Plateau of the central west the flow of water picks up tons of loess, a windblown fine dust that renders the water yellow in color, hence, the name of the river. Some of the earliest records of the civilization were discovered in Henan Province along the Yellow River bank. Several cities on the Yellow River, such as Xian, Anyang, and Luoyang had been capitals of ancient empires for thousands of years.

The longest river in China is the Yangtze. With its source in the Tanggula Mountains and its outlet in Shanghai, the biggest city on the east coast, the Yangtze River runs a course of 3,915 miles long meandering across nine provinces including Qinghai, Tibet, Sichuan, Yunnan, Hubei, Hunan, Jiangxi, Anhui, and Jiangsu. The cultural impact of the Yangtze River touches the daily life of millions of people. As an example, it divides China into two worlds with different customs. People would stereotypically fit themselves into two categories — the "northerners" and the "southerners," the cultural connotations of which are of great complexity.

Given the geographical configuration, the climate varies greatly from north to south. In most areas, the climate is continental with distinct seasons. Extreme temperatures hit the north and the west where deserts and mountains are abundant. The weather turns monsoonal in the south and in the east especially in provinces by the Pacific Ocean. From north to south there are basically three temperature zones: The cold zone, the warm zone, and the tropical zone. The temperature in the northeast could reach as low as -18.04 °F in January. Winters may seem endlessly long with deep snow and cold wind blowing from Siberia. Summers are hot and short; springs and autumns are short but charming seasons. In provinces along the southern borders, such as the Hainan Province, the weather is typically tropical with rainy, hot, and humid seasons. The temperature remains at about 97 °F for an extended period of time, where as many as four crops could be harvested throughout the year.

Administrative Divisions

Similar to the fifty states in the United States, China is divided into twenty-three provinces. Provinces are the highest local administrative units. However, unlike the American federal system, the Chinese provinces are executive units of the central government answering to the State Council. In addition to the provinces, there are five "Autonomous Regions," four "Directly Governed Municipalities" and two "Special Administrative Regions" (SARs), all of which belong to the same level as the provinces.

Provinces

The history of the provincial system dates back to the Qin Empire (221-206 B.C.). Qin's founding emperor devised the system in order to avoid separatism. The system worked effectively in preventing local power build up: Instead of assigning dukedoms as gifts to military generals and the kinship, the Qin emperor divided the country into thirty-eight commanderies governed by his handpicked officials on a rotating basis. These commanderies were predecessors to the current provinces. Today's provinces are subdivided into cities, counties or autonomous prefectures. A county is further divided into townships or national minority townships and towns. Autonomous regions subdivide in a similar fashion. Apparently, with the economic transition, local administrative entities are gaining more autonomy in determining what is good for themselves.

The Law of Local Organizations, first promulgated by the National People's Congress (NPC) in 1979 and later revised in 1982 and 1986, stipulates that provincial level governments are elected every five years by the local NPC. The primary function of provincial level governments is to implement policies of the central government and set up local policies. The State Council may override local policies.

The following table shows the provinces and their populations:

Provinces	Population (Million)
Anhui	59.86
Fujian	34.71
Gansu	25.62
Guangdong	86.42
Guizhou	35.25
Hainan	7.87
Hebei	67.44
Heilongjiang	36.89
Henan	92.56
Hubei	60.28
Hunan	64.40
Jiangsu	74.38
Jiangxi	41.40
Jilin	27.28
Liaoning	42.38
Qinghai	5.18
Shaanxi	36.05
Shandong	90.79
Shanxi	32.97
Sichuan	83.29
Taiwan (and Nearby Islands)	22.28
Yunnan	42.88
Zhejiang	46.77

(Source of data: The 5th National Census)[2]

Taiwan

While Taiwan is officially the 23rd province, Taiwan's sovereignty has been a sensitive issue since 1949, particularly during the Cold War when American military protection was preponderant. The 13,900 square miles of total area includes the Penghu Islands and some eighty smaller islands. Taiwan was under Japanese occupation for fifty years before the Nationalist government under Jiang Jieshi gained control in

1945. On the eve of the communist victory, the Nationalist Party (KMT) retreated to Taiwan and restored the Republic of China. In 1954, the Taiwan government signed the "Mutual Defense Treaty" with the United States. In 1979, with the resumption of the Sino-U.S. diplomatic relationship, the U.S. government recognized the People's Republic of China as the sole legitimate government and terminated the "Mutual Defense Treaty."

Since early 1980s, the Chinese government has stepped up efforts of reunification by urging negotiations over the "one country, two systems" plan under which Taiwan would be allowed to maintain its current socio-economic system as long as it agrees to give up separatism. In September 1981, the Chinese government released the "Nine-point Policy" which laid down a roadmap to reunification. The nine points are 1) talks should be held between the two governments; 2) people on both sides of the Taiwan Strait should be allowed to communicate; 3) Taiwan will enjoy a high level of autonomy under the status of special administrative region after the reunification; 4) Taiwan's socio-economic system and its way of life, will remain unchanged; 5) Taiwan government may send representatives to assume positions in the central government; 6) the central government will provide financial aid to Taiwan if needed; 7) Taiwan people will be allowed to settle down in the mainland and enjoy privileges; 8) Taiwan businesses are welcomed to invest in the mainland; 9) all efforts towards reunification are encouraged. In 1983, Deng Xiaoping further emphasized the "one country, two systems" policy by promising Taiwan the right to keep its own judicial and military systems. Taiwan's reactions have been cold and hostile at times. In response to the escalation of tension in the Taiwan Strait, the U.S. congress conveyed in the past its determination to maintain peace in the region through diplomacy, without excluding military measures, if necessary.[3]

Apparently, with the development of trade across the Taiwan Strait, both Taiwan and the mainland government are looking for a peaceful solution. Compared with the situation in 1987 when only a handful of retired veteran soldiers were allowed to visit their hometowns in the mainland, much progress has been made in the improvement of cross-strait relationships. Today, approximately 60,000 Taiwanese reside in China on a long-term basis.[4] Approximately seventy billion U.S. dollars have been invested by Taiwanese firms.[5] The economic and cultural tie between Taiwan and the mainland is perceived as growing stronger daily on both sides. Officials of the Taiwanese government admit that the strong economic interests involved will more likely lead to unification rather than separation, although current public opinion favors maintaining the status quo.[6]

In answer to the speeches of President Chen Shuibian of Taiwan that frequently carry separatist tendencies, President Hu Jintao maintains the standpoint of zero tolerance for Taiwan independence. President Hu reiterated his firm stand of "unswervingly adhering to the principle of one country, two systems"[7] at the time of the presidential inauguration in March 2003, taking up the Taiwan issue as a primary item on his agenda.

Autonomous Regions

Autonomous regions are different from provinces in two aspects: 1) Autonomous regions have a high concentration of minority ethnic groups. For instance, almost all Uygurs live in the Xinjiang Uygur Autonomous Region which covers more than 660,000 square miles, or approximately one sixth of China's total landmass. Although the Han, the Kazak, the Hui, the Mongol, the Kirgiz, the Tajik, the Xibe, the Ozbek, the Manchu, the Daur, the Tatar, and Russians cohabit in Xinjiang and share the Muslim religion, the Uygurs are by far the largest ethnic group in the region.[8] 2) Different from the provincial election process, the governor of an autonomous region must be elected from the dominant ethnic group.[9] Representatives of the ethnic group must also form the standing committee of the local NPC. Government employees are primarily hired from the ethnic group as well. The level of autonomy is not only reflected in the personnel structure, but also in decision making. As long as the *Constitution* is followed, the local government has the right to run the local economy according to local conditions. The local government may also make changes to general policies issued by the central government, if these policies do not conform to local conditions. Such changes, however, are subject to approval particularly when the interests of the State or those of neighboring ethnic groups are at stake. Another important autonomous privilege is represented by the right to use local languages: The government of an autonomous region may choose to use the language of the dominant ethnic group as the primary language in civil service, publication, and education. Obviously, the primary condition for the wide adoption of an ethnic language is population concentration. The following table lists the five autonomous regions and their populations according to the 4th National Census of 1990.

Autonomous Regions	Population (Millions)
Inner Mongolia (Mongol)	23.76
Guangxi (Zhuang)	44.89
Ningxia (Muslim)	5.62
Tibet (Tibetan)	2.62
Xinjiang (Uygur)	19.25

(Source of data: The 4th National Census) [10]

Special Administrative Regions (SAR)

Special Administrative Region (SAR) is a recent administrative unit developed by Deng Xiaoping in the late 1970s. The policy paved the way for the return and smooth integration of such regions as Hong Kong, Macao and Taiwan. The word "special" refers the "one country two systems" policy whereby the special regions, once returned to China, would be allowed to continue with their own socio-economic systems instead of having to adopt the communist system.

The 1982 *Constitution* has the following stipulation in Article 31: "The state may establish special administrative regions when necessary. The systems to be instituted in special administrative regions shall be prescribed by law enacted by the National People's Congress in the light of the specific conditions." [11] In 1997 and 1999, Hong Kong and Macao became SARs respectively.

Special Administrative Regions	Population (Millions)
Hong Kong	6.78
Macao	.44

(Source of data: The 5th National Census)

Hong Kong became a British concession after the first Opium War. In 1842, the Qing Government signed the "The Treaty of Nanking" whereby the island was ceded to the British as a trading port. During the Second Opium War, the Qing Government signed the "Treaty of Peking" in 1860. The treaty ceded the southern end of the Kowloon Peninsula. Finally, in 1898 the Qing Government signed the "Convention for the Extension of Hong Kong Territory" leasing the northern end of the Kowloon Peninsula, and extending a 99-year lease of Hong Kong until 1997.

Macao used to be a trading port frequently used by the Portuguese traders in the 16th century. In 1887, as part of a series of territorial concessions the government was forced into after the Opium War, the "Draft Agreement of the Sino-Portuguese Meeting" was signed, followed by the "Sino-Portuguese Treaty of Peking." Since then, the 6.757 square miles trading port had been ceded to Portugal until 1999.

In light of the principle of "one country, two systems," the Chinese government adopted the *Basic Law of Hong Kong Special Administrative Region of the People's Republic of China* in 1990 and the "Basic Law of the Macao Special Administrative Region of the People's Republic of China" in 1993. Both laws stipulate that the SARs will maintain the current economic structure, government, and social system for a certain period of time. For example, Article 5 of the Hong Kong Basic Law stipulates: "The socialist system and policies shall not be practiced in the Hong Kong Special Administrative Region and the previous capitalist system and way of life shall remain unchanged for 50 years."[12]

Municipalities

While most cities fall under their respective provincial jurisdiction, a few large cities, due to their political and economic importance, are directly managed by the central government. In addition to their paramount impact in the national economy, these cities typically have gigantic populations, well-developed infrastructures, and a high concentration of educational institutions. In ranking, the municipality sits at the same level as the province and the autonomous region. The following table shows the municipalities and their population figures according to the 5th census conducted in 2000.

Municipalities	Population (Millions)
Beijing	13.82
Chongqing	30.90
Shanghai	16.74
Tianjin	10.01

(Source of data: The 5th National Census)

Population

According to census reports, the total Chinese population was 12.95 billion in 2000,[13] which includes Taiwan's 22.28 million, and Hong Kong's 6.78 million and Macao's 440,000. 36.09 percent live in cities and towns. Age and gender structures show that the Chinese population is young and balanced, despite the impact of family planning implemented since the early 1970s.

Ages	%
0-14	22.89%
15-64	70.15%
65 and above	6.96%
Female	48.37%
Male	51.63%

(Source of data: The 5th National Census)

Family Planning

The family planning policy, also known as the "one-child policy," restricts urban families to one child and families in rural and pastoral areas to a maximum of two children.[14] A government report released earlier in 2001 claimed that the policy had effectively curbed the rapidly growing population. According to Information Office of the State Council, without enforcing family planning, China would have added 300 million people by 2001, more than the entire U.S. population.[15] Benefits of family planning, according to the government, include better life for the people, liberation of women from frequent births, and the availability of more educational opportunities.

Back in the 1950s, the government encouraged population growth and downplayed warnings of population explosion. The issue of family planning was only brought up again in the 1970s and major cities started to urge population control. The policy was only forcefully implemented after the National People's Congress in 1980 called for building family planning into China's long-term development strategy. In the same year, the *Marriage Law* was revised to restrict the minimum age of marriage to twenty-two for men and twenty for women. The *Law* also encourages late marriage and late childbearing. The 1982 census revealed that the population had crossed the one billion mark. Until then, the Chinese government had rejected "population explosion" as a real and significant threat to the national economy, the prevailing ideology had been that more people would generate more productivity and hence, making a more powerful nation. Later on, Article 25 of the *Constitution* of 1982 was formulated to state, "The state promotes family planning so that population growth may fit the plans for economic and social development."

Since the implementation of family planning, the average fertility rate has dropped from six children per family in the 1970s to about two per family by the beginning of the year 2001. This is largely attributable to abortion that has since been made widely available and the compulsory use of long-term birth control devices such as IUDs. Financial punishment has been forceful as well: Violators pay a heavy fine equivalent to $300 in some areas and lose all benefits allocated to qualifying families which typically include food subsidies and cash bonus.

The "one child policy" met tremendous resistance, especially before the 1990s. The traditional concept of having a son to carry on the family name is deeply rooted. Rural people still harbor the traditional concept of family happiness -- the more children the better. Violent protests often broke out in rural areas where 800 million Chinese live. Because the policy was never formalized into law, local officials have had wide latitudes in carrying out the policy, resorting to brutal force at times. Measures such as coerced abortion and sterilization were among the most widely condemned by international human rights groups.

As the market reform gains momentum, and as population ageing grows into a real pressure in the late 1990s, the government has started to reform the stiff population pragmatism. In large cities, such as Shanghai, an experimental policy allows single-child couples to have two children. Some cities allow couples to have two children, as long as the births are five years apart. In rural areas, some villages abolished birth permits (a quota system) allowing couples to decide on their own when to have a baby. The government also encourages local officials to initiate and fund their own pilot projects on family planning, expecting to achieve both population reduction and stability.

Changes are happening in the market of birth control devices as well. Notably since 2000, a variety of birth control pills and devices are put on the market as alternatives to IUDs. The prospect of profit is attracting both state-owned and private enterprises. It is not rare for newspapers, media and educational materials prepared by government agencies to include graphical instructions on the use of contraceptives that used to be frowned upon before. Analysts suspect, however, that the policy change may actually reflect recent governmental effort in dealing with consequences caused by the overly harsh practices in the past. These consequences include gender imbalance, rapid population ageing, workforce deficiencies, and symptoms of a single-children society. In fact, in a report published in 2000, a group of Chinese demographic scientists estimated that a "two-children plan" could be safely implemented in the entire China. Clearly, while the government continues to implement its principles, family planning today is undergoing significant changes. For some people, this forbidden area has transformed from a simple arena of law enforcement to attractive market opportunities.

Ethnicity

China has fifty-six ethnic groups on the record. The ethnic group with the largest population is the Han, representing 91.59 percent of the total population. According to the 4th National census of 1990,[16] the following are minority ethnic groups with populations above one million and their primary residing provinces:

Ethnic Groups	Population (Millions)	Residing Provinces
Bai	1.59	Yunnan, Guizhou
Bouyei	2.54	Guizhou
Chaoxian (Korean)	1.92	Jilin, Liaoning, Heilongjian
Dai	1.02	Yunnan
Dong	2.5	Guizhou, Hunan, Guangxi
Hani	1.25	Yunnan
Hui	8.61	Ningxia, Gansu, Henan, Hebei, Qinghai, Shandong, Yunnan, Xinjiang, Anhui, Liaoning, Heilongjiang, Jilin, Shaanxi, Beijing, Tianjin
Kazak	1.11	Xinjiang, Gansu, Qinghai
Man (Manchu)	9.84	Liaoning, Jilin, Heilongjiang, Hebei, Beijing, Inner Mongolia
Miao	7.38	Guizhou, Hunan, Yunnan, Guangxi, Sichuan, Hainan, Hubei
Mongol	4.8	Inner Mongolia, Xinjiang, Liaoning, Jilin, Heilongjiang, Gansu, Hebei, Henan, Qinghai
Tujia	5.72	Hunan, Hubei
Uygur	7.2	Xinjiang
Yao	2.13	Guangxi, Hunan, Yunnan, Guangdong, Guizhou
Yi	6.57	Sichuan, Yunnan, Guizhou, Guangxi
Zang (Tibetan)	4.59	Tibet, Qinghai, Sichuan, Gansu, Yunnan, Xinjiang
Zhuang	15.55	Guangxi, Yunnan, Guangdong, Guizhou

(Source of data: The 4th National Census, 1990)

Ethnic groups with less than one million population include: Lisu, Va, She, Gaoshan, Lahu, Shui, Dongxiang, Naxi, Jingpo, Kirgiz, Tu, Daur,

Mulam, Qiang, Blang, Salar, Maonan, Gelo, Xibe, Achang, Pumi, Tajik, Nu, Ozbek, Russian, Ewenki, Deang, Bonan, Yugur, Jing, Tatar, Drung, Oroquen, Hezhen, Moinba, Lhoba, Jino.

The fifty-six ethnic groups were registered in the 1950s by the central government in a large-scale multi-year survey with the help of hundreds of linguists and social scientists. The criteria used for identifying and classifying ethnic groups at the time were much influenced by the Soviet system, which, in many cases, was hardly applicable to the Chinese reality. While physical appearance, language, geographical location, and life style were among the most important yardsticks. In general, these standards were hardly effective uniformly. Consequently, except for a few ethnic groups, such as the Tibetans, the Mongols, and the Uygurs due to their distinct physical appearances and languages, other ethnic groups are not intuitively distinguishable from the Han Chinese. Most ethnic groups have long been sinified through marriage and cultural integration. The Chinese speaking Muslims or the Hui, for example, have long ceased to be physically distinguishable from the Han. Their ancestors were Muslim Arabs and Persian merchants of the Islamic faith who traveled to China during the Tang (618-907) and the Song (960-1279) eras to conduct trade. After more than a thousand years of cultural and ethnic integration the most eminent marks of identity are the high concentration of the Chinese Muslim population in the Ningxia Autonomous Region, as well as their Islamic belief that has weathered political movements that were hostile to their religious practice. Another example is the Manchu residing in the northeast and the northwest Xinjiang. With a population of 9.84 million, the Manchu ethnicity is only kept in family records. Having governed China for two and a half centuries, the Manchu were finally integrated into the Han culture. Today, people of Manchu descent would have to resort to family records as the only proof of their lineage.

Close-up: The Yao, the Dai and the Zhuang

More than two million Yao people reside in southern provinces such as Guangxi, Hunan, Yunnan, Guangdong, and Guizhou. Regional variations are often shown in costumes and customs. In general, men wear blue jackets buttoned in the middle or to the left with a wide belt. Women wear colorful embroidered head covers, collarless jackets, and short or long skirts often with a long opening on one side. The Yao are known for their communication through singing, particularly between young men and women in dating ceremonies. The King Pan Festival is a grand celebration for Yao's ancestor King Pan. The festival is held on the 16th day of the 10th lunar month. Activities include singing, dancing, sculpture display, religious services and day-long banquets.

The Dai is a smaller ethnic group with a population of one million residing primarily in Xishuangbanna and Dehong autonomous districts that are located at the southern tip of the Yunnan Province. Dai tribal villages are built along rivers and streams with houses constructed on stilts. Women wear short dresses and sarongs. Men wear collarless tight-sleeve short jackets with an opening at the front or along the right side, long baggy pants, and black or white turbans. Tattooing is common for men. The Dai believe in Buddhism, have their own language, their own calendar, and a history of approximately one thousand years according to their tradition. The Dai New Year is celebrated during five days in the late sixth month or the early seventh month by the Dai calendar, which corresponds to the month of April in the Western calendar. The celebration by the name of the Water-Sprinkling Festival is a grand carnival where people of all ages step onto the streets, dressed in the most colorful costumes, and splash water onto one another. The level of one's popularity and good fortune is reflected in how much one gets soaked. The more one gets soaked the luckier one is. Fireworks are set off at night. Young men and women throw embroidered pouches at each other as a dating invitation.

Residing in Guangxi, Yunnan, Guangdong, and Guizhou, the Zhuang is the most populous minority with more than fifteen million people. Most people reside in the recently founded Zhuang Autonomous Region in Guangxi Province. Men typically wear black jackets, colorful headbands, and wide belts with hanging decorative objects, mostly of the cutlery category. In history, the Zhuang has a long relationship with the Han Chinese. Documents engraved on copper or rock drums date back more than a thousand years. The Zhuang have inherited a wide range of cultural traditions from their ancestors. The Zhuang folk literature, songs, and operas constitute the main body of the southern minority's culture. The singing tradition of the Zhuang is more ancient and their skills more diversified than those of other southern minorities. The Singing Festival is held on the third day of the third lunar month to celebrate the singing goddess Sister Liu. Singing competitions are held among teams of tribal villages. Dragon and lion dances are performed all day long while embroidery gifts are passed by lovers. Both are traditions shared by most southern ethnic groups.

(Data source: China National Tourism Administration, "Ethnic Groups Southwest China.")

Language

The official Chinese language is "Putonghua (the Common Speech)," better known as the "Mandarin Chinese." Mandarin is a dialect along with more than 120 Chinese dialects. It is defined as the combination of the pronunciation of the Beijing area and the vocabulary of the northern dialect group. Beijing pronunciation has been the standard for the official speech for about a thousand years. Poets and singer song composers had already adopted the Beijing dialect, known as "language of the central region," in their artistic creations.[17] This tradition was reinforced during recent times. Since the May 4th Movement of 1919 that promoted vernacular speech, Mandarin Chinese has been routinely used in films and theater arts. As early as the 1920s, the Beijing pronunciation had gained the prestige of "national pronunciation" in the National Language Unification Movement.[18] Any art form that is not presented in Mandarin are referred to, sometimes with prejudice too, as "local."

The promotion of the Mandarin has been part of a long-term government plan since the 1950s. Although minority regions are allowed to maintain indigenous languages, these languages tend to be replaced by the Mandarin in the long run. While a few major ethnic languages remain intact, backed by larger populations and more distinct cultures, such as Tibetan, Mongolian, and Uygur, smaller languages are clearly heading toward extinction. As an example, the Xibe language, a dialect of the Manchurian language still spoken today in a Manchu community in Yili County of Xinjiang Autonomous Region, is actually reduced to a "kitchen language." Apparently, the Xibe vocabulary is being replaced by the vocabulary of neighboring northern Chinese dialects, as the Xibe people are constantly sinicized through marriage and job-related relocations.

The tonal system is a general feature of the Chinese language. The dialects have a range of three to eight tones. Mandarin, for example, has four tones. The same syllable may represent different meanings when pronounced under different tones. Therefore, a syllable under four different tones may represent four sets of words. Intimidating as this may appear, the tonal system is only a secondary distinctive feature, next to the accurate pronunciation of the syllable. Word order and larger context typically provides clues to the meaning as well. In other words, one could nevertheless communicate without handling the tones perfectly. In the worst case, by producing the tones wrong one may get mistaken as a "provincial."

The writing system may cause the wrong perception of how unapproachable the Chinese language is. Actually, the writing system is nothing but a script system that records the language. The Chinese language, with respect to its syntax and semantics, is no more difficult than any other language in the world. One common question is how many characters there are in all, "character" being a distinct written unit. The Kangxi Dictionary, compiled in 1716 carries 47,035 characters. The Hanyu Da Cidian (The Big Chinese Lexicon) which was published in the late 1980s in eight volumes, included 56,000 characters. However, only 3,000 characters or so are believed to account for ninety-nine percent of those used in modern books and newspapers. Some linguists estimate that 400 characters of the 3,000 have the highest frequency.[19]

The Chinese script was first used in documents of the Shang Dynasty, around 16th century B.C. The characters were inscribed on turtle shells or animal bones known as "oracle bones." Archeologists believe that ancient witches heated bone pieces with fire to induce cracks on the surface. They engraved oracle scriptures reflecting their interpretations of the cracks.

Simplification of the Writing System

As complex as they may look, Chinese characters are formed by a limited number of components called ideograms and phonograms. These components are further divisible into a dozen or so distinct strokes. After several phases of simplification over thousands of years, the original pictographs lost their original designs and became the standardized written symbols of today. Nonetheless, in the past, learning the writing system required much effort and resources that not everyone could afford. It was thus considered a major barrier to literacy. To wipe out illiteracy, the Chinese government has devoted tremendous efforts since the 1950s in simplifying the system. Characters with twenty or more strokes, for example, were gradually reduced to less than ten strokes resulting in the "simplified version" of the script. The non-simplified version, also known as the "full version," remains in use primarily in overseas Chinese communities.

The simplification movement met strong resistance, however, from intellectuals, artists, and politicians who pride themselves to be guardians of the traditional culture. Typically, they blame the Chinese government for destroying the traditional graphic structure, the elegance of which supposedly preserves a great deal of cultural and artistic spirit. The government's opinion holds that the writing system, as a vehicle of information, has little significance in and of itself. Hence, it must serve more important goals such as promoting literacy. In addition, it is a widely held opinion that the Chinese writing system has always been simplified since the moment of its creation. A persistent divide has resulted based on these perspectives.

Government and Election

The *Constitution* of the PRC requires that the central government be comprised of six components: The National People's Congress (NPC), the Presidency of the PRC, the State Council, the Central Military Commission, the Supreme People's Court, and the Supreme People's Procuratorate. The structure of the NPC is illustrated in the following chart.

National People's Congress (NPC)			
NPC Standing Committee			
President of the People's Republic of China			
State Council	Central Military Commission	Supreme People's Court	Supreme People's Procuratorate

The president and the vice president of the PRC are elected by the NPC for a five-year term, with the possibility of serving a maximum of two consecutive terms. Candidates must be lawful citizens of above age forty-five. Domestic functions of the president include declaring laws passed by the NPC, nominating candidates for State Council positions, and declaring the marshal law under unusual circumstances. The president's international responsibilities typically include meeting with foreign diplomatic and government officials, implementing diplomatic procedures, such as dispatching/recalling ambassadors, and signing international treaties.

The New Leaders

During the First Plenum of the 10th National People's Congress held in March 2003, Hu Jintao was elected president of the People's Republic of China. His predecessor, Jiang Zemin, remains Chairman of the Central Military Commission. In the Chinese system, high-ranking administrators tend to occupy top political positions as well. Such a tradition represents an eminent characteristic of the dual system where administration and party-control are not separated. Hu also holds the highest leadership position of the CPC as General Secretary of the CPC Central Committee.

Born in 1942 in Anhui Province, Hu witnessed the hardship in ordinary people's lives, which fostered his populist focus. Hu graduated from Tsinghua University and received an engineering degree in the area of water conservancy. In the 1980s, Hu rose to take the party secretary position of the Gansu provincial government. He was soon promoted to the central government to be in charge of the

Communist Youth League. In the early 1990s, Hu assumed the position of the CPC Secretary of Tibet before he was appointed to the Political Bureau of the CPC. Hu's chairmanship had been widely expected due to his pro-reform political tendency, his effectiveness and age advantage. Hu vowed to deepen the reform started by Deng Xiaoping and to continue with the implementation of the open-door policy.[20]

The Tenth NPC elected Wen Jiabao, a geologist by training, to be China's premier. Born in 1942, a native of Tianjin, Wen grew up in urban environment and received a good education that included a post-graduate degree from Beijing Institute of Geology. He worked in the Gansu Provincial Geological Bureau in the late 1970s before assuming the position of Vice-minister of Geology and Mineral Resources. Starting in the late 1980s, Wen steadily moved up the ladder in the political arena. By 2002, Wen had become a member of the most prestigious Political Bureau of the CPC Central Committee. He was also member of the Secretariat of the CPC Central Committee, deputy premier of the State Council, and Secretary of the Financial Work Committee of the CPC Central Committee. In his inauguration ceremony, Premier Wen vowed to forge ahead with the economic reform, particularly with the reform of state-owned enterprises, and continue to open up China to the world. Among the items of higher priority, the Premier Wen promised to seek solutions to alleviate unemployment, rural poverty, and problems in providing social security to the broad masses of low-income people.[21]

System of Election

In general, for each congressional term, approximately 3,000 deputies are elected into the NPC from all occupations for a five-year term. The *Constitution* of 1982 and *The Electoral Law* of 1979 both stipulate that any lawful Chinese citizen of eighteen years of age or above, regardless of ethnicity, gender, occupation, education, property ownership, family background, or religious belief, enjoys the right to elect or to be elected.

According to the *Electoral Law*, deputies to people's congresses at the county and township levels are directly elected by voters; deputies above these levels are elected indirectly by deputies of the next lower level. The final deputies to the NPC are elected by people's congresses of provinces, autonomous regions and municipalities. Elections are conducted through secret ballot. Once elected, the deputies will represent their respective administrative regions at the grand NPC congress held in Beijing once every five years.

The number of candidates is normally greater than the number of elected deputies by between one fifth to one half. All political entities and people's groups may jointly or separately recommend candidates in the phase of indirect election. Ten or more county-level deputies may also recommend candidates. With respect to Taiwan's representation, a bill was passed by the Eighth NPC in 1992 approving thirteen seats to be filled by candidates from 34,000 citizens currently residing in China of Taiwan origin.[22]

Functions of the NPC

Functions of NPC include amending the *Constitution*, passing new laws, supervising the administration through auditing work reports, appointing or removing officials who serve at the State Council, approving and monitoring state budgetary programs, and declaring war on foreign nations. Because of its gigantic membership, it is inconvenient for the NPC to convene assembly meetings frequently. Hence, a Standing Committee with approximately 135 members is put in place to handle current issues. Composed of the chairman, the vice-chairmen, and the secretary-general, the Standing Committee executes routine responsibilities within the principles of the current NPC. Its functions would normally include the following:

1. To enact and amend statutes with the exception of the ones that should be enacted by the NPC general meeting.
2. To enact, when the NPC is not in session, partial supplements and amendments to statutes enacted by the NPC, provided that they do not contravene the basic principles of these statutes.
3. To interpret the *Constitution* and statutes.
4. To annul administrative rules and regulations, decisions and orders of the State Council that contravene the *Constitution* or the statutes.

5. To annul local regulations or decisions of the organs of state power of provinces, autonomous regions and centrally administered municipalities that contravene the *Constitution*, the statutes, or the administrative rules and regulations.

Members of the Standing Committee may not hold office in any of the administrative, judicial, or procuratorial organs of the state. The Standing Committee is elected for the same five-year term as the National People's Congress. Normally, the Committee meets once every two months.

The State Council

The State Council is the highest administrative organ headed by a premier and a number of deputy premiers. The premier has a comprehensive responsibility for both the daily work and the making of far-reaching decisions. Commissions, ministries and ministry level bureaus carry out detailed administrative responsibilities. The number of ministries and bureaus varies following the ever-changing structure of the national economy. For example, the State Economic Planning Commission is responsible for drafting the five-year plans; the National Bureau of Statistics conducts national census and monitors economic development; the Ministry of Information Industry regulates the Internet use and communication policies. Since each ministry represents an important sector of the national affairs, new ministries are constantly added while old ones are eliminated following the NPC's recommendations. In fact, structural revision is an important item on the agenda of every NPC plenum. The premier briefs the NPC of economic development and proposes the establishment or removal of new branches of the State Council.

Close-up: High Level Government Offices

Ministries:

Ministry of Foreign Affairs
Ministry of National Defense
State Development and Reform Commission

Ministry of Education
Ministry of Science and Technology
State Commission of Science, Technology, and Industry for
    National Defense
State Ethnic Affairs Commission
Ministry of Public Security
Ministry of State Security
Ministry of Supervision
Ministry of Civil Affairs
Ministry of Justice
Ministry of Finance
Ministry of Personnel
Ministry of Labor and Social Security
Ministry of Land and Resources
Ministry of Construction
Ministry of Railways
Ministry of Communications
Ministry of Information Industry
Ministry of Water Resources
Ministry of Agriculture
Ministry of Commerce
Ministry of Culture
Ministry of Health
State Population and Family Planning Commission People's
    Bank of China
National Audit Office: Auditor-General

Organizations:

Commission of the State-owned Assets Supervision and Administration
    General Administration of Customs
State Bureau of Taxation
State Environmental Protection Administration
Civil Aviation Administration of China
State Administration of Radio, Film, and Television
State Sports General Administration
State Statistics Bureau
State Administration for Industry and Commerce

State Press and Publication Administration
State Forestry Bureau
General Administration of Quality Supervision, Inspection, and
    Quarantine
State Drug Administration
State Intellectual Property Office
National Tourism Administration
State Administration for Religious Affairs
Counselor's Office under the State Council
Bureau of Government Offices Administration
State Administration of Work Safety

Offices:

Office of Overseas Chinese Affairs
Taiwan Affairs Office
Hong Kong and Macao Affairs Office
Legislative Affairs Office
Information Office
Research Office

Institutions:

Xinhua News Agency
Chinese Academy of Sciences
Chinese Academy of Social Sciences
Chinese Academy of Engineering
Development Research Center
National School of Administration
State Seismological Bureau
China Meteorological Administration
China Banking Regulatory Commission (CBRC)
China Securities Regulatory Commission
China Insurance Regulatory Commission
State Electricity Regulatory Commission (SERC)
National Council for Social Security Fund
National Natural Science Foundation

Administrations and Bureaus under Ministries and Commissions:

State Grain Bureau

State Tobacco Monopoly Industry Bureau

State Bureau of Foreign Experts Affairs

State Oceanography Bureau

State Bureau of Surveying & Mapping

State Postal Bureau

State Bureau of Cultural Relics

State Administration of Traditional Chinese Medicine

State Administration of Foreign Exchange

(Source of data: The State Council)[23]

The Constitution

Since 1949, four constitutions have been promulgated respectively in 1954, 1975, 1978 and 1982. Each of the four versions represents significant changes. The 1975 *Constitution* eliminated the position of the Chairman of the State as well as the whole section of the Supreme People's Procuratorate that existed back in the 1954 *Constitution*. Both items were reinstated in the 1978 *Constitution* and continued into the 1982 *Constitution*. Article 37 of the 1982 *Constitution* stipulates, with respect to the Supreme People's Procuratorate, "No citizen may be arrested except with the approval or by decision of a people's procuratorate or by decision of a people's court, and arrests must be made by a public security organ."

The current *Constitution* has four chapters and 138 articles defining general principles, rights and duties of the citizen, the structure of the state, the national flag, and the national emblem. Many important amendments have been made since the promulgation reflecting a rapidly changing society. For example, the 8th NPC of 1993 added the following to the Preamble in Amendment Two:[24]

China is at the primary stage of socialism. The basic task of the nation is, according to the theory of building socialism with Chinese characteristics, to concentrate its effort on socialist modernization. Under the leadership of the Communist Party of China and the guidance of Marxism-Leninism and Mao Zedong Thought, the Chinese people of all nationalities will continue to adhere to the people's democratic dictatorship and follow the socialist road, persevere in reform and opening to the outside, steadily improve socialist institutions, develop socialist democracy, improve the socialist legal system and work hard and self-reliantly to modernize industry, agriculture, national defense and science and technology step by step to turn China into a socialist country with prosperity and power, democracy and culture.

The 1999 Amendment added the following lines to Article Six:

During the primary stage of socialism, the State adheres to the basic economic system with the public ownership remaining dominant and diverse sectors of the economy developing side by side, and to the distribution system with the distribution according to work remaining dominant and the coexistence of a variety of modes of distribution.

Both amendments reflect the situation of a transitional society where the market economy is gaining ground while the socialist state planning system is being maintained at a growing disadvantage. The few core principles of the *Constitution*, however, have remained unchanged. The nature of the State, for instance, has always been defined as "a socialist state under the people's democratic dictatorship." Clearly, while the reform has brought about a sea of change in the national economy, the Chinese government remains under the CPC alone. To handle political discrepancies of this sort, the *Constitution* advocates multi-party cooperation instead of multi-party competition. Nonetheless, the smaller political entities, such as the "democratic parties," have never been significantly influential.

The Chinese People's Political Consultative Conference (CPPCC) is the most popular channel for other parties to voice their opinions. The major democratic parties are listed below.

Democratic Parties	Representation	Founding Year
China Revolutionary Committee of the Kuomintang	Former Kuomintang members	1948
China Democratic League	Intellectuals of prestige	1941
China Democratic National Construction Association	Economists	1945
China Association for Promoting Democracy	Educators, scientists, publishers	1945
Chinese Peasants and Workers' Democratic Party	Specialists of public health and labor protection	1930
China Zhi Gong Dang	Overseas Chinese	1925
Jiu San Society	Scientists and educators	1944

National Flag, Emblem, and Anthem

The national flag of the People's Republic of China figures a red colored rectangular base with five yellow stars on the left upper corner. The red color represents communism; the five yellow stars represent the working people united around the Communist Party. The national emblem features a background of a red flag with five stars, the Tiananmen Gate, ears of wheat, and a cogwheel, symbolizing the government's representation of the laboring people.

The national anthem is adapted from a song composed in 1935 by poet Tian Han and composer Nie Er. The song, entitled *The March of the Volunteers*, first appeared in the film *Sons and Daughters in Times of Storms*. The film praised the determination of young people marching to the front to battle Japanese invaders. To commemorate the Anti-Japanese War and the heroism demonstrated by the Chinese people, the CPPCC adopted the song as the national anthem. The lyric reads as follows:

Arise, those who refuse to be slaves!
With our flesh and blood,
Let us build another Great Wall.
This is the final moment of the Chinese nation.

Everyone is forced to shout out the last battle cry.
Arise, arise, arise!
Let us tens of thousands be united as one.
Braving the enemy's fire,
We march on, we march on, and we march on!

---

[1] *The CIA World Fact Book* 2003 <www.cia.gov/cia/publications /factbook/geos/us.html> (13 February 2004); and "Status of Natural Resources," National Bureau of Statistics of China, 1999, <www.stats.gov.cn /tjsj/qtsj/hjtjzl/> (13 February 2004).

[2] "Communiqué of Core Data of the 5th National Census," no 2, National Bureau of Statistics of China, 15 May 2001, <www.stats.gov.cn/tjgb/rkpcgb /qgrkpcgb/200203310084.htm> (11 June 2003).

[3] Kerry Dumbaugh, "CRS Report for Congress," 18 March 1996, <www.fas. org/man/crs/96-246f.htm> (11 June 2003).

[4] Jing Luo, "Notes of a Visit to Taiwan," *Laiyin Forum*, no. 5 (München, Germany: October 2003): 38-41.

[5] Rob Gifford, *National Public Radio News (NPR)*, 10 March 2004.

[6] Jing Luo, "Notes of a Visit to Taiwan," *Laiyin Forum*, no. 5 (Müchen: October 2003): 38-41.

[7] "Party Chief Hu Jintao on Taiwan Issue," *The People's Daily*, 12 March 2003, <english.peopledaily.com.cn/200303/12/eng20030312_113135.shtml> (11 June 2003).

[8] "Ethnic Minorities," <www.china.org.cn/e-groups/shaoshu/index.htm> (12 June 2003).

[9] Pu Xingzu, Ding Rongsheng, Sun Guanhong, Hu Jinxing, et al., *Political System of the People's Republic of China (zhong hua ren min gong he guo zheng zhi zhi du)*, (Hong Kong: Joint Publishing Co., LTD., 1996): 365.

[10] "Communiqué of the 4th National Census," 14 November 1990, no 3, <www.stats.gov.cn/tjgb/rkpcgb/qgrkpcgb/200204040084.htm> (11 June 2003).

[11] *Constitution of the People's Republic of China*, 4 December 1982, <english.peopledaily.com.cn/constitution/constitution.html> (12 June 2003).

[12] *The Basic Law of the Hong Kong Special Administrative Region of the People's Republic of China* (Hong Kong: Joint Publishing Company HK CO. Limited, 1997): 6.

[13] "Communiqué on Major Figures of the 2000 Population Census," no. 1, 28 March 2001, <www.stats.gov.cn/english/newrelease/statisticalreports /200204230084.htm> (13 June 2003).

[14] *Family Planning in China*, (Beijing: Information Office of the State Council of the People's Republic of China, 1995).

[15] Ibid.

[16] "Communiqué of the 4th National Census," no 3, 14 November 1990, <www.stats.gov.cn/tjgb/rkpcgb/qgrkpcgb/200204040084.htm> (13 June 2003).

[17] Shirong Xu, *Putonghua Phonetics* (Beijing: Language Reform Publishing, 1980): 20.

[18] John De Francis, *Nationalism and Language Reform in China* (New York: Octagon Books, 1972).

[19] Joel Bellassen, Zhang Pengpeng, *Méthode d'initiation à la Lanugue et à l'Écriture chinoise*, tome 2 (Paris: La Compagnie, 1989): 17.

[20] "Hu Jintao Pledges Wholehearted Service to Nation," 18 March 2003, <www.chinadaily.com.cn/highlights/nbc/news/318hu.html> (17 June 2003).

[21] "Premier Preoccupied with Rural Areas, Unemployment, Poverty," 18 March 2003, <www.chinadaily.com.cn/highlights/nbc/news/318rural.html> (17 June 2003).

[22] Xingzu Pu et al., *Political System of the People's Republic of China*, 141.

[23] "The State Council." *The People's Daily On-line Edition*, <english. peopledaily.com.cn/data/organs/statecouncil.shtml#Ministry> (17 June 2003).

[24] *Constitution of the People's Republic of China, 1982.* <english.peopledaily. com.cn/constitution/constitution.html> (9 December 2003).

2
Overview of History

From Legends to Dynasties

Little evidence has been unearthed as of today attesting the time when humans first settled down in the Yellow River Valley. The earliest written records known date back to the Shang Dynasty (1600-1100 B.C.). The text-bearing oracle bones provide a rich record of the structure and activities of a mature agricultural society. The earlier stage, known as the Xia Dynasty (2100-1600 B.C.), remains legendary due to absence of written records and inadequate archeological finds. As more and more archeological evidence is unearthed, the colorful pre-history pans out, revealing the dawn of the Chinese civilization.

Early Residents

In the late 1920s, scientists found early human remains in Zhoukoudian, a hilly village to the southwest of Beijing. The remains were identified as belonging to *Peking Man,* a *Homo Erectus* species dating back over 500,000 years. These hominids were capable of using fire, creating stone tools, hunting, and possibly had a language. *Homo Erectus* as a species is dated from 200,000 to 1.5 million years ago. Its brain capacity of is about two-thirds of that of modern humans. It is known that until 200,000 years ago *Homo Erectus* lived throughout the temperate zones of Africa, Europe, and Asia.[1]

Some 20,000 years ago, residents in eastern China had learned to use composite tools, projectile points, and animal decorations. About 10,000 years later, the food gathering and scavenging style of life was replaced by agriculture. An eminent agricultural society seemed to have emerged around 6,000-7,000 years ago, as revealed by the discovery of Yangshao Culture that spreads across the Shaanxi and the Gansu provinces. The society at this time was already at an advanced agricultural stage. Villages were divided into dwelling areas, kiln centers, and cemeteries. Farmers planted millet, raised pigs, dogs, and silkworms. People lived in semi-subterranean dwellings. Painted pottery containers were widely used as cookware and storage purposes.[2]

Yangshao pottery was typically hand-built and hand-painted in black color on a reddish base. Designs included animals, plants, and fertility symbols. Compared with earlier potteries of 12,000 years ago that were made of coarse paste and decorated with impressions of cord-wrapped sticks and paddles, Yanshao pottery represents a significant leap in craftsmanship.

The Longshan Culture unearthed across today's Shangdong Province dates back to over 2000 B.C. Longshan Culture demonstrates a further refinement of the agricultural culture. Large rectangular rammed earth foundations suggest that administrative centers and cities were constructed within strong walls. Early cities enclosing royal palaces appeared in the primitive horizon. The occupation-based segregation system reveals primitive social stratification and work divisions. The orderly layout of the city plan implies that the authority was capable of effective organization.

The Longshan black pottery shows an impressive craftsmanship achieved through using machinery. The shiny and sometimes very thin walls of the pottery are evidence of smaller kilns and higher temperature.[3] The black pottery is obviously polished and decorated with a highly artistic taste. It was around this time that an ideographic writing system was used. However, the early writing was lost due to the lack of durable medium. The problem with document preservation was solved around the 16th century B.C. when witches and craftsmen engraved oracle scripts on animal bones, such as turtle shells and animal shoulder blades. Because most of the scripts unearthed carry oracle predictions related to routine activities, the oracle bones are a valuable archive of the Shang history.

Legends

The pre-Shang history did not completely fall into oblivion. Some of the events were passed down through oral literature, most of which was written down finally during the Zhou Dynasty (1050-771 B.C.). Mystical and legendary in nature, as most oral literatures are, the pre-Shang legends maintain an impressive coherence and artistic elegance. They vividly depict details of daily life, religious beliefs and practices, and moral value systems of the primitive people. These legends reveal an early understanding of the origin of the universe and about how natural phenomena such as thunder, lightening, rain, wind... come about. Some stories describe the haunting death world and the great fear that death would invoke. What particularly stand out, however, are stories about the deeds of great warriors who conquer natural disasters and control ferocious beasts that generated such devastations. The following are a few examples.[4]

The Origin of the Universe

The sky, the earth, and a man by the name of Pangu were enclosed in a chicken egg. Pangu had lived in the egg for 18,000 years when the eggshell cracked open. The white became the sky, and the yoke formed the earth. With each day passing the sky grew ten feet high and the earth ten feet wide. After 18,000 years, the sky was broad and the earth wide, and Pangu had turned into a giant. It was at this time when three sacred kings arrived.

The Origin of Natural Phenomena

After Pangu died, his head became the four mountain ranges, his eyes became the sun and the moon, his body fat became rivers and seas, and his hairs became forests.

Heroes and Heroines

Once upon a time, the four pillars supporting the sky broke down and the nine continents sank into the ground. The sky could not cover the ground and the ground could not stay afloat. Wild fires engulfed lands and forests, floods inundated vast lands, wild beasts preyed on innocent people. Vultures attacked the weak and the elderly. Goddess Nuwa created stones of five colors with which she mended the sky. She cut the legs of the turtle and made four pillars out of them to hold up the sky. She killed the black dragon to stop the floods in the state of Ji, and she used reed ashes to block the flooding water.

The Origin of Man

Since there were no people in the world when the sky and earth separated, Nuwa shaped yellow clay into humans. Exhausted by the toil and growing impatient, Nuwa whipped the clay with a rope. The bits of clay that splashed around turned into humans as well. Therefore, the rich and the wise were handmade by Nuwa; the poor and the mediocre were created under Nuwa's whip.

The Story of Kuaifu the Giant

In the grand wilderness, there was a mountain by the name of Chengduzaitian. There was a man who carried two yellow snakes on his head above the ears and held two yellow snakes in his hands. His name was Kuaifu. He overestimated his grand martial prowess and raced with the sun. Stranded in the sun's valley, dying of thirst, Kuaifu emptied the Yellow River. As the Yellow River was not enough to quench his thirst, Kuaifu walked toward the grand marshes and died on his way.

Houyi Shooting the Suns

In the time of Yao, ten suns appeared in the sky scorching crops and forests. People were starving while wild beasts roamed the land and dined on people. Yao commanded the great archer Houyi to shoot down the extra suns and to kill the beasts that raised floods and fires. People were relieved. They worshipped Yao as the Son of Heaven.

These legends are informative in many ways about the primitive times. One eminent feature is that the gods and goddesses in the Chinese context are more of empowered humans, with their weaknesses and strengths, rather than all mighty creators. They die (Pangu), they cut corners in their work (Nuwa), and out of their macho ego, they race against the sun and die of human limitations (Kuaifu). These powerful figures are not only creative, but also work hard to maintain order. The interpretation of the origin of the rich and the poor, here, suggests that the story was created at a time when socio-economic hierarchies were already clearly drawn and were even disturbing to some. Transpiring from these legends is the worship of the powerful human. It is the all-mighty human, but not any spiritual source, that is at the center of the universe. The legendary figures represent an extension of human imaginations, those of putting everything in order and with hard work. Apparently, the belief holds that since human beings are the most powerful in the universe, they are entitled to controlling everything on land. At least, the coexistence of man and nature does not presume that man is necessarily inferior.

Apparently, the trend of an atheist tradition had already dawned by the time of these legends. But why did the primitive Chinese demonstrate such a remarkable engaging attitude towards natural disasters while in most other civilizations running away from deluge were the preferred choice?

An explanation might lie with the prevalent way of life of which the agrarian activities were the core. As early as 7,000 years ago millet was grown in Zhangzhai and Banpo of the Shaanxi Province. These cereals were domesticated along the Yellow River bank and spread later to the rest of China.[5] Unlike hunter-gatherers who are sensitive to the constraint of resources, agrarians are assured of a yield proportional to efforts spent on attending the crops. In general, barring severe weather conditions, the harvest is very much predictable based on the amount of the work put in. Harvesting more crops is almost a matter of having more labor and vice versa.[6] *Odes:July*, for example, provides a detailed list of farm work to be done for each season. As such, a practical attitude might have been nurtured at a very early time. Furthermore the pursuit of social hierarchy dates back to the early times as well, as agrarian communities typically form stratified societies, and power struggles and the compromise of power through the founding of empires are hallmarks of agrarian civilizations.[7]

However, this generally reliable equation is disturbed when natural disasters do occur. Why would the Chinese remain in their locations at times of natural disasters trying to fix them rather than escaping in vessels? While geographical determinism is clearly simplistic, there is room to believe that environment plays an important role in forming the spiritual predisposition of a people.[8] Here, geographical situation may indeed hold a clue.

The early Chinese civilization is formed along the Yellow River bank, in particular, along its segment inside today's Shaanxi and Henan Provinces. The geographical situation shows a topology primarily of a vast plain washed out by the flooding of the Yellow River, covered with a deep layer of the fertile loess. Unlike in mountainous regions where people have the choice of running to higher grounds when floods hit, the primitive residents here were practically stranded. Moreover, agrarian way of life dictates a strong bonding between farmers and their land. Particularly, short of resources for hunting-gathering, the geographical situation seems to leave no other choices. Under such constraint, people are forced to maintain their way of life in farming. Being forced to be "plumbers" and "roofers" may have been the most important factor that nurtured a general atheist attitude.

It remains to be indicated, however, that the speculation on how an atheist spiritual predisposition may have been formed based on the agrarian way of life and the environmental impact is one of many approaches to the issue. The actual evolution of the civilization into its modern stage is an infinitely complicated process. It is obvious, however, that the prevalence of atheism, once established, suppressed the rise of religious beliefs from the beginning. It is a fact that none of the world's major religions was born in China. This is not to imply that religious beliefs did not exist at all. Daoism as a religion was, in effect, quite influential. The dimension, however, did not become the mainstay. It is estimated that ninety-five percent of the Chinese population today are atheists. The remaining five percent are divided among Christians (three to four percent), Daoists, Buddhists, and Muslims (one to two percent).[9]

The primitive legends reveal much of the early understanding of the universe. For the Chinese ancestors, the sky was a dome upheld by four pillars, the way a palace hall was. The roof would leak for the same reasons an old house would. Conveniently, the earth was flat like the floor of a house, and cracks may occur due to natural wearing. When the earth sank, floods would happen; when the sky leaked, torrential rain would fall. To the early Chinese, natural disasters were fully understandable and hence, fixable. If the old house can be fixed, so can the universe. Hence, since the early times, the belief that man can conquer the Nature has been a dominent belief.

Other legends demonstrated similar "great man" tendency. Shennong or the "divine farmer", for example, delivers the knowledge of agriculture. He was accredited with the invention of the plow and the hoe. Fuxi, the legendary ox tamer, teaches skills of domesticating animals. Fuxi was also accredited with inventing and promoting the very core unit of the society, the family. Huangdi, or the Yellow Emperor, is credited with the founding of the Chinese Empire in the year 2697 B.C. on the Yellow River plain. To secure the Yellow River plain for his people, Huangdi won multiple legendary battles against Chiyou, the "Horned Emperor" who dominated the south, and Yandi, the "Red Emperor" who ruled over western China. Huangdi is accredited with the invention of bows and arrows, boats, wheels, the writing system, and silk. Yao, Shun and Yu are the beginning emperors of the legendary Xia Dynasty. These well-famed predynastic emperors brought the calendar, court rituals, and flood-control techniques to their people. Emperor Yu was succeeded by fifteen emperors; the last emperor, Xia Jie, was a tyrant known for his uncontrollable cruelty. The absolute corruption leads to the replacement of Xia by the Shang Dynasty, concluding the legendary lineage.

The *Odes (shi)*

While there are epics of the legendary figures, there is also a wealth of realist literature that truthfully reflects the life of the early times. The ancient singing poems in *The Book of Odes (shi)*, for example, record year-round farming activities with painstaking efforts. Social relationships, wars, families, and marriages also leave their traces. One hears travelers chanting their roads, farmers praying for a good crop, and lovers courting. The compiling of the *The Book of Odes* is accredited to Confucius. An admirer of ancient virtuous societies, Confucius states that the very nature of the *Odes* is "purity and sincerity."

A good portion of *The Book of Odes* is composed of songs of lovers. The following is presumably sung by a young woman at a dating ceremony to extend an invitation. The tradition continues today in many southern minority communities.

Plums

Plop fall the plums; but there are still seven.
Let those gentlemen that would court me
Come while it is lucky!

Plop fall the plums; but there are still three.
Let any gentleman that would court me
Come before it is too late!

Plop fall the plums; in shallow baskets we lay them.
Any gentleman who would court me
Had better speak while there is time.[10]

Sorrow

He's to the war
for the duration;
Hens to wall-hole,
beasts to stall,
shall I not remember
him at night-fall?

He's to the war
for the duration,
fowl to their perches,
cattle to byre;
is there food enough
by their camp fire? [11]

The Dynasties

The Shang and the Zhou

The early Chinese civilization follows a sequence that is common to the pre-historic world, though the Chinese Stone Age is one of the longest. The Paleolithic Era started around 100,000 ago and lasts into the Shang Dynasty. The Shang (1600-1100 B.C.) carried features of both the Neolithic and Bronze ages, the evidence being that the cookware unearthed shows with its immature artistic designs, and that the metal in general was only sparingly used to forge production tools. Due to agricultural development and the use of a combination of refined stone tools and bronze tools, however, the Shang population rose and cities emerged.

The organizational capability of the Shang court was impressive in many ways. The Shang controlled Henan, Shandong, Anhui, Hebei, and Shanxi provinces. Zheng Zhou and Anyang were Shang capitals. Archeological finds showed chariots used around 1200 B.C. pulled by two to four horses. The city wall of Zheng Zhou was constructed in a solid rammed earth structure. It is sixty feet wide, thirty feet high, 2,385 feet long, surrounding a settlement area of about one and a quarter square miles. It is estimated that to construct a wall like this would take 10,000 workers to work more than two decades.[12]

Much different from the time of legends, under the Shang Dynasty, "Shang-Di" was worshipped as God of the supreme power. "Shang" means "superior," and "Di" means "king." It is possible that Shang-Di referred to divinity in general rather than a single divine figure. A proof to this speculation is the functionality of the idol: Shang-Di commands a variety of smaller deities of natural powers, as well as remote ancestors.

During the Shang, religious power and administrative power merged to create the absolute king. The Shang kings possessed the highest religious power. Oracle bones unearthed in Anyang show that Shang kings typically led worship ceremonies in which they received the divine wills. The typical trouble with authoritarian systems surfaced: the king's errors and weaknesses were maximized, resulting in devastative social unrest.   In effect, the Shang Dynasty was overthrown by the Zhou primarily because of the king's abuse of power.   However, it was not until the time of the Zhou Dynasty, some 500 hundred years later, that the king of China was finally and permanently associated with the sacred title of "The Son of Heaven."

Oracle Bones

The earliest Chinese writing system was discovered in Anyang of the Henan province dating back some 2,600 years from today.   While this record pales in front of the world's earliest record in writing systems discovered in Mesopotamia dating back to 3300 B.C., and the Egyptian hieroglyphs dating back to 3000 B.C., the common belief is that a much earlier predecessor could have existed.   The Chinese script was inscribed on animal bones, typically ox shoulder blades and turtle shells.   Approximately two hundred thousand pieces of inscriptions have been recovered from looting or controlled excavations, accounting for roughly five to ten percent of the original corpus of inscribed pieces.   The vocabulary of the inscriptions has been estimated at about 5,000 logographs, of which forty percent are recognized, according to the Academia Sinica of Taiwan.

Oracle ceremonies were conducted routinely in the court on a variety of issues, including hunting, marriage, birth, burial, weather, and war.   Questions asked by the diviner were inscribed on the bone shells, and then heat was applied to induce cracks on the surface.   The heat-induced cracks served as signs of divination that only the Shang kings had the right to interpret.   Because of its practical nature, oracle scripts include a rich account of events at the time, allowing historians to peek into the functions of an early authoritarian government.   From these scripts of divinity archeologists were able to assemble a profile of the broader society.

In general, a complete oracle record includes four segments:[13]

1. Preface: the time of divination and the name of the person executing the divination.
2. Charge: the question asked at the divination.
3. Prognostication: the predictions of the Shang kings based on the divined omen.
4. Verification: the actual outcomes.

The following is an example of a complete oracle record inscribed on a piece of turtle shell currently preserved by Academia Sinica of Taiwan, section *bing* #247:

> On the day of *jiashen*, the diviner asked: "Fuhao will soon give birth. Is this good?" The King interpreted the revelation stating: "If she gives birth on the day of *ding*, this is good. If she gives birth on the day of *geng*, this is auspicious." After thirty-one days, Fuhao gave birth on the day of *jiayin* to a girl. This is inauspicious.

From an artistic point of view, oracle scripts demonstrate the simplicity and elegance of a matured writing system. Judging from its consistency, balance, and stroke fluency, archeologists and artists today agree that the Shang script had long become a conventional system. Presumably, for a script to serve as a conventional vehicle of information, hundreds of years of exploration would have been necessary. Unfortunately, earlier scripts may have been written on less durable materials that eventually left very few fragments. A recent find revealed a record dating back to 8,600 years where the character for "eye" was almost the same as that found in records of 13th century B.C.[14]

Although unearthed clay utensils reveal some symbols from time to time, such records were found too sketchy and poorly preserved to carry much information. The fact that durable materials such as cooking and ceremonial ware were rarely engraved with scripts suggests that it might have been conventional to avoid such medium at the time, probably due to its rarity. Utensils, however, became popular document carriers by later Zhou times when an abundance of high quality pottery became available. There is no doubt, however, that the Shang oracle script is the source of the modern Chinese script.

Human Sacrifice

Animals and humans were sacrificed to royal ancestors or gods. Subordinates would accompany their superiors to their death to demonstrate loyalty and obligation. Slaves and captives of war were also sacrificed. Headless corpses have been unearthed both in royal tombs and in the foundations of buildings, sometimes in rather large numbers. Tomb Number 1001 in Anyang, for example, houses the ruler, ninety followers, seventy-four human sacrifices, twelve horses, and eleven dogs. Judging from the ornaments and weaponry lying next to the corpses, the male and female followers clearly included royal guards, officials, and servants.[15]

Lady Fu Hao's tomb in Anyang was probably the most complete tomb, one of the few that had never been looted. The burial site shows a human sacrifice of sixteen male and female children and adults. A wealth of burial objects was found that included 460 bronze objects including weapons and a full set of ritual goblets, tripods and basins. The collection offers the most comprehensive view of the Shang bronze. Also unearthed were 750 jade objects, seventy stone sculptures, and 6,900 cowry shells that may have been used as money. It is speculated that Lady Fuhao may have been one of King Wuding's wives. The oracle text cited in the section "Oracle Bones" most likely concerned her pregnancy.[16]

Age of Bronze

Bronze is an alloy of copper and tin that does not occur in nature. In ancient times, lead was commonly used and may have been intentionally added to copper to increase the hardness of the metal, which resulted in bronze. There is also speculation that bronze may have resulted from the impurity of ores that contained both led and copper. Both metals could be conveniently mined within the vicinity of Anyang of the Honan Province. The earliest bronze objects, discovered in Erlitou of the Henan Province, date back to 1700-1600 B.C. Cups, goblets, steamers, and cauldrons are the most common forms of the Shang bronze. Some items weigh up to 200 pounds. To pour such heavy objects, according to some scientists, the melted bronze would have to be led to the cast through a heated pathway, a technology that is considered impressive even from today's standards.[17]

Early Shang bronze carried realistic and vivid designs of beasts and birds. By the late Zhou times, the designs became more abstract and refined. One characteristic was animal designs being no more explicit.[18] By this time, a new function, probably a more important one, was added to the bronze art: document preservation. Records of important events were inscribed on or inside of bronze objects. Inside one of the winery objects believed to be crafted around 1050 B.C., the following scripture was found:

> King Wu campaigned against Shang. It was in the morning of the day of *jiazi*. King Wu performed *su* and *ding* sacrifices and announced that his army had routed the Shang. On the day of *xinwei*, the King was at Jian encampment and awarded the *General Deputy* title to Duke of Zhan. A vessel made of the Li metal was crafted as the reward.[19]

Engraving scripts onto bronze surface required special tools that had an impact on the style of strokes; meanwhile, the official nature of these inscriptions resulted in a canonized documentary style. Both elements led to the creation of *jinwen*, or the "metal scripture style." Different from oracle bone scriptures in which angular strokes and unequal sizes of characters are the norm, *jinwen* are refined showing rounded contours and uniform sizes. Although the characters still show signs of pictographs, significant abstraction has already been made. *Jinwen* represents an important step towards a standardized writing system that was finally put in place by the Qin Dynasty. In fact, the wide use of bronze was of such a tremendous significance that the Shang and the following Zhou dynasties are known as China's "Golden Age," whereby "golden" refers to both the bronze art and the prosperity of philosophies which will be introduced in the next chapter.

The Shang Government

There were five capitals during the Shang Dynasty, of which Anyang was the last one. Although no detailed record of the Shang government legacy has been unearthed, some oracle inscriptions allowed historians and archeologists to reconstruct a profile. It is believed that the Shang kings typically ran a kingdom in a patriarchic style. They gave orders, patrolled the territory, conducted hunts, and led religious ceremonies. The royal army was 3,000 to 5,000 soldiers strong, consisting of footmen and horse drawn chariots. While the Shang kings had tremendous authority, his status was not associated with the highest power the way the kings of the Zhou Dynasty were. The Shang kings were not yet "Sons of Heaven."

Royal succession was hereditary as a matter of a most widely adopted primitive convention. This tradition was strictly followed in Shang time. The throne was normally passed on to a son of the royal house. In rare occasions, it was passed to the brother of the legitimate heir. It is also known that the "feudal system" of the Shang was essentially a tribute system based on the hierarchy in which the Shang kings rewarded their relatives and generals, often on meritorious grounds, with fief domains. In return, these lords of the fiefs paid tribute to the royal house, both as a symbol of loyalty and as material subvention to the court's expenses.

The lords collected tributes from the farmers that farmed their land. Farming was the work of entire villages rather than individual households. Eventually, farmers started to gain their own land while working for their lords. Families became the predominant farming units by the mid to late Zhou Dynasty. War captives had a tragic fate in a slavery society as such where, in addition to being labors they were also sacrificed in frequent worship ceremonies dedicated to Shang-Di, family ancestors, and in funeral ceremonies.

Farmers' dwellings were round or rectangular semi-subterranean houses from nine to fifteen feet in diameter. The entrance opens to a flight of descending steps. Millet, rice and wheat were planted with hoes, spades, and stone sickles. The water buffalo was added to the list of domesticated animals that already included pigs, dogs, cattle, sheep, horses, and chickens. A palatial building was excavated in 1977 at Zhengzhou of the Henan Province, dating from the 16th century B.C., was probably used by courtiers. During the laying of the foundations both human beings and animals were ritually killed and interred. About 100 human skulls, mostly sawn off across the eyebrow and the ear, reveal a highly stratified society in which slaves and prisoners of war were used in worship ceremonies.[20] Human sacrifice lingered until the 5th century B.C. when Confucius condemned such ritual practices.

As more territory was added to the limited monarchy, the government lost its effectiveness and authority. The lords were becoming disobedient, as they constantly enlarged their fiefdoms through wars with their neighbors. In the meantime, the Shang kingdom was sinking into corruption and extravagance. The last Shang king, King XinZhou, was allegedly obsessed with women and the use of cruelty against dissidents. The popular novel *The Romance of the Eastern Zhou States*[21] relates that in order to make his most favored concubine, Baosi, smile, King XinZhou set off battle-alert signals and called in frontier troops to his rescue. When the troops arrived at the palace, King XinZhou told them that nothing had happened. Lady Baosi finally cracked a smile, amused with the frustration on the faces of the dumfounded generals. When finally the troops of the Zhou Kingdom arrived from the west to overthrow the Shang Dynasty, none of his generals answered to his stress calls.

Zhou Dynasty

The succeeding dynasty, the Zhou (1100-256 B.C.), was primarily a Bronze Age society marked by a wider usage of bronze tools and weapons. This transition opened a new world indeed. Under the Zhou Empire, not only productivity gyrated, but also and particularly an ideological leap forward took place, which was represented by the emergence of the classic Chinese philosophies.

The Zhou was possibly a tribal community roaming between the Qiang (proto-Tibetan) communities and Shang's domains. Their history indicates that their ancestors may have lived among pastoral communities in the north before relocating into the upper region of the Wei River, in what is now the province of Shaanxi. The Zhou people possessed advanced agricultural skills and became a formidable power on the western border of the Shang kingdom. Although the Shang controlled the entire Central Plain, Zhou quickly became a serious threat. Finally, worn out by the military campaigns launched against the nomadic tribes along the northern borders and plagued with corruption, the Shang Dynasty was destroyed. Under the new Zhou regime, China's feudal system went into a more mature stage.

Son of Heaven

The Zhou Dynasty was founded by King Wen (11th century B.C.) who successfully expanded Zhou's territory by acquiring regions west and northwest of the Shang kingdom. After his death, his son, King Wu, defeated the Shang in a surprise attack. The new capital was established at Haojing, near the modern Xian City. King Wu made it clear to the nation that the Zhou people shouldered the "Mandate of

Heaven (*tian ming*)" to conquer the corrupted Shang regime. Thereafter, Zhou King became the son of heaven. Zhou King constantly warned his people that the mandate of Heaven may be taken away from them if they would fail to deserve such a trust. Zhou's military campaigns, therefore, were backed by justice and particularly by the higher order. Much of King Wu's declaration is preserved in the *The Book of Documents (Shangshu)*. The Duke of Zhou, following the successful conquer by King Wu, was able to consolidate the newly founded kingdom and expand the territory eastward, bringing the entire Yellow River plain under control.

As mentioned earlier, the newly acquired title "Son of Heaven," as illustrated on the right, entitled the Zhou kings more than ever to an absolute power. In reality, the "Heaven" of the Zhou Dynasty was similar to Shang Dynasty's idol "Shang-Di" which literally means "the Lord above," or a conglomerate of deities. Notice that the character for "Heaven," *tian* is the combination of the pictograph of a "big man" with arms stretched wide and a "cover" over his head represented by the symbol "—." While the idols were similar, the tie between the king and the supreme religious figure was a powerful invention of the Zhou kings. The practical  significance is evident: on the one hand, with the backing of the "Mandate of Heaven" the Zhou conquered the Shang and consolidated the new regime with relative ease; on the other hand, from this time on, interpretation and implementation of the Heaven's mandate will be solely the business of the kings. This is a double-edged sword, indeed. Given the heavenly power, good kings will be able to accomplish good deeds, while bad kings will have their way, too.

Being aware of human weaknesses, the founders of the Zhou developed a code called *li* (the Code), the literary meaning of which is "courtesy code." The principles of *li,* however, were not limited to rules of good manners. In fact, they were essentially about defining the boundaries in ranking, protocol, and behavior. Since *li* served as a constraint to the nobles, it is fairly comparable to a constitution at an early stage.

Li, as a code of conduct, involved fundamental principles of justice as well as arts of administration. However, "equality in front of the law" was not acceptable at the time. To the commoners the system of *xing* or "penalty" was applied. The old rules stipulated that *li* was not for the commoners, nor was *xing* applicable to the nobles. Confucius considered *li* as guiding principles for an ideal society and urged people to model their conduct accordingly. Confucius stated, "Whatever is not compliant with *li* should not be looked at; whatever transgresses *li* should not be allowed in behavior."

Well-field System

During the Zhou Dynasty, the feudal system that germinated under the Shang regime was further developed. First of all, rulers of fiefdoms were gaining more independence, as they possessed not only political and economic authority over their domains, but also military forces, all of which made them *de facto* independent states. Rewarding the kinship and high-level officials with fiefs was originally a system aimed at rallying loyalty. As the degree of freedom of the fief domains increased, the system started to decline. Eventually the fiefdoms transitioned step by step into full-fledged states leaving the central government in isolation and leading the country into constant bloody conflicts.

With the Zhou Kingdom disintegrating, farmers living under the fief lords gained more freedom. Instead of working primarily in larger work units, farmers became mostly "landlords" paying duties to the duke of the fiefdom. Under a system as such, the lord-vassal ties declined, which led to an unreliable inflow of tribute to the court. The Zhou court imposed, thus, the *Well-field System* in which four or five families had the obligation of farming a privileged farmland dedicated to the tributary purpose. The system was diagrammed with two Chinese characters — "well" and "field," as illustrated above, hence the *Well-field System*. The system allowed farmers to keep the surplus to themselves after paying tribute to the court. The reduction of crop yield at the time, due to over farming, was also a factor that prompted the court to enforce the *Well-field System*. The impact of the system on loyalty attrition was eminent: it shifted the vassal-lord relationship from the feudal kinship bonding to a materialistic relationship. This new kind of relationship was an important disintegrating factor that led to the collapse of the feudal system.

Western Zhou, Eastern Zhou and Warring States

While there are more than one ways to divide historical periods, there appear to be two distinct periods of the Zhou Dynasty: the Western Zhou (1105-770 B.C.) with its capital city in Haojing, near modern Xian, and the Eastern Zhou (771-256 B.C.) with its capital city in Luoyang. The conventional names of "Eastern Zhou" and "Western Zhou" resulted from the shift of the capital location that occurred in 770 B.C. under the pressure from ethnic groups in the west. The new capital was located to the east of the previous one.

The Western Zhou is further divisible into two periods:

1) The period from 771 B.C. to 402 B.C. was a relatively peaceful time during which some 150 states coexisted. This period is also known as the "Spring and Autumn Era," a name taken from a Confucian classic "Spring and Autumn Annals" which recorded the history from 722 to 481 B.C..

2) Between 403 B.C. and 211 B.C. China was plunged into a bloodbath. During approximately 200 years, states fought against one another in a wide-scaled civil war. These years were conventionally called the "Warring States Era," a name taken from a well known book recording events of this period, *The Intrigues of the Warring States.* As conflicts intensified during the entire period of 192 years, the number of adversary states was reduced to a dozen or so toward the end. The Zhou house was destroyed in 256 B.C., marking the official end of the Zhou Dynasty. Continued fighting further reduced the number of states to seven: the Qi, the Chu, the Yan, the Han, the Qin, the Zhao, and the Wei. Shortly afterward, China was reunified by the state of Qin in 221 B.C.

While the Warring States was an era of sufferings and bloodshed, it was also a time of heroic deeds and a treasure trove of literary and philosophical masterpieces. During this period, classic philosophies arose from the chaos, and science and technology advanced by leaps and bounds. This was a rare moment in the Chinese history when the Chinese ingenuity and dynamism, under the challenge of constant life and death struggles, offered a most brilliant show that would never be surpassed by later generations.

Civil Service and Public Education

The Zhou Dynasty had a much more refined government than its predecessor, which was reflected in its sophisticated bureaucracy. Government positions could be sought in three ways: inheritance, recommendation, and examination. Higher positions were primarily inherited. Some positions were occupied by the wise and competent who were recommended to the court. Using examinations to select civil servants was embryonic at the time of the Zhou, but it gained predominance by the time of the Sui (A.D. 589-618) and the Tang (A.D. 618-907) dynasties. On the other hand, there was clear consciousness of the importance of maintaining a healthy and effective government, as the *Code* (*li*) stipulated that offices must be occupied by competent people. Officials at the county level had the obligation of identifying the wise and competent and recommending them to the court. Failing to do so would result in punishment and even removal from office.[22] Zhou's school system was based on public education at various administrative levels. The system is divisible into four basic categories: *xiao, xu, yang, xue* as illustrated in Chinese writing on the right. *Xue* referred to the royal university operated by the court, taught by government ministers, and attended by the offsprings of noble descent. The other three types of schools, *xiao, xu,* and *yang,* were local schools at the village level. According to the *Code* or the *li,* in addition to assuming administrative duties and responsibilities, officials must be qualified educators as well. The qualities of a governor and those of an educator were not to be separated, because a good governor must be a competent teacher at the same time. The society was mainly divided into four occupational categories including officials, farmers, artisans, and soldiers. Vocational training schools existed for every category. Local schools were held in public squares to attract people to education, or to give education a prominent place in public life.[23]

Time of the Classics

The Zhou time is often referred to as China's golden age of ideas. Philosophers traveled from state to state preaching their insights and ideals to kings and lords who eagerly sought ways to conquer, to survive, or simply to improve their own well-being. While Confucius promoted the philosophy of righteousness and engagement, Lao Zi and Zhuang Zi preached Daoism according to which the non-action would be the ultimate course to happiness. Mencius based his theory of benevolence on the good nature of the mankind, which was against Xun Zi's Legalism that arose from the belief that because human nature is vicious, "reward and punishment" would be the way to order. Sun Zi's theory on military maneuver offered guidance to winning without bloodshed. A more detailed narrative of these theories follows in the next chapter.

The Qin (221-206 B.C.)

Centuries of fighting reduced the number of Zhou states from over 150 to only seven. The Qin, the westernmost state protected by rough terrain, secretly prepared itself for a reunification war while other states were fighting among themselves. In addition, Qin emperors employed legalist administrators, such as Li Si and Shang Yang, to strengthen the legal system. The legalists drastically reformed the government by cutting bureaucracy and by rigorously applying the rule of law. All government positions were assigned based on competence alone, excluding influence from nobility and kinship. Punishment was served according to the law to any violators including the higher strata. Corruption was eliminated. Qin's healthy and dynamic government guaranteed a successful reunification campaign.

On the other hand, the Qin society was transformed into a police society in which reporting on any anti-government actions was rewarded with jade and gold. Similarly, those who dared to transgress would receive the most severe punishment. Cruel and inhumane as the system may appear, the legalist reforms provided the most useful advantages that had assured the final victory over the lower six states long before any military action was launched.

The opportunity of reunification finally arrived when a young and competent prince of only nine, Ying Zheng, came to power in 247 B.C. After two and a half decades of preparation and military campaigning, in 221 B.C., Qin reunited China. From the founding of the Qin Dynasty until 206 B.C., a legacy of dictatorship was established. Qin's authoritarian tradition was passed down from one generation to another almost unfailingly, and eventually came to the hands of Mao Zedong, the ultimate Chinese communist leader of the 20th century. Mao, a self-declared worshiper of the Qin Emperor since his youth, was a ruthless practitioner of dictatorship. Under Mao, China plunged into decades of political strives at the cost of millions of lives.

Jun-xian System

Sima Qian in his famous *The Records of the Grand Historian* recorded much of the Qin regime. Qin's administration best modeled after the theoretical structure that had been brought forth by legalist philosophers during the 4th century B.C. According to the legalist model, the rule of law must be above all; priority must be given to state interest; individuality must be suppressed. The law would know no violators, neither would the King's words. To achieve this end, the Qin government adopted several policies that all became part of the authoritarian legacy.

The division of the country into twenty-three provinces today, for example, traces back to the Qin time. The Qin Emperor, drawing a lesson from Zhou's feudal division of the country that finally resulted in warring states, decided to adopt the *Jun-Xian System* or the "commandery/county" system. China was divided into thirty-six commanderies accordingly, and each commandery was further divided into counties. Governors of the commanderies were assigned by the central government and rotated on a regular basis to avoid accumulation of individual power. By so doing, the emperor ingeniously solidified his control over local regions.

Standardization

Another measure adopted to guarantee the unification was to standardize measure, road track, and writing in order to maximally keep out local variations. Before Qin's reunification, different states used different measuring systems. The ounce, for example, weighed differently from one state to another; the road tracks for horse-pulled carts were in different widths. Similarly, writing systems varied widely, some regions using the *big cursive*, some using the *small cursive*, while other variations existed. For a unified country under one government, this situation posed an inconvenience for tax collection, transportation, and particularly, administrative management. As a way of strengthening the control, the Qin government implemented a standardized system including a standard measure system, a unified road track system, and a standardized writing system that was based on the *small cursive*.

Bao-Jia System

Strict control was a hallmark of the Qin Empire. Lawbreakers were punished without mercy. As reported by Sima Qian in his *Records of the Grand Historian*, severance of hands and feet was common punishment for small crimes, to the extent that people maimed one way or another could be seen everywhere in Capital Xianyang. To facilitate control, residential areas were organized into the *Bao* (a five-family community) and *Jia* (a ten-family community) systems. Within these communities, members of families had the responsibility of watching and reporting on their neighbors whenever they detected suspicious actions or speeches. The crime reporter would be rewarded generously; the perpetrator would be punished without mercy. In addition to "neighborhood watch," a secondary function of the *Bao-Jia System* lies in its mobility in responding to military emergencies. Every community would turn into a military unit almost immediately when called upon.

Arms Control

Tradition has it that after the unification war was over, the Qin Emperor ordered to have weapons collected from every household, melted, and cast into eight gigantic statues. These statues were said to have been erected in the capital city of Xianyang. Ordinary people were not permitted to possess weapons. Five families were allowed to share one kitchen knife that had to be chained.

Brainwashing and Ideological Control

It was first prescribed by the legalist theory that law books should be used as educational material, and teachers should come from the rank of county officials or law enforcement officers. The Qin Emperor feared liberal opinions more than tens of thousands of enemy forces. To control people's thoughts, the emperor ordered to have all books confiscated and burned, with the exception of "useful" books such as manuals of farming and engineering. Moreover, the emperor had 460 recalcitrant scholars from all over the country buried alive, setting an example to those who would dare to denigrate the emperor's authority.

Building the Great Wall

Once reunification was accomplished, the primary concern of the Qin was shifted to defending its northern borders from the devastations caused by Xiongnu and other northern minorities. Tens of thousands of farmers and penal laborers, some say 300,000, were drafted. They were sent to construct rammed earth walls to connect the old city walls left by the conquered northern states. The Great Wall stretches 3,750 miles from its eastern end, the Shanghai-Guan Pass, to its western end, the Jiayu-Guan Pass inside the Gansu Province. Its main strategic function was to defend China from frequent invasions by northern nomadic tribes. How effective could the Wall have really been in achieving the intended goal has been a debated issue ever since. The story goes that when the Chinggis Khan first saw the Great Wall, he remarked that the Great Wall would be no stronger than the men behind it. Indeed, the Mongols later crossed the Great Wall and dominated China for a century.

The "First Emperor"

The Emperor of Qin, Ying Zheng, labeled himself *shi huangdi* or "the Founding Emperor." Being the founding emperor, he managed every detail of the state affairs, reading five cartloads of documents (books made of bamboo strips) daily, and inspecting the realm on a regular basis. Having survived three assassination attempts and being concerned about his weakening health, the emperor became obsessed with secrets of immortality. He allegedly sent a trusted official by the name of Xu Fu and hundreds of young males and females out to the sea in search of the mythical Penglai Mountain where longevity secrets could be found. He had tens of thousands of farmers drafted to build the most pompous royal palace in Xianyang and the grand Lishan Tomb. Guarding the tomb were thousands of live size terracotta warriors lined up in battle formations. The king died in 210 B.C. at the age of forty-nine during his last patrol to the east. The emperor's body was transported back to Xianyang secretly. To cover the odor of the emperor's decaying body, dead fish were loaded in the mortuary cart, as reported in Sima Qian's *Records of the Grand Historian* .

After Emperor Yingzheng died, the Qin Empire disintegrated in short order. The second Prince Hu Hai usurped the throne after having his brother, Prince Fu Su, the legitimate heir, murdered. The incompetent new emperor came into power at a chaotic time when people were on the brink of rebellion after having endured years of harsh treatment under the founding emperor's reign. It was by coincidence, however, that a group of draftees heading for their frontier assignment were delayed in a downpour. Knowing that they would be beheaded for missing the deadline, they killed the commanders and revolted. They were joined by thousands of people. Eventually, in the year 206 B.C., a leader of a peasant revolt, Liu Bang (r. 202-195 B.C.), declared himself emperor of the Han and founded the Han Dynasty. Changan or the modern Xian City was chosen to be the capital city of the Han.

Close-up: The Emperor's Mausoleum

Recent discoveries showed that the Qin Emperor was the first in Chinese history to construct a mausoleum city, coffin chambers, and even palace halls in the mausoleum. The emperor also started the ritual of building chambers for those buried alive to keep him company. Archeologists were surprised, however, that the mausoleum did not include a tomb chamber for the empress.

The 2,200-year-old burial structure houses some 7,000 terracotta horses and warriors. Located in Xi'an, the site covers 2.13 square kilometers. The four-layered mausoleum, like a well-structured city, includes an underground palace located in the inner city and an outer city. During forty years of excavation, archeologists identified constructions over hundreds of square kilometers and more than 600 tombs built for a massive human sacrifice.

The ramparts of the inner city and outer city measure twelve kilometers long in total, similar to that of Xian city in time of the Ming Dynasty (1368-1644). The underground palace lies under the grave mound in the south of the inner city symbolizing the emperor's real palace when he was alive. The structure occupies two thirds of the southern part of the inner city which is populated with burial chambers of the emperor's concubines.

In the area between the inner and outer cities, archeologists discovered a chamber for horses, thirty-one chambers for birds and rare animals, forty-eight tombs for imperial concubines buried alive, and three burial sites for gardeners and temple guards. Outside the outer city, along with the well-known terracotta horses and warriors, archeologists found ninety-eight chambers for small stables and more tombs for court servants. The gates of the inner and outer cities in both the west and the east were built in the form of courtyards. The city wall in the mausoleum has cloisters on both sides with turrets at the four corners.

(Source of data: Xinhua News Agency)[24]

The Han (206 B.C. - A.D.220)

The Han government learned a good lesson from Qin's failure and governed in a benevolent manner. Han's founding Emperor Gaozu Liu Bang (r. 202-195 B.C.) took to heart the Daoist admonition, "If men are not afraid to die, it is of no avail to threaten them with death."[25] Building a benevolent government, however, was by no means easy. In several ways, the Emperor Gaozu managed to exercise a strong control and yet without resorting to undue harshness. One measure adopted was to establish a government office called the "Music Bureau" to collect folk songs. The band of the royal palace would later perform these songs before the emperor and his ministers. The intention was to detect the mood of the people by listening to their songs. The *yuefu* or the "Music Bureau's Collection" became a most treasured literary heritage. Credit should be given to Confucius whose theory became a source of moral guidance for the Han government. Confucius once said, "The hungry sings his belly; the traveler sings his road."

Another measure adopted by Emperor Gao Zu was to drastically reduce taxes and government-imposed corvee three years in a row to let the war-torn economy recover. In order to speed the recovery of agricultural production, he reduced conscription and ordered officers, soldiers, and refugees to return home, providing them with houses and farmlands. He also enacted a law to release slaves and restricted the merchant classes from building private gardens on farmlands. For these reasons, Emperor Gao Zu's reign was lauded to be a successful "ruling through non-action." Untroubled by wars and natural disasters, the people lived in peace. This resulted in an increase in the population and the development of manufacturing industries and commerce.

Continuing with Gao Zu's legacy, Emperor Wu Di, or the "Martial Emperor" (r.141-87 B.C.), further curbed the influence from aristocracy and rich merchants whose plans often meant pressure on farming. Moreover, the emperor levied a heavy tax on inheritance, forcing the rich to pay their share to the state. Nevertheless, industries and commerce demonstrated prosperous growth. The court monopolized the production of trading of iron, salt, and liquor whereby guaranteeing the needed flow of income.

With the economy effectively recovered, Emperor Wu Di was able to do what a Chinese emperor typically had on his mind: territorial expansion. Han's control was extended over vast regions from Korea in the east to Central Asia in the west and Vietnam in the south. Garrisons were established in remote regions that later became trading settlements or cities.

Emergence of Civil Service Examination

During the Han, Confucianism became the state philosophy under the reign of Emperor Wu Di. The Imperial Academy was established. Scholars were hired by the Academy to research on the five Confucian classics — *The Book of Changes (I-ching), The Book of Documents, The Book of Odes, The Book of Rites,* and *The Spring and Autumn Annals.* Confucianism contributed tremendously to stabilizing the society with its principles of ritual observation, filial piety, respect, devotion, learning, and moral virtues. These principles were promoted to the height of moral guidance for both nobles and commoners. For the first time, Confucianism became the blueprint of an ideal society.

In administration, Han inherited Qin's official appointment system that had proven to be effective in curbing aristocracy. The fief system continued to be used on the side to reward generals and royal family members. However, a new channel of recruitment through civil service examination was gaining popularity. Later, the system became the main venue to officialdom during the Sui Dynasty (589-618). Presumably, the emperor was eager to seek the truly talented to serve the country and to avoid resurgence of family politics.

The rise of the civil service examination was partly due to the failure of the recommendation system. In a decree of 196 B.C., Emperor Gao Zu had urged officials at all levels to recommend the wise and the virtuous (fang zheng xian liang) to fill government positions. Punishment would be assessed to those who failed to follow the order. The recommendation system, however, was soon found exploited by corrupted officials to fulfill their own interests. Offices were taken by relatives and cronies of high officials, most of whom did not have the least qualification. A folk song at the time complained, "The doctorate candidate can't read. The virtuous candidate abandons his parent. The moral candidate has his greedy thoughts disguised. The future generalissimo is as coward as a fly."[26] Apparently, the recommendation system needed to be fixed.

In the year 132 B.C., a proposal from a literary official by the name of Zuo Xiong prompted the court to implement examinations as a measure to stop the loophole. Test subjects focused on "family rules" that were primarily Confucianism-based principles. In addition, writing skills, administrative skills, martial arts, and military knowledge were in the test batteries. The new selection system represented a progress in the direction of an equality and competence-based civil service system. It provided the much-needed motivation to talented candidates to serve the country. For the Han dynasty to become one of the longest and strongest dynasties in Chinese history, the reform in civil service recruiting system played a crucial role.

The Silk Road

The Han suffered from raids by the Xiongnu in the north. By the time of Emperor Wu Di, the proto-mongol nomadic tribes had organized themselves into a confederation. The Xiongnu gloried themselves for horse riding skills and fast military attacks. As early as Qin Dynasty, the Xiongnu had begun to devastate the northern border causing significant damage. In 213 B.C. the Qin had to send General Meng Tian and 100,000 troops into the Ordos region to attack Xiongnu. A year earlier, the Great Wall was built to defend the northern border as a result of the instability, but had proven to be largely insufficient.

The Han government's approach was more tactful. Emperor Wu Di first used the conciliatory strategy, delivering gifts and goods to Xiongnu tribes periodically. The strategy of feeding the enemy, however, not only failed to secure the northern border, but also led to more devastating invasions, one of which reached as close as a hundred miles from the capital city Changan.

Military actions became the next choice. However, Emperor Wu Di was not satisfied with simply chasing the Xiongnu forces into Siberia. The emperor came up with a long-term plan that aimed at forcing the Xiongnu out of their habitat. In 139 B.C., the emperor sent Ambassador Zhang Qian to the Western Region, or today's Afganistan region, to seek alliance. One of Xiongnu's enemies in the west was the Yuezhi tribe whose king was killed by Xiongnu. Yuezhi was certainly eager to be Han's ally and to take revenge on Xiongnu for the long accumulated hatred.

Zhang Qian's mission opened up the history of trade between Changan and the Western Region. Along the 4,350 miles, the Silk Road passed Batria and the Ancient Afganistan. Through this road, the Persians and Europeans traveled a long way into China to trade horses for silk. Zhang Qian made a detailed description of countries and cities along the Silk Road, one of which was Ferghana that grew wheat and grapes for wine, and had fine horses that sweated blood. By 44 B.C., the year Caesar died, silk products from China had already reached Rome. In the opposite direction, the Silk Road opened the door to Western arts, music, sports and religions. One example is the import of Polo, a Central Asian game popular in Iran. Archeologists have discovered figurines of polo players, for example, in Han tombs.

In 55 B.C., the Xiongnu Confederation broke up. Some tribes surrendered and became Han's tributary states, delivering tribute gifts and hostages; others migrated west into Eurasia. The northern border was eventually secured. Later on, Emperor Wu Di controlled the northeast wielding strong political and cultural influence over Korea and Japan. From Indochina up to the Red River Delta was also annexed.

Prosperity of Arts and Science

The Han Dynasty was not only known for military expansions, but also famed for a great prosperity of arts and scientific inventions. In the second century, Zhang Heng invented quantitative cartography which was used to map geographical locations on a grid system similar to the Cartesian system. Zhang Heng was also the inventor of the first seismograph in A.D 132. The mechanism was given the name the "seismic weather coq." The barrel-shaped instrument consists of a bronze barrel with a central pendulum triggering system and eight dragonheads on the outer wall pointing to eight directions. In every dragon's mouth is a bronze ball waiting to drop into the open mouth of a bronze toad sitting underneath. When an earthquake strikes, the pendulum causes one of the dragon heads to drop the metal ball into the toad's mouth, which would yield a loud alerting sound. This way, the observer would be able to estimate the direction of the epicenter accordingly.

During the Han Dynasty paper was invented. The earliest paper dates between 87 B.C. and A.D. 140. Cai Lun was credited with producing the first paper from hemp fiber. The fiber was ground to make pulp that was applied to a flat surface to dry. While paper played a more and more important role in life, paper clothing having been discovered from Han tombs, bamboo strips continued to be a trusted medium for documentation in conjunction with silk. In addition, the calligraphy written on bamboo strips represented an artistic style with a unique elegance.

Excessive military expansion prompted navigational technology to answer the challenges of transporting troops. Rudders and masts were invented between the first and the second century of the Christian era. Blood circulation was discovered in the second century B.C., about two thousand years earlier than William Harvey's discovery in 1628. The *Yellow Emperor's Manual of Corporeal Medicine*, accredited to the legendary Yellow Emperor and written down around the early Han, describes the human body as having two circulation systems — the blood and the *Chi*("air"). The vascular system was found to be channels of blood pumped by the heart. The *Chi* was described as propelled by the lungs.

In the area of arts and literature, *Records of the Grand Historian (Shiji)* authored by Sima Qian (145-85 B.C.) was the first comprehensive and systematic history book in 130 chapters that cover from the legendary emperors to Emperor Wu Di of the Han Dynasty.

Han's Fall

Primary factors that contributed to the downfall of the great Han Empire included adversary impact from the warfare against Xiongnu, the internal crisis caused by factions among members of the aristocracy, and the interference of eunuchs in politics. As the central government weakened, a dominos effect started: civil wars and famine became the routine of daily life. Hungry peasants finally rebelled against the court and replaced a variety of short-lived government forms, the first of which was known as the Three Kingdoms (220-256). These three local powers, the Wei, the Shu and the Wu, respectively belonged to three strong warlord families. The Wei eventually defeated the Shu and the Wu, and founded the Western Jin Dynasty (256-316).

However, stability did not last long before China was divided again, and this time, by the natural demarcation line, the Yangtze River. In the north, five ethnic groups including Xiongnu, Xianbei, Jie, Di and Qiang ruled in sixteen kingdoms (304-439). In the south, five short-lived Chinese dynasties ruled in succession. These Chinese courts were the Eastern Jin (317-420), the Song (420-479), the Qi (479-502), the Liang (502-557), and the Chen (557-589). Once again, chaos was followed by unity. The Sui (589-618) pieced together a fragmented state and paved the way to yet another long-term prosperity of the Tang Dynasty (618-907).

Era of Poetry

The Sui Dynasty was a short-lived regime. Under the reign of Emperor Wen Di Yang Jian (r.581-604), China was unified with its capital settled in Luoyang. By this time, a profound cultural change had taken place. Buddhism that was introduced to China during the first century of the Christian era had become widespread. The incoming religion added an important dimension to the Chinese thinking, which will be discussed in the next chapter. The first ruler, Emperor Wen Di, was a Buddhist patron himself. His effort in promoting the religion won him the title the Great Cakravartin King.

As usual, the period of peace led to a fast economic recovery. Once again, instability interrupted the economic rebound. Emperor Wen Di was soon assassinated by his ambitious son Yuang Guang who became Emperor Yang Di (r.604-618). To guarantee tax flow, Emperor Yang Di ordered the Grand Canal to be built to link Luo Yang, the capital city in the north, to Yangzhou city on the Yangtze River. Thirst of territorial expansion, the emperor sent an army to invade *Tuyuhun,* a Tibetan-Xianbei state in Northern Tibet. In the south, the Sui controlled up to northern Vietnam. In 612, the emperor dispatched a large army of a million men to conquer Korea. Wars against Korea's Koguryo Kingdom had such a disastrous impact on Sui's own economy that the emperor had to call off the military campaign. In 615, the Sui was badly defeated in the west by the Eastern Turks. The empire started to disintegrate. Emperor Yang Di eventually fled from the capital, and was soon assassinated in 618.

Rebel troops led by Li Yuan and his son Li Shimin established the Tang Dynasty in 618. Li Yuan or Emperor Gaozong (r.618-626) and Li Shimin who succeeded him to be Emperor Taizong (r.626-649) were both known as rulers of great achievements in history.

The Grand Canal

The Grand Canal, a 1,200-mile long manmade river, was constructed due to political and economic necessity. The first phase of the project was completed during the Sui between 605-609 that linked Luoyang to Yangzhou. The second phase was completed during the Tang Dynasty. The new segments extended the Canal to Beijing in the north and Hanzhou in the south. While the project was considered extravagant and blamed for being inhumanely labor-intensive at the time, its economic benefit was tremendous. The Canal not only served the emperor's goals, but also benefits the economy today. The most unique value of the Grand Canal lies in the fact that unlike all major natural rivers that flow from the west to the east following China's geo-configuration, the Grand Canal is the only waterway of economic importance to link the north and the south.

Civil Service Examination

The civil service examination was started in the Han Dynasty as a result of a reform in 132 B.C. Before this time, officials were recommended based on moral qualities, clean personal records, and a good reputation. During the Sui Dynasty, written examinations were standardized and adopted by the court as a primary venue to becoming government officials. Candidates were tested at the county level first, and then, again at the provincial levels. Candidates who survived provincial tests were finally tested at the royal palace. Test topics were mostly drawn from the Confucian classics. The ultimate goal of the civil service examination was to select officials on the basis of their merit rather than affiliation or kinship. A system like this was inspired by the fundamental principles of Confucianism. Nevertheless, because schooling was not available to every commoner, most winners were from the noble and the rich strata.

Cultural Prosperity of Tang (618 - 907)

During the first few years of the Tang Dynasty, a laissez-faire policy, similar to Han Emperor Gao Zu's "non-action," encouraging farmers to ramp up production. As the economy pulled off the ground, the Tang China soon became the most powerful nation in Asia. One aspect of Tang's prosperity was reflected in its variety of liberal arts. Poetry writing and appreciation became the most fashionable intellectual activity. The best poets would be given the most prestigious positions at the Royal University. As a matter of pre-requisite, high-level officials must possess poetry-writing skills as well. In this sense, the Tang was indeed the most poetic dynasty in Chinese history.

The Grand Canal was extended for about 1,200 miles reaching Beijing in the north and Hanzhou in the south. The extension of this north and south bound waterway allowed the government to access a wider range of income resources. To increase the bandwidth of transportation, an imperial road was also paved along the Canal. Taking advantage of new transportation facilities, large cities rose in the north and in the south. The increased variety of urban life, in return, pushed various Tang arts to a new height. The climax of poetry, for example, was directly related to the prosperity of urban culture.

The Tang maintained good economic and diplomatic relationships with Central Asian states, many of which became Tang's satellite states. Deploying an array of strategies including strengthening fortifications, marriage diplomacy, trade, and split-and-conquer, the Tang Empire assumed over-lordship along the Silk Road in the mid 7th century. The Tang subjugated the Eastern Turks and the Western Turks by 648, pushing the Turkish groups westward into West Asia and Europe. By marrying out a princess to a Tibetan prince in 641, the Tang government was able to maintain its control over one of the most unreachable and rebellious ethnic groups. By the 7th century, Korea, Japan, and Vietnam became tributary vassal states. Tang's influence was extended over a vast area from Southern Siberia to Southeast Asia, and westward through Tibet and Central Asia to the Caspian Sea.

An open society must first be an orderly society. The Tang government was a vanguard in systematically addressing the issue of building a legal system. The code of 653 had more than 500 articles specifying penalties on a long list of crimes. However, within a dictatorial system, due to the unavoidable existence of classes above the law, the rule of law has its limit. For that reason, the Tang code was essentially a penal code system, rather than a code of rights and responsibilities. Amid the glory of expansion was hidden the onset of the downfall. After suffering a disastrous defeat in 751 by the Arabs at Talas, north of Ferghana, Tang's suzerainty in the west collapsed. In 755, An Lushan, a frontier general trusted by Emperor Xuanzong, led a rebellion aimed at destroying the corrupt government. The civil war lasted for eight years before the rebel troops finally took Luoyang and Changan, causing the emperor to flee to Sichuan. During the flight, Emperor Xuanzong's guards executed Yang Guozhong and Yang Guifei. The former was a corrupt but trusted high-level official, while the latter the emperor's most favorite concubine.

The Tang Dynasty did not perish because of the coup. However, financial crisis, internal power struggle, and a peasant rebellion that took place in 874 led by Huang Chao, an unsuccessful palace examination candidate, finally doomed the regime. The rebel army entered Changan City to found the kingdom "Da Qi." Emperor Xizong (873-888) was forced to escape to Chengdu. Although the rebels were finally put down by royal troops that came to the emperor's rescue, Tang's pomposity was destroyed in these civil wars. From 907 to 960, the Tang was replaced by ten warlord kingdoms and five ephemeral dynasties. Once again, after a period of strife, the unity of the country was resumed, this time by General Zhao Kuangyin who founded the Song Dynasty (960-1276).

Cultural Prosperity

The Tang was a cosmopolitan empire. The variety of cultural life reflected a society that was tolerant and open to the outside world. Emperor Taizong was lauded for his tolerance of different opinions. When Wei Zheng, a minister and one of the most outspoken critics of the emperor, passed away, Emperor Taizong was deeply saddened. He compared Weizheng to a mirror and was grateful to him for correcting his faults. "With the passing of Wei Zheng I lost a mirror," the Emperor stated.

Changan welcomed performing artists from central Asian countries, and received cultural ambassadors from Japan. The Japanese scholars who came to Changan to study Buddhism and Tang arts carried home the Chinese writing system. Art forms from India, Iran, and Central Asia were performed in the Tang court. Foreign delicacies were also served on the royal tables. Envoys, merchants, and pilgrims from Central Asia came to Changan. Believers from foreign countries were allowed to practice their own religions, including Islam, Judaism, Manichaeism, Zoroastrianism, and Nestorian Christianity. The variety of cultural life in Changan was reflected in handcrafts, paintings, poems and novels.

Poetry writing was given the highest privilege during the reign of Emperor Xuan Zong (r.712-756). Poets were given high positions in the Imperial Academy and often higher seats in the court as well. In addition to the five classics, poem writing became an integral part of civil service examinations. Li Bai, Bai Juyi, Du Fu were among the most famous poets. Their masterpieces became the must-read for all generations.

Li Bai was the most venerated romantic poet at the time. Influenced by Daoism and good wines, Li Bai was able to display the wildest and the most beautiful imaginations in his poems expressing his love for the nature. Du Fu, a good friend of Li Bai, belonged to a different style, one of realism. Du Fu's poems were centered on social issues, filled with compassion for the poor and the unprivileged. Du Fu condemned the rich who enjoyed their daylong banquets while homeless people were starving to death on the road. He expressed profound sympathy for the chagrin felt by military families whose sons were fighting in the frontier. Li Bai and Du Fu developed romanticism and realism to the highest artistic level.

Close-up: Poems of Li Bai and Du Fu

Moon over the Mountain Pass

By Li Bai

The bright moon rises from the Tianshan Mountain,
Immersed in a sea of clouds.
The far-reaching wind stretches tens of thousands of miles,

Blowing across the Jade Mountain Pass.
The Han Dynasty had guarded the Baideng Path,
When the barbarians tempted to invade the Qinghai Bay.
From this ancient battlefield,
Few soldiers had ever returned.
When faraway border towns appeared at the horizon,
Sadness must have covered soldiers' weary faces.
Standing on top of the watchtowers as the dusk closed down,
The men should have been homesick through dawn.

To Old Friend Wei

By Du Fu

Rarely could old friends a meet again;
Easily did we separate as stars apart.
What a wonderful night tonight,
Allowing us to share the candlelight!
The youthful years did not last, helas;
Our hair has turned gray in no time.
Half of the friends have passed away.
The greetings are all the more heartfelt when the living ones meet.
Twenty years having flown by,
How could I have dared to expect a reunion?
You were single, my dear friend, when we bid goodbye.
Standing in line are your children greeting me tonight.
Politely they paid respect to me, and
Inquiring from which place I came.
Before I was able to extensively answer,
The children had poured fragrant liquor.
In the night rain you cut the spring chives,
And cooked the most tasty rice.
Ten times we toasted and toasted,
Over the precious moment of sitting next to one another.
The ten bowls of wine were not enough to make us drunk,
As we lost ourselves in reminiscence of the past.
The following day, yet again, we were separated by valleys and ridges,
And we will not hear from one another for a long long time.

The Song (960 - 1276)

In 960, warlord Zhao Kuangyin (r.960-976) reunited the country under the Song Dynasty. The capital city was Kaifeng in today's Henan Province. While the Song Dynasty was every bit as brilliant as the Tang in arts and literature, it was a much weaker state in other aspects. The Song was not able to dominate the neighboring states as the Han and the Tang did. In fact, starting from the year 1004, the Song had to buy peace from the Liao, a powerful northern minority, by submitting quantities of silk and silver annually. In an effort to protect the northern border, the Song stationed 1.25 million troops along the northern and northwestern borders between 976 and 1041. The costly military buildup proved to be worthless when the Jurched (the Jin) swept across the northern border and seized Song's capital city in 1127, ending Northern Song's unity. During the following 150 years, the Chinese fled to the South to set up the capital in Lin An ("temporary peace") which is today's Nanjing City. The dynasty tradition continued until 1276 the year the Mongols took over the southern half of China. Due to the southward migration, the second half of the Song Dynasty was also known as the Southern Song Dynasty.

In general, the Song followed the pattern of every new dynasty in the past in which a quick economic recovery led the way. Cities with multi-million population emerged. The economy expanded from the north to the south. According to one source, China's population increased from eighty-seven million in the year 755 to 119 million in 1110.[27] With the increase of typical southern industries in the areas of silk, bamboo products, paper, and textile, commerce gained the momentum for fast development. This resulted in paper money first being used in the 1120s.

The advance of metallurgical technology contributed to a rapidly rising productivity. Iron was produced in abundance with the introduction of the hydraulic blower. Farming instruments made of iron enhanced agricultural production, meeting the demand of a fast growing population. Shipbuilding, lacquer, ceramics, silk, and printing technology all reached high levels of perfection.

The Song government, however, was comparable to a rusty machine. A heavy bureaucracy plagued the Song government from the very beginning. To fill the abundant offices, civil service examination reached its zenith. While during the early 11th century there were only 30,000 candidates taking the examinations, by the end of the century, the number rose to 80,000. The promise of high paying positions, the prestige of being above the common herd, and the tax-exempt status fuelled the rush to testing centers. The emergence of the gentry's class or the class of office holders had its negative impact. The phenomenon was a sign of a bureaucracy-congested government. Rampant briberies and the typical inertia of government offices rendered the government inefficient. The fact that gentry's families controlled local industries and businesses while being tax-exempt posed a heavy pressure on government's income. Moreover, the gentry were resistant to any governmental reform that would hurt their interests. Faced with an imminent invasion by the Jurched in the northeast, the Song was apparently incapable of revitalizing its dormant system. Song's defeat was certain.

The Reform

In an effort to rejuvenate the government, Emperor Shenzong (r.1067-1085) attempted the reform. The emperor adopted Chancellor Wang Anshi's reform plan that included installing a gradual tax system to make rich people pay more taxes. Other items on the agenda included curbing tributary income by eliminating items of luxury, reforming civil service examination by deleting non-essential subjects, setting up a state loan system to curb money lenders' profits, and converting labor service into taxes payable in cash. The gentry and the nobles immediately opposed these measures. The reform failed and Wang was ousted from office. Consequently, the Jurched seized the opportunity to grow into a strong military power. They established the Jin Dynasty in 1115, conquered Khitan Liao in 1125, and occupied Song's capital city Kaifeng in 1126. Emperor Huizong (r.1100-1126) was captured by the Jurched and later died in captivity.

By the time of the Southern Song, the Jurched in northern China had been engaged in years of conflicts both with the Chinese and with other ethnic groups. Eventually, stretched thin by their own military campaigns, the Jurched fell prey to a group known for its agile horse riders, the Mongols. Before long, the Mongols wiped out the Jurched, took over China, and founded the Yuan Dynasty.

The Yuan (1276 - 1368)

In 1260, Khubilai Khan came to power. After defeating the Jurched, Khubilai moved the capital city from Karakorum, known as Dong Du or "the Winter Capital," to today's Beijing. He named the new capital Da Du, or the "Grand Capital." In 1275, Mongol troops crossed the Yangtze River and occupied southern China. In 1276 Khibilai Khan declared the founding of the Yuan Dynasty.

The rise of the Mongol power was unarguably much indebted to Chinggis Khan, Khubilai's grandfather, a talented and tough leader. According to a legend, the dynastic title "Yuan" was chosen by Chinggis Khan, from the classic oracle book *Yi Jing (The Book of Changes)*, the meaning of the word being "eternal source of power." Chinggis Khan assured the solidarity of his domain first by subduing the Tartars, Kereyid, Naiman, Merkid, and some Turkic tribes. The great Khan secured loyalty of his subjects as well as the unity of the Mongol confederation in multiple ways, one of which was to implement a hostage system forcing the sons of his higher commanders to serve in the royal bodyguard regiment. Meanwhile, Chinggis Khan founded an army of 150,000 tough fighters. This swift army galloped through much of Eurasia in the 13th century without meeting significant resistance.

Many factors contributed to the impressive military achievements of the relatively small Mongol army. Without a doubt, a clear discipline assisted with severe punishment and generous reward was an important key to victory. Robbery and adultery were punishable by death; deserters were beheaded. As a typical military strategy, the Mongols used cruelty to psychologically deter resistance. Any resistance would be dealt with mercilessly, which often meant butchering of towns and villages.

The Mongols did not concern themselves with governing the conquered territories during their early military campaigns until Khubilai Khan's occupied China. The goal of the Mongol conquerors had typically been attacking and looting, which was best served by the strength of a horse-riding army. Lack of experience in governing, unfamiliar with Chinese language and culture, and struggling to adapt to the agricultural way of life, the Mongols soon found themselves engaged in a mission impossible. The Mongol regime soon engaged themselves in a series of conservative policies that only intensified the Chinese resistance. Of these policies was the race-based administration system.

The Racial Divide

The strength of the conqueror soon became the weakness of the occupier. Kubilai Khan's race-based privilege system deprived the Chinese of their participatory rights. The consequence was that, by excluding the Chinese from the administration, the Mongols alienated themselves as well. According to the system, the Mongols were superior to the *semu* group (color-eyed people). The *semu* included Europeans and Central Asians, such as Turks, Uighurs, Persians, Tibetans, and Tanguts. The third level, the "Northern Chinese" or the "sinified Chinese" primarily referred to the Jurched and the Khitan. The indigenous Chinese constituted the lowest class. The Chinese were forbidden to own weapons and were prohibited from dealing in anything that may be used to make weapons.

By the beginning of the 14th century, the Mongols appeared to have been culturally adapted. The Yuan government started to offer civil service examinations to the Chinese literati. This was done, however, on a small scale, given the fact that the Mongols remained vigilant toward the Chinese. On the other hand, civil service examinations were not as attractive to the Chinese as it was under the Chinese dynasties. Many Chinese literati remained unwilling to serve in the foreign court. For example, in his captivity, Wen Tianxiang, a poet and anti-Mongol general, refused to cooperate with the Khubilai government and was executed. To make a living while being recalcitrant, many Chinese literati supported themselves by doing odd jobs; some became playwrights.

The Yuan Dramas

Dramas topped the performing arts during the Yuan, similar to poems and songs that dominated the Tang and the Song. Presumably, art forms of on-stage performance was an accessible literary genre to

Mongols who generally had little Chinese literacy. Out of the 160 dramas that have survived, most were written simply to entertain the audience. The content dealt with trifles of life, hence the name "za ju" or "dramas of all kinds." One example is the anonymous comic drama "The Battling Doctors" which tells the story of two con-artists who use conflicting medications to keep the patient barely alive.

The Yuan dramas gained higher literary taste under the pen-brush of Guan Hanqing. Guan authored some sixty plays some of which became masterpieces of all time. *The Story of the Injustice to Dou E* is one of his representative works. In the play, the heaven proved the innocence of a wrongfully convicted woman by sending a snowfall on a warm summer day of June after the woman was executed. The Yuan dramas are appreciated more as a reading literature today than a performing art. However, the popular Peking Opera and many local operas have all tremendously benefited from the Yuan dramas one way or another. In a sense, the legacy of the Yuan dramas is carried on by modern dramas.

The Ming (1368 - 1644)

The Yuan Dynasty collapsed in the midst of peasant rebellions. Zhu Yuanzhang (1328-1398), a talented rebel general gained control over China and founded the Ming Dynasty. Nanjing was chosen to be the capital city. During the Ming, Beijing was constructed into a magnificent capital city to which the court relocated during thirteen years. It was during the Ming that the Chinese, for the first and the last time, embarked on a maritime exploration and reached Africa.

During the latter half of the Ming Dynasty, the Japanese became a major threat in the east. Japanese pirates aided by Chinese rebels frequently robbed the east coast. The Japanese occupied Korea and made it a springboard for further invasion into China. To control the situation, the Ming military defeated Japanese forces both at the sea and on land in Korea. These military campaigns cost heavily to the Ming government that was already plagued with internal crisis.

Eventually, the collapse of the economy resulted in famine and peasant rebellions. In 1636, Li Zicheng and Zhang Xianzhong's rebel forces controlled the area between the Yellow River and the Yangtze River. In 1644, the rebels marched toward Beijing and Emperor Chong

Zhen committed suicide. Ming general Wu Sangui sought military assistance from the Manchu confederation in the northeast. The Manchu forces crossed the Great Wall on fast horses and quelled down Li Zicheng's rebel troops in short order. Once the mission was accomplished, the Manchu settled down in Beijing and founded what would be known as the Qing Dynasty (1644-1911).

The rise and fall of the Ming, however, was not a simple repetition of the past patterns. The first half of the Ming was mixed with a tightened administrative control on the one hand, and a dynamic economic recovery on the other. After driving out the Mongols, the Chinese returned to their traditional way of ruling. Unfortunately, the Ming was one of the darkest periods in history known for its abundant internal feud.

Emperor Zhu Yuanzhang or Taizu (the founding emperor) was a ruthless emperor who would not hesitate to use extreme cruelty against dissidents. The emperor's way of dealing with plotters, for example, was merciless. The punishment would not only befall the perpetrators, but also their family members. In 1380, the emperor had his chief minister executed. More than 30,000 people, including kinship and associates, were also massacred. This was followed by another 70,000 or so lives taken in various subsequent investigations. Lives were apparently worthless to the emperor, as long as he could maintain the absolute control.

Suspicious, shrewd, and constantly alert were adjectives often used to describe Emperor Taizu's personality. It is speculated that the emperor's humble background may have contributed to his highly sensitive and defensive character. During his childhood, famine and epidemic killed both of his parents. Zhu Yuanzhang joined a Buddhist monastery and had to beg from village to village for a living. Smallpox infections left facial scars on him, subjecting him to insensitive ridicules. Even after he became emperor, some audaciously sarcastic painters painted his royal portrait with emphasis on facial details. During his vagabondage, Zhu Yuanzhang joined the White Lotus Society that preached the coming of the Metreya (the "Ming Wang," in Chinese, after which the emperor named his dynasty) to liberate the Chinese from the Mongol occupation. He soon proved to be a brave soldier and a competent commander. Throughout his life, however, Zhu Yuanzhang was haunted with fear and suspicion.

After Zhu Yuanzhang died, his 4th son usurped the throne and became Emperor Chengzu Yongle (r.1403-1424). Emperor Yongle transferred the capital city from Nanjing to Beijing during over thirteen years. The Grand Canal was extended to link Beijing to the Shandong province. The economy grew fast. The population reached 200 million.

Among the many features of the Ming court under Emperor Yongle, the broad employment of eunuchs was probably the most eye-catching. In the history, eunuchs were typically assigned to inner-court services that were labor intensive. It was not uncommon for ambitious eunuchs to take advantage of their proximity to the royal family, higher-level officials, and even the emperor himself, to place their influence. Powerful eunuchs were able to influence policies, shield information, and seek huge profits for themselves. For that reason, Emperor Taizu had imposed the ban on involvement of eunuchs with state affairs.

Under Emperor Yongle, however, the ban was lifted. The eunuchs made up a large part of the staff of the imperial household. The imperial household itself was headed by the Directorate of Palace Attendants and divided into different directorates and services whose responsibilities were to administer the staff, the rites, food, documents, stables, seals, gardens, state-owned manufactories and so on; still their responsibilities remained small. However, this soon changed when power struggle intensified. To monitor officials, Emperor Yongle established a eunuch Secret Service. In addition to spying on officials, these agents would occasionally monitor civilians as well. They meddled in court affairs and even exercised unauthorized power to arrest citizens and use torture in the emperor's name. Wang Zhen, Liu Jin, and Wei Zhongxian, for example, were among the most infamous. However, some were capable of accomplishing great deeds. Zheng He, for example, conducted the first maritime expedition to the outer world, which was rather unusual for what has been an ancient and, so far, sedentary civilization.

Maritime Expeditions and Science Manuals

Ming's maritime expedition in 1405-1433 covered a tremendous distance. Headed by Zheng He, a Muslim eunuch serving in the court of Emperor Yongle, the first journey involved 27,000 sailors on sixty-two large and 225 small ships. The largest vassal was 440 feet long. The expedition traveled along the east coast of China, passing by India and Persia, and reached as far as the African coast. The purpose of these expeditions was primarily to increase the number of tributary nations as well as to explore opportunities of trade and commerce. There are speculations that the Ming fleets discovered North America ahead of the discovery of Christopher Columbus, which, if proven reliable, would certainly add to the grandeur of these explorations.[28]

Despite the tremendous investment in the first expeditions, the success did not result in further maritime projects, nor did it open China's door to the outer world. The most plausible reason was that the Japanese and local pirates intensified their devastations of the east coast at the time, rendering further maritime expeditions untimely. Some argue that the successful maritime ventures, indeed, strengthened the confidence of the court in its superiority. The success, however, directed the emperor's attention to a different endeavor, one of creating science manuals to summarize and preserve the Chinese experience.[29]

At any rate, reference projects did enter the most prosperous era during the Ming. Song Yingxing's *Industrial Handbook* was a comprehensive collection of techniques for manufacturing paper, porcelain, boats, and a variety of industrial products. Li Shizhen's *Medical Handbook* recorded thousands of herbal and animal-based prescriptions. The Yongle Encyclopedia (Yongle Dadian) was a royal project consisting of 22,877 volumes in 11,095 books, compiled by 3,000 scholars from 1403 to 1407, and prefaced by the emperor himself. The reference project was an enormous collection of materials from the Pre-Qin period (before 221 B.C.) to the Ming Dynasty. Experts estimate that only about 400 books survived, less than four percent of the original work.[30]

Eight-Legged Prose

Ming was a bureaucratic empire with a huge official system full of redundancy. Part of the problem was generated from the supervisory tradition left by the founding emperor. Ming's civil service examinations became more sophisticated than previous dynasties. However, the new features were more about stylistic mannerism rather than the usefulness of the content. Essays, for example, had to be written in a fixed style called the "eight legged prose." This style strictly requires the writer to include eight segments in the writing regardless of the relevance of the formality. Hence, participating in a civil examination was more about competing in rhetoric than in problem solving.

Literati were given special privileges: *shengyuan* or those who passed county tests, for example, were exempt of labor service. *juren* or those who succeeded in the provincial tests were given lower level government posts. *jinshi* or those who succeeded in the most prestigious palace examinations were granted government posts at the palace. Studying for the civil examinations, once again, became one of the most the respected hardships to endure.

Idealism and Romantic Literature

During the Ming Dynasty, a famous Confucian scholar, Wang Yangming (1472-1528), enriched the theory of Neo-Confucianism which first appeared during the Song Dynasty. The founders, Zhu Xi (1130-1200) and Lu Xiangshan (1139-1193), picked up a traditional topic of morality and subjectivity. Zhu Xi's *lixue* or the "School of Principles" stressed rationalism, while Lu Xiangshan's theory of introspection emphasized on subjectivity. Wang Yangming's *xinxue* or "School of Mind" was a systematic extension of the introspective theory.

According to Wang Yangming, the highest knowledge of the truth comes from constant reflection and self-examination. In this process, one develops or recovers the fundamental goodness of one's nature. The premise of this theory advocates that sagehood is innate, and the principles of the universe exist in man's conscience. Thus, to find the true goodness, one does not proceed by investigating the objective world; but rather, one should eliminate desires and concentrate on introspection. Wang Yangming eloquently argues in the following passage, that the good is within oneself rather than elsewhere. For that reason, his theory was labeled "idealism."

> What one calls 'moral principles' in an event or object, 'righteousness' in our adapting ourselves towards it, and 'good' in nature, are differently designated on account of the things to which they refer, but in reality are all manifestations of my *hsin* [mind]. There is no good that lies outside the mind. When my mind regards events and objects purely from the viewpoint of moral principles (li) and without any falsity, there is good. This is not fixed in events and objects, and can be sought for in a definite place. Righteousness means to adapt oneself properly to objects; it refers to my mind having done what is appropriate. For righteousness is not an external object, which one can seize and take over. To 'investigate' means to investigate this, to 'extend' means to extend this. To insist on seeking the supreme good in every event and object is to separate what is one into two things. Yi-Ch'uan (Ch'eng Yi) has said, if you use that you would know this, meaning that this and that are not to be distinguished in nature, or principle or goodness. As to what you say about how to make efforts to understand the good, how to begin such efforts, whether there are definite steps towards the attainment of sincerity, and what is sincerity all about, these show that you think there is a special effort for the understanding of the good and for the attainment of sincerity. But according to my idea, the understanding of the good is itself the effort of attaining sincerity.[31]

Wang Yangming's idealism is believed to have inspired the romantic literature of the Ming era. *The Water Margin* and *The Romance of the Three Kingdoms* both by Luo Guanzhong, *The Journey to the West* by Wu Chengen, and *The Golden Vase* by Li Yu are considered masterpieces of the trend. Tang Xianzu's romantic plays such as *The Dream of Han Dan* and *The Peony Pavilion* depicting the individual pursuit of love between young men and women that transcends social strata are among the representative theater arts at the time.

Exploration of emotion and imagination was characteristic to the literature of this time. *The Journey to the West*, for example, relates the trip of Xuan Zhuang, a Buddhist monk of the Tang Dynasty, who travels to India to collect Buddhist sutras. Protected by a magical monkey and three other magically empowered figures, Xuang Zhuang is able return to the Changan Capital, with the sutras that he has acquired, but not without having survived ninety-nine life-threatening encounters with monsters along the journey. Romanticism, despised from the Confucian point of view as yielding to human weaknesses, became the main literary trend of the time.

The Qing (1644 - 1911)

The rise of the Manchu in northeastern China was by no means a coincidence. On the one hand, the fall of the Mongol empire and the weakening of the Chinese empire provided an ideal window for the Manchu to develop into a dominant power. On the other hand, living on hunting, fishing, and farming, the Manchu life style was closer to the Chinese than the Mongols' and those of other "barbarians" in the past. While the opportunity of expansion was ripe, someone had yet to seize it. The man who seized the opportunity and prepared the Manchu for the 300 years of ruling in China was Nurhachi.

The credit of founding the Manchu state was attributed to Nurhachi (1559-1616) who united scattered Manchu tribal groups into four primary and eight peripheral banner-camps, hence the "banner system." Nurhachi was also credited for creating the Manchu writing system based on the Mongol alphabet. Nurhachi's eighth son, Hong Taiji (r. 1626-1643) became the founder of Qing Dyasty. The dynastical title "Qing," meaning "clearance," is popularly believed to have been chosen by Hong Taiji to imply the intention to invade China.

In 1644, after having suppressed rebel Li Zicheng, the Manchu settled down and chose Beijing to be the capital city. The three emperors who reigned during the early stage, Kanxi (r.1662-1722), Yongzheng (r.1722-1736) and Qianlong (r.1736-1795), laid a solid foundation for the long lasting stability of the Qing Dynasty.

The Manchu emperors were different from the past emperors of foreign origins in that they were well versed in Chinese classics. Emperor Kangxi, being a scholar of Chinese classics himself, was on good terms with the Chinese literati. Under his reign, the Kangxi Dictionary was compiled and remained in use until mid 20th century.

While assuring higher administrative positions to Manchu's inner circle, Emperor Kangxi was successful in absorbing Chinese literati officials in the government. The emperor also hired Jesuit missionaries to be palace tutors, and encouraged them to introduce western science and technology. Christianity was welcomed along with other religions, the condition being that the practitioners would allow converts to pay respect to their ancestors. After the Vatican representative Maillard de Trounon ruled against ancestral rites, Emperor Kangxi started to expel Christian missionaries.

Emperor Yongzheng's contribution included curbing the power of Manchu nobles and forcing them to return the money that they had borrowed from the government. Such borrowing was a widespread corruption at the time. Most borrowers not only turned delinquent by the terms of their loans, worse yet, they had no genuine intention to return the money at all. Emperor Yongzheng's effort in fiscal reform financially guaranteed the financial backing of Emperor Qianlong's reign for the next forty-nine years.

Emperor Qianlong, following the footsteps of his grandfather, was an expert on Chinese culture. He was famed for having published over 42,000 poems. His calligraphy remains visible today engraved on stone steles in many scenery spots. Nevertheless, Emperor Qianlong was merciless in punishing anti-Manchu dissidents regardless of their learning. Many Chinese literati who dared to belittle his government were beheaded. In addition, some 2,000 titles were searched out from *The Complete Books of the Four Treasures* compiled in the Ming Dynasty, due to the overt or covert despise of "barbarians." These volumes were torched.

During the reign of Kangxi, Yongzheng, and Qianlong, China's territory was expanded to include Chinese Central Asia (Zongar area), Mongolia, Tibet (1720), and Taiwan. Taiwan was acquired in 1683 from the occupation of Zheng Chenggong, a Ming general, who had freed Taiwan from the Dutch control in 1662. Qing government sent a naval expedition to Taiwan and claimed the island part of the Fujian prefecture.

Maritime trade with Europe developed rapidly in the early 18th century. Government-recognized monopolies, such as the British East India Company, and the Co-hong, an official Chinese merchant guild in Guangzhou, handled most of the trade. A total of 400,000 pounds of tea was exported to England in 1720. The figured reached 23 million pounds in 1800. In the opposite direction, silver inflow rose from three million ounces in 1760, to 16 million ounces in the 1780s. The British soon discovered that the trade imbalance was not easily reversible, because none of the industrial gadgets, such as scientific instruments, carpets, knives, and plate glasses could find a market in China.[32]

The Opium War of 1840-42 resulted from trade conflicts between Britain and China. The British pushed trade on opium in exchange for silver and tea, a practice that the Chinese government was determined to stop. Opium had been mostly used as a painkiller in China. The use of opium for its narcotic effects was never popular until opium flooded the market. Opium consumption increased drastically after the East India Company increased its opium export to China from 200 chests in 1729 to 23,570 chests in 1832 (A chest averaged 140 pounds). Millions of taels of silver flowed out of China. Suddenly, opium had become a major threat to people's health and the cause of much social instability.

British Sales of Opium	
Year	Number of chests
1729	200
1750	600
1773	1,000
1800	4,570
1810	4,968
1816	5,106
1823	7,082
1828	13,131
1832	23,570

(Source of data: Jonathan Spence, *The Search for Modern China, 130*)[33]

In view of the situation, the court dispatched Commissioner Lin Zexu to Guangzhou in 1839 to stop opium trade. In his appeal to Queen Victoria, the commissioner condemned the British for seducing Chinese people into buying and smoking opium:

How can you possibly consent to forgo it for a drug that is hurtful to men, and an unbridled craving after gain that seems to know no bounds! Let us suppose that foreigners came from another country, and brought opium into England, and seduced the people of your country to smoke it, would not you, the sovereign of the said country, look upon such a procedure with anger, and in your just indignation endeavor to get rid of it? [34]

By all means, Commissioner Lin was able to expel British merchants from Guangzhou and confiscate their opium stock. In response, a British fleet left India in 1840 with sixteen warships and some supply boats. The fleet bypassed Guangzhou that Lin Zexu had reinforced with newly installed cannons and attacked Ningbo and Tianjin. The Qing government agreed to negotiate. The demand was a surprising six million Mexican silver dollars of indemnity to cover the British expedition costs. In addition, the Treaty of Nanjing signed in 1842 included the following terms:

a) Payment of 21 million ounces of silver
b) Abolishing government monopoly agency Co-hong
c) Ceding Hong Kong to Britain and opening five treaty ports that were Guangzhou, Xiamen, Fuzhou, Ningbo, and Shanghai
d) Adopting a fixed tariff of five percent
e) In case of dispute, British subjects in China would only be answerable to British law
f) Under the "most favored nation" status, Britain would be automatically granted the same privileges granted to other nations [35]

Taiping Rebellion (1850 - 1864)

The loss of the Opium War was a heavy blow to the Chinese gentry class as a whole. Many questioned the Confucian tradition and blamed it for suppressing science and democracy, and for nurturing a broad-based bureaucracy. The ultimate blame, however, was put on the corrupted Manchu government. A direct reaction was the Taiping Rebellion, "Taiping" meaning "grand peace." The uprising was started from the Guangxi province in 1851 led by Hong Xiuquan, a disgruntled examination candidate. The rebels soon spread over sixteen provinces and ransacked 600 cities. By the time of its failure in 1864, twenty million lives had been lost.

The Taiping Rebellion had a complex background involved with Christianity. Hong Xiuquan, having read some Christian tracts and the Old Testament, believed himself to be the messiah entrusted with the mandate to eliminate "foreign demons," a term referring to both the Manchu and the Western forces occupying in China. Hong labeled himself the King and his uprising "The Heavenly Kingdom of Grand Peace" (Taiping Tian Guo). Faced with the powerful coalition of the Manchu and the Westerners, however, the rebels had no chance of winning. Although the uprising failed, it marked the beginning of a series of rebellions that would finally lead to the downfall of the Qing Dynasty in 1912.

The Boxer Rebellion (1900)

Since the Opium War of 1840, a nationalist mood accumulated in the background. The Boxer Rebellion arose in June 1900 trailing the footsteps of the Taiping Rebellion, targeting foreigners residing in large cities. The "boxers" were originally martial art practitioners in central provinces who joined the organized training primarily for doing exercises and exchanging martial art skills. These groups were in a nationalist and revengeful mood at the time and were indignant against foreign occupiers. They were later transformed into a secret anti-foreigner society. The Qing government was clearly aware of their existence and demonstrated sympathy for their cause. The boxers soon rallied peasants from the most impoverished regions in the Shandong and the Hebei provinces, looted businesses, and killed missionaries in Tianjin and Beijing. The Boxers' slogan was "supporting the Qing and wiping out foreigners" (fu qing mie yang).

Taking advantage of the situation, the Manchu government secretly supported the rebellion and used the event to curtail British expansion. On 14 October 1900, the alliance formed by Japan, Russia, Britain, the United States, France, and Germany sent 20,000 troops to Beijing and put down the rebellion. The *Boxer Protocol* was signed in Peking between the Chinese government and the allied forces. According to the *Protocol*, the Chinese government had to pay an indemnity for war losses of 450 million taels of silver. In addition, official examinations were to be suspended for five years in the cities where foreigners were killed or mistreated.

Learning from the West

The Opium War served as a wakeup call to Chinese intellectuals and statesmen. They came to the realization that the Western industrial civilization differed in many ways from the Confucian tradition, and that the mentality that the Middle Kingdom was superior needed to be revisited. They started to examine the many differences between the foreign culture and the Chinese tradition. To many, understanding the West and learning from the West soon became a mission. Foreign books and maps were translated. Factories, arsenals, and railways were built. This was known as *yangwu yundong* or the "Foreign Enterprise Movement" that started in the mid 19th century.

A charismatic and entrepreneurial statesman behind the modernization movement was Li Hongzhang. He was trusted by Empress Dowager Cixi, and posted to northern China in the dual capacity of governor-general of Hebei and commissioner of trade for the northern ports. Li's vision was to develop China's own capacity in key areas of industry such as shipbuilding, mining, weaponry production, and the building of railroads. To develop China's navigation industry, Li founded China Merchant Steamship Navigation Company in 1872. The project was followed by the opening of Kaiping Coal Mine in 1877 near Tianjin. In 1878, Li founded the first textile mills in Shanghai and developed arsenals in Tianjin two years later. The new arsenals, for example, acquired Remington's technology and started to produce Remington rifles. Li's formula was "government supervision and merchant management," which effectively encouraged local entrepreneurs to creatively develop local industries.

Li Hongzhang was clearly aware that industrial development must be backed by educational reform. Under his influence, a group of young children aged twelve to fourteen were sent to Hartford, Connecticut, followed by more in 1875.[36] In 1905, Empress Dowager Cixi sent a government envoy to tour Europe, Japan, and the United States to inspect foreign governmental models, in the expectation of reforming the Chinese government. In the same year, the civil service examination was abolished. Cixi adopted the plan that would lead to a constitutional system to be phased in over a period of nine years. While the Qing court engaged in self-reform at a slow pace, revolutionaries grew more and more impatient. Sun Zhongshan, for one, was eager to see the Qing Dynasty gone and the 5,000-year old dictatorship regime disappear without further delay.

Sea Change (1900 - 1949)

The Republic

After the Opium War, regime change rose to the top priority on the revolutionary agenda. Tens of thousands of lives had been lost in the struggle to overthrow the Manchu rule. It was not until Sun Zhongshan (1866-1925), however, that revolutionaries finally realized what was good for China and how to achieve it.

Sun Zhongshan was educated in missionary schools in Hawaii. He went to Hong Kong later on to receive his medical degree. A worshiper of the American system, Sun decided to bring a similar government to China. Sun's revolutionary theory, better known as the "Three Principles of the People," included nationalism, democracy, and people's livelihood. Sun's nationalist goal was primarily to free China from the Manchu rule. By "democracy," Sun aimed at founding a constitutional government headed by a president and monitored by a parliament composed of representatives from the provinces. The power would be shared by five branches: executive, legislative, judicial, examination, and censorial. Sun's "People's livelihood" referred to improving people's living conditions without, however, equalizing property ownership. These principles clearly distinguished Sun's republican system from any regime in the Chinese history. To initialize the new system, Sun planned for a tutelage phase during which a strong military government would be installed to teach people their rights and duties. Thereafter, democracy would be phased in gradually.

In 1905, Sun founded the Revolutionary Alliance, the predecessor of the Nationalist Party or the Kuo Min Tang (KMT) to implement the plan. In 1911, an accidental explosion at an underground arsenal in Hankou led to an open rebellion later known as the "Xinhai Revolution." The Revolution ended the two and a half century old Manchu Dynasty. The Revolutionary Alliance elected Sun the Provisional President of the Republic of China. Sun assumed office on 1 January 1912. Emperor Puyi resigned on 12 February 1912 and trusted full power to Yuan Shikai to form a provisional government on behalf of the court in Beijing.

Restoration and Instability

The regime's easy collapse caught the revolutionaries unprepared. Sun Zhongshan and his comrades lacked experience in dealing with the actual transition. Sun primarily proceeded by the book. He ceded the provisional presidency to Yuan Shikai on 13 February 1912 on the ground that Yuan represented the outgoing regime, and that the new system would start with a democratic transition. To insure the democratic process, Sun had a provisional constitution drafted on 11 March 1912, which laid down procedures for electing a legitimate president.

Under the rules of this constitution, there would be a Parliament with two chambers: a Senate with 274 seats and a six-year service term. Members of the Senate would come from provinces and overseas Chinese communities on the basis of ten representatives for each province. The other chamber was the House of Representatives with 596 seats and a three-year term. Members of the House would be drawn based on one delegate for every 800,000 people. Sun did not anticipate, however, that Yuan had no genuine intention to play by these rules in the first place.

In January 1913, the first national election resulted in a clear victory for the Nationalist Party, which won 269 seats out of the 596 total in the House of Representatives, and 123 out of 274 total seats in the Senate. Yuan assassinated the key Nationalist presidential campaign organizer Song Jiaoren and forced the newly elected Parliament to elect him President for a five-year term. At rejection, Yuan dismissed the Parliament. After Song Jiaoren's murder, Sun Zhongshan had escaped to Japan to avoid assassination. In January

1916, Yuan declared himself Emperor Hong Xian (Emperor of the Grand Constitution). The republican revolution ended in failure. Witnessing the restoration of the empire, provinces such as Guanxi, Yunnan, and Guizhou declared independence. Many close allies of Yuan abandoned him once he put himself on the throne. Foreign powers refused to lend support. Yuan died of uremia on 6 June 1916. The succeeding Provisional President Li Yuanhong, a republican by heart, was overthrown by a powerful warlord Zhang Xun. A firm loyalist to the Manchu emperor, Zhang Xun put the Ex-emperor Puyi, age eleven, back on the thrown. Before the Beijing residents hung up the royal flag, however, Zhang Xun was driven out of Beijing by other warlords. From then on, China became a conglomerate of warring states.

May 4th Movement

One event that marked an important turning point of the modern history was the May 4th Movement in which Chinese intellectuals bashed Confucianism and promoted science and democracy, as they saw in it the best hope for a new China. The movement, therefore, was a cultural revolution by nature. It was an unsuccessful student demonstration, the May 4th Demonstration, which brought the movement to the open.

During WWI, China joined the Allies in 1917 by sending 140,000 laborers to France. Instead of rewarding China for the contribution to the victory of the allies, the Versailles Treaty of April 1919 rewarded China's Shandong Province to Japan. The decision was made without the Chinese government's agreement. Students from Peking University manifested in Tiananmen Square on 4 May 1919 shouting patriotic slogans, protesting against the unfair treaty, and condemning the "spineless" Chinese government. Police arrived and soon dispersed demonstrators. One student was killed. Though the student demonstration was suppressed, the event aroused a profound cultural introspection.

To some people, clearly, the Confucian tradition failed to make China a strong nation in the world. The republican revolution also failed to bring any hope. China continued to be divided and humiliated by foreign nations. The question awaiting an urgent answer was, which way should China head for?

Intellectuals dug into the Chinese tradition in search of sources of weakness. Chen Duxiu started the "New Culture Movement" in 1915. The same year he published the journal *The New Youth*. Chen was born into a wealthy family in the Anhui province. Having failed the provincial examination, he spent much time traveling to Japan and France. Chen ardently criticized the Confucian bureaucracy and the civil service examination system; he enthusiastically promoted individual freedom, science, democracy, and emancipation of women.

Another direction of the May 4th Movement was *The Vernacular Language Movement* started by Hu Shi, a professor at Peking University. Having studied in the United States, Hu Shi believed that promoting the vernacular or the colloquial language was necessary to promoting the mass education. In answering to Hu's initiative, Lu Xun (1881-1936) was the first novelist to write articles and novels in the vernacular language. Lu Xun's *The True Story of AQ* showed bitterness and humor. The sarcastic story depicts a man by the name of AQ who is a failure in everything he does, but is always able to declare moral victory over his enemies. AQ is finally executed for a theft that he did not commit. The story is an irony on the traditional attachment to Confucian moral principles but detachment from the reality.

Birth of the CPC

At the moment when Chinese intellectuals were desperately searching for a way out for the nation, the success of the 1917 Bolshevik revolution turned on the light at the end of the tunnel. Revolutionary intellectuals were excited with the new hope. Li Dazhao, head of Peking University Library, immediately applauded the Bolshevik revolution in the journal *The New Youth*. Chen Duxiu resigned his position of Dean at Peking University and went to Shanghai to join a Marxist study group. The Soviet-led Comintern (Communist International) sent representatives to direct the founding of the Communist Party of China (CPC).

Following the guidance of the Comintern representatives, thirteen members representing fifty-seven Marxist activists secretly held the founding conference on 1 July 1921 in Shanghai. Mao Zedong, as representative of Hunan Marxist activists, attended the meeting. The party adopted the policy of achieving the ultimate goal of the revolution by stages. Rather than launching an all out assault on reactionaries, the CPC decided, as the first step of revolution, to cooperate with the Nationalist Party in wiping out warlords. The newly founded CPC encouraged its members to join the Nationalist Party as individuals. The concept of building a communist China in which the working poor become masters of the country immediately won support from the people. In particular, after the failure of the republican revolution, many intellectuals believed that they found in communism the ultimate way to save China.

Nationalists vs. Communists

The paramount revolutionary leader Sun Zhongshan died in 1925 without being able to realize his will of wiping out warlords and reuniting China under the republican government. He left the project of the Northern Expedition to Jiang Jieshi (1887-1975), a long-time follower.

CPC members participated in the Northern Expedition, some even at the leadership level, and fought heroically. Meanwhile, the troops led by Communists not only spread the communist idea, but also equalized property along the way, whereby gaining the much needed popularity.

Growing wary about the communist movement, Jiang Jieshi decided to purge CPC members from his army. Jiang had many Communists murdered in Guangzhou in April 1927. Jiang's pretext was that the Communists staged a coup to sabotage the Nationalist Government. Immediately, the CPC withdrew from the Northern Expedition and went into hiding in the mountains of the Jiangxi province where they founded the Red Army on 1 August 1928.

From 1926 to 1928, the Northern Expedition subjugated three major warlords in central and northern China, reuniting the country under the Nationalist government. Nanjing, once again, was chosen to be the capital of the new government. Jiang Jieshi became the chairman of the State Council in addition to being the Chairman of the Nationalist Party. According to Sun Zhongshan's "Five Power

Constitution," the government was divided into five branches, called "yuan" or bureaus.

Born in Ningpo, Jiang Jieshi studied military science in Japan. He loyally followed Sun Zhongshan whom he called "teacher." Sun later appointed him to be head of the Huangpu Military Academy, which proved to be of crucial importance to his career. Huangpu graduates became key military leaders and loyalists whom Jiang Jieshi would rely on during his life-long struggle against the Communists.

The Long March

Once the CPC and its troops withdrew into the Jiangxi mountains, Jiang launched incessant military campaigns, bombing the red base and cutting off its supply lines. The Red Army eventually broke out of the blockade and went on the Long March in the fall of 1934. The Long March put the newly founded Red Army to its first harsh test. In October, 80,000 troops broke out leaving behind 20,000 wounded soldiers and family members. After marching 6,000 miles through terrains of the harshest conditions, the Red Army arrived in Yan An of the Shaanxi province in spring 1935. Only 8,000 Red Army soldiers survived the journey. Mao Zedong, now Chairman of the CPC, declared that the Long March was a great victory for the Communists in the sense that it spread the message and rallied support from the people. Mao lauded the Long March as a manifesto, a propaganda team, and a seeding machine.

The Long March saved the Red Army from perish and proved Mao to be a brilliant leader and an unsurpassed military strategist. After the Zunyi Meeting of 1935, Mao won the top position of the party. From then on, Mao stabilized his control over the CPC for the rest of his life.

Anti-Japanese War (1937 - 1945)

Since the Ming Dynasty, Japan had been a major military threat to China. Japan rose to a strong military power only after the mid 19th century. Similar to China, Japan had been closed to the outer world until 1854, when American warships forced the Japanese government to open multiple ports for trade. During the Meiji period (1868 -1912), the feudal system was abolished. Western ideas gained wide acceptance. In the parliament established in 1878, the military party began to push the idea that expansion to the continental Asia was more important than the domestic socio-economic reforms. This led to the Sino-Japanese War in 1894. The Chinese lost and ceded Taiwan to the Japanese. Later on, after defeating the Russians in the Russo-Japanese War in 1905, the Japanese occupied Korea.

In 1915, Japan gained economic privileges in China under Yuan Shikai. Furthermore, under the "Twenty-One Articles" imposed to the Yuan regime, Japanese armies were allowed to station in Manchuaria. Japanese troops occupied Shenyang in 1931 and attacked Shanghai in the following year. Meanwhile, the Japanese Government set up a puppet regime "Manchukuo" in the northeast under the ruling of Pu Yi who stepped down from the throne back in 1912.

Faced with an imminent invasion, Jiang Jieshi's generals urged him to temporarily stop pursuing the Communists and to get ready for the war against Japanese invaders. The Communists called upon the Nationalists to form an anti-Japanese coalition. Jiang Jieshi, however, persisted on wiping out the "internal enemy" before dealing with outside invaders. Eventually, in a military coup that took place on 12 October 1936, better known as the "Xian Event," Jiang Jieshi was forced into establishing an anti-Japanese coalition with the Communists by two of his most trusted generals. The coalition started in 1937 with both the Red Army and the troops of KMT under the command of Jiang Jieshi. The coalition disintegrated in 1941 when Jiang Jieshi ambushed the New Fourth Army division of the Communists and killed more than 3,000 troops.

On 7 July 1937, under the pretext of searching for a lost soldier, Japanese troops crossed the Marco Polo Bridge in Peking, which marked the beginning of the eight-year Anti-Japanese War. After taking Peking and Tianjin, Japanese troops headed toward Shanghai where they met a heroic defense that lasted for three months. After Shanghai fell, Japanese troops attacked Nanjing, the capital of the Nationalist government on 13 December 1937. According to an estimate, as many as 300,000 Chinese civilians and soldiers were killed, some 20,000 women were raped. The siege of Nanjing was also known as the "Rape of Nanjing."

Flying Tigers

After Nanjing fell in December 1937, the Nationalist government relocated to Chongqing of the Sichuan Province. As the Japanese had destroyed most of the Chinese industrial bases during the bombing campaigns, supplies had to be flown in from Burma to Chongqing. The Chinese needed an air force to defend the Burma supply line. This mission was accomplished by the American Volunteer Group (A.V.G) or the "Flying Tigers" under the commandment of General Claire Lee Chennault. As early as 1937 Gerneral Chennault had arrived in China at Generalissimo Jiang Jieshi's invitation to secretly survey the Chinese air force. He later provided training to Chinese fighter pilots.

In addition to answering to China's persistent request for help, one strong motivation for General Chennault's involvement was his distrust for Japanese endeavors in Asia and in the world. In a letter dated 8 Octover 1942 to Ken Willkie, Special Representative to President Franklin D. Roosevelt, General Chennault stated that the Japanese military could be defeated in China through air attacks, and that such action must be taken earlier rather than later to avoid American casualties, should the war expand. General Chennault eloquently made his case:

> I speak with confidence, but, I believe, not with egotism. The reason for my confidence is based on the fact that since 1923 I have believed firmly in the possibility of Japan making war on the United States; I have devoted the best years of my military life to the study of this subject; I have for five years been unofficial adviser to the Chinese Air Force; in this capacity, I made war against Japan for over five years; for the last year I have commanded first the A.V.G., then the China Air Task Force; at no time in China have I had as many as fifty fighting planes in operation to meet the full fighting air force of Japan; as Commander of the A.V.G. and the China Air Task Force, I have never lost an air battle against the Japanese...[37]

The Pearl Harbor Attack on 7 December 1941 led to the declaration of war on Japan by President Roosevelt. Until then, fighter pilots led by General Chennault were recruited as civilian volunteers. The pilots, flying the shark-faced P-40 Tomahawks (the Chinese called them "flying tigers" or Feihu), inflicted heavy damage on the Japanese in late 1941 and early 1942. As reward, the Chinese government paid a $500 reward for every Japanese plane downed or destroyed on the ground. By July 1942 when the A.V.G. went out of service, the Flying Tigers had achieved an impressive battle record of downing 299 Japanese planes, possibly destroying 153, and with a loss of twelve P-40s in combat and sixty-one on the ground.[38]

Close-up: Way of a Fighter (Excerpt)

Preliminaries dispensed with, the Generalissimo turned to Mow and in sharp staccato Chinese began to quiz him on the condition of the air force. Madame Chiang and I stood to one side as she translated for me.

"How many first-line planes are ready to fight?" Chiang barked at Mow.

"Ninety-one, Your Excellency," Mow replied.

Chiang turned turkey red, and I thought he was going to explode. He strode up and down the terrace, losing long strings of sibilant Chinese that seemed to hiss, coil, and strike like a snake. Madame stopped translating. Color drained from Mow's face as he stood stiffly at attention, his eyes fixed straight ahead.

"The Generalissimo has threatened to execute him," Madame Chiang whispered. "The Aero Commission records show we should have five hundred first-line planes ready to fight."

Never in the eight years that I have known him have I seen the Generalissimo so mad. Finally, as his anger ebbed, he turned to me and asked in Chinese: "What does your survey show?" Madame interpreted.

"General Mow's figures are correct," I replied.

"Go on," urged Madame, "tell him all of the truth."

Thus encouraged, I went on to describe conditions as I found them. As Madame translated my remarks, the pace of the Generalissimo's striding slowed. I must have talked for twenty minutes when Madame signaled a halt. The Generalissimo abruptly left the porch and disappeared inside the bungalow. Mow retained his head intact. Madame got the authority she needed to oppose the Aero Commission, and I laid the foundation of a reputation for absolute frankness. That session at Kuling established the tone of my relations with the Generalissimo. He came to rely on me for bald facts no matter how unpleasant they might be, and he always allowed me to have my way if I could convince him whatever I proposed would help the war. In all my dealings with him that seemed to be his sole standard — whether it would help the war.

(Source: *Way of a Fighter* by Claire Lee Chennault)[39]

Civil War (1946 - 1949)

After eight years of heroic struggle, the Chinese people defeated the Japanese invaders in 1945. Once Japan surrendered, however, the internal conflicts between the Nationalists and the Communists resumed. The United States made every effort to avoid a potential civil war by pushing for a coalition government. Under American influence, Jiang Jieshi finally agreed to negotiate with Mao Zedong. In August 1945, escorted by American Ambassador Henry Hurley, Mao arrived in Chongqing. Jiang, however, had no genuine intention to negotiate.

After the failure of the Chongqing negotiation, the U.S. made every effort to airlift the Nationalist troops to key positions. U.S. Marines were also sent to help defend major cities, such as Peking and Tianjin. The maneuver proved to be futile. From 1946 to 1949, Mao relied on the support that the Communists had built up during years of Land Reform to gain the much-needed manpower. In the Land Reform movement conducted in controlled rural areas, the Communists confiscated wealthy landlords' property and gave it to the poor, thereby winning the trust of the majority. Mao brilliantly deployed the strategy of stretching thin the enemy's frontline and overwhelming the enemy with forces that were often ten times that of the enemy. Mao was correct in predicting that while the Nationalists had the superior manpower and the best weapons, they would eventually lose the war due to the absence of support from the majority of the people.

On 1 October 1949, Mao declared the founding of the People's Republic of China. By this time, Jiang Jieshi and his Nationalist government had moved to Taiwan, escorted by American Navy forces. Chinese history turned a new page.

In a sense, the communist victory had already been assured at the moment of the founding of the CPC in 1921. The communist victory did not happen overnight, but rather came as a natural result of the extreme discrepancy between the rich and the poor that had lasted for thousands of years. Unfortunately, communism equalized ownership as promised but failed to improve people's lives. The pompous communist ideal was simply impeded by many of its innate problems the worst of which was equalization itself.

China after 1949

In his article published in June 1949, "On People's Democratic Dictatorship," Mao Zedong defined New China as a regime that exercises dictatorship against the enemy and serves democracy to its people. In reality, however, the distinction between enemy and people proved to be of such a complexity that it generated waves of disastrous political campaigns. These campaigns were aimed at potential enemies, resulting in tens of thousands of innocent people being persecuted or murdered. As such, the traditional social relationships disintegrated, the economy collapsed, the society turned into a McCarthyist network. The system was finally reversed after Mao's death in 1976. Since then, China has been firmly engaging in reform under the leadership of Deng Xiaoping, Jiang Zemin, and the current leader Hu Jintao. The economic strength of the nation, as well as the quality of people's lives, have been on a rising trend ever since.

Political Campaigns in the 1950s

Starting from the moment the new socialist state was founded, prevention of possible sabotage by open and covert enemies was high on the agenda of the new government. Consequently, the first measures taken by the CPC were aimed at flushing out internal "bad elements." In 1951, the "Anti-Counter-revolutionary Campaign" was launched targeting potential enemies — those who had served under the Nationalist regime or who had cooperated with Japanese invaders. Those who "had blood on their hands" in the past from killing the

Communists were executed; others with lesser crimes were either jailed or exiled. During this campaign, weapons were collected from neighborhoods. In the Guangdong Province alone, 50,000 rifles were collected.

In the same year, another cleansing campaign by the name of "Three-anti Campaign" was launched in parallel. This campaign particularly addressed the issue of corruption within the party, as many communist cadres were found receiving briberies once they were trusted with high-level administrative power in cities.

The new leadership was keenly aware that, just as defined in the classical Marxism, private property ownership and the communist system would not belong together. In January 1952, the "Five-anti Campaign" was launched targeting five vices including bribery, tax evasion, stealing state economic secrets, cheating on government contracts, and theft of state assets. Workers were organized into unions that were empowered to monitor the management. Factory owners were soon forced to confess their crimes or business wrong doings. In reality, by targeting these vices, urban property was under the control of the government. Confiscation and selling at a "fair price" to the State were the only choices available to company owners. By April 1953, the government called off the Five-anti Campaign and declared that the "basic victory" against the five vices had been achieved. What this meant was that almost all of the private urban enterprises had been transformed into government properties.

The initial political campaigns ensured domestic security, at least psychologically so, while China was involved in the Korean War (1950-1953). The Korean War put the new government to the test. During the War, Mao Zedong lost his son, Mao Anying, who was born in 1922. An estimated total of 700,000 to 900,000 Chinese troops were killed, although the actual figure was never released. The U.S. casualties reached 160,000, with 54,000 dead, 103,000 wounded, and 5000 missing. South Korean casualties were estimated to be 400,000; the North Korean figure was approximately 600,000.[40] International confrontation had always been helpful in strengthening domestic solidarity. The Chinese people, once again, were united around the central government firmly believing in the goal of "Resisting American invasion, and safeguarding the motherland."

Intellectuals or the "Number Nine"

Ideological control had always been of primary importance to the new communist regime. For that reason, intellectuals were not considered as reliable as the working class. Those who had been trained in the West soon found themselves to be frequent targets of scrutiny, an interesting parallel to the rampant McCarthyism in the United States. Mao once jokingly ranked intellectuals "number nine," or the lowest in social strata, with the factory workers being the highest in rank.

In 1957, when Mao Zedong called on the nation's knowledge class to voice their opinions on the party and the government, intellectuals from every walk of life brought forth their harsh criticisms. Some condemned the lack of democracy, others revealed flaws in the election processes. All of these criticisms turned out to be the least that the new government would genuinely want to hear. This event is more popularly known as the "Hundred Flowers," a term taken from Mao's words "Let one hundred flowers bloom, let one hundred schools debate." Without further delay, Mao launched a counter-attack, known as the "Anti-rightist Campaign," in which he labeled the critics "poisonous weeds" and sent them to remote regions to receive "re-education" through hard labor. The rightists were only to be rehabilitated in 1978.

People's Commune

During the Civil War (1946-1949), through the Land Reform, poor peasants were allocated equitable plots of land. In return, the Communists gained support from the peasants. New China having been founded, de-privatization in the country became a necessary procedure. Agricultural collectivization had actually already started in the early 1950s. The process was planned as a gradual change through several stages. At the beginning stage, "mutual-aid-teams" were formed in which families living within a close range would pool together land and labor. This form of collectivization actually dates back to the time of the Civil War (1946-1949) in liberated northeastern China. During 1952-1953, Mutual-aid-teams developed into "cooperatives" involving a few dozens of families per unit. The combination of cooperatives soon resulted in larger units called "High-level cooperatives." Finally, by 1958, cooperatives joined force to form "People's Communes" or collectivized villages that normally covered 200 to 300 households.

Clearly, private land disappeared in the process of reorganization. Not every farmer gave up the land happily, however, the propaganda work by the government work teams was simply irresistible. Grudges were swept under the carpet, as a popular Chinese saying goes, "There is no damp firewood in the hot flames!" Agricultural collectivization was reversed in 1978 when the party decided to give land back to peasants in exchange for higher sense of responsibility and better productivity.

Great Leap Forward

The year 1958 is not only known for dissident-purging and de-privatization campaigns, it is also remembered for the economic exuberance called the "Great Leap Forward." During this campaign, Mao Zedong called on the farmers to help the nation by doing two things: increasing agricultural production by opening more land, and producing abundance of steel and iron in every possible way to support the national defense. The slogans were "Catch up with Britain and America in fifteen years" and "Liberate Taiwan."

To answer Mao's initiative, commune after commune reported unprecedented bumper crops. Agricultural production increased from 1,000 percent to 10,000 percent. No one lagged behind in reporting higher yield. In reality, the storage of grain was running low due to the fact that strong laborers were sent to open new farmlands or to steel-producing projects, leaving women and the elderly working on the existing farmlands. Unfortunately, the new farmlands were not immediately productive while the old farmlands were under-productive. To make things worse, sparrows were killed off to save grains, which, ironically, induced heavier damages caused by grasshoppers and other insects. As a result, the famine was looming. Marshal Peng Dehuai and other higher-level officials warned Mao of possible consequences if the current movement were to continue, but only found themselves reprimanded. Marshal Peng was dismissed from his position of Defense Minister.

The steel-producing front was immersed in the same frantic spirit. Doorknobs, window frames, and cooking utensils were melted into iron ingots and submitted to the state, dressed in red silk. Every iron and steel production site was in a festival mood. Flags were flying in the work fields; revolutionary songs were broadcast through loudspeakers all day long; people worked enthusiastically. The workers lived a communal style of life. The workers had their free meals in public restaurants. Children were sent to daycare centers. Family members rarely saw each other, but no one openly complained. It was found out later that the metal produced in such a manner was of low quality and little use. This was, however, the least to be concerned about, because it was more important to follow Mao's call. As such, crucial economic signals were ignored. The Great Famine struck.

When natural disasters occurred, the consequence was immediately catastrophic. The three years from 1959 to 1961 were called the "Three Years of Hardships" or the "Three Years of Famine," during which twenty-four million people died of hunger and diseases. Relief came only after Mao broke away from "Big Brother" Khrushchev in 1960 whom he accused of "revisionism." As the Sino-Soviet trade was discontinued, the grains originally to be exported to the Soviet Union in exchange for weaponry was allocated to famine relief. The Soviets withdrew their engineers, and left projects unfinished.

One outcome from the Sino-Soviet rift was the change of China's world status: from an ally of the Soviets, China went independent. Because of this change, the world was never the same anymore.

Battling the Soviet Revisionism

The "peaceful transition" theory of Nikita Khrushchev was an explosive concept within the communist block. At the Bandung Conference in 1956, Khrushchev told his followers that, unlike what classic Marxism had predicted, war against capitalism was "not fatalistically inevitable." Khrushchev further elaborated that Communists might very well change the society by winning the majority of seats in a capitalist parliament. Khrushchev's remarks sent chills to Mao Zedong at a time when the Korean War was freshly concluded and China was bombing the Quemoy Island.

To exacerbate the situation, the Soviets extended economic support to India with which China had territorial disputes, and to Indonesia where Chinese communities were ravaged in ethnic violence. In 1960, Mao Zedong declared that China was departing from the Soviet Block. Mao called upon the Chinese people to be ready to fight both the American imperialists and the Soviet revisionists. Meanwhile he urged people to tighten their belts in front of the economic sanctions. "Self reliance and hard struggle" was the fundamental strategy that Mao handed down to the nation. Once again, the famine-shattered country was closely united around the CPC. People were ready to tough it out. China's door to the outer world was shut down.

Political Investigation and Socialist Education

The Famine that had caused millions of deaths tarnished the party's image. Confused by the communist promise, people complained that they had never in the past suffered as much as they did now in the New China. Across the land, the morale was low, and questions arose with respect to the nature of the regime.

To brush up the party's image, Mao launched the campaign of "Political Investigation and Socialist Education" from 1962 to 1963. Through the investigation, the party aimed at cleaning up problems in the spheres of accounting, food supply, distribution of work points, and property accumulation. Corrupted officials were stripped off the party membership and labeled "class enemies." On the other hand, through socialist education, the party introduced communist values formulated into the "three threes," which were three sets of concepts, each containing three elements. The first of these was to promote three "isms" that were collectivism, patriotism and socialism. The second was to avoid three bad styles which included the capitalist, the feudal, and the extravagant styles. The third was to implement the three necessities including building socialism, loving the collective, and operating the communes effectively. The brainwashing campaign effectively saved the party's image, but failed to appease the internal feud. Conflicts between Liu Shaoqi who was the President of the State and the CPC Chairman Mao Zedong intensified. Poignant blames were lashed out from Liu's camp on Mao's mismanagement that eventually led to the big famine. Mao's dictatorial work style was also a flaming target. To answer his political opponents, Mao launched a powerful counter-attack known as the "Great Cultural Revolution."

Great Cultural Revolution

From 1966 to Mao's death in 1976, the Great Cultural Revolution ravaged the country even more profoundly than the big famine of the late 1950s. Originally, the campaign was intended to rid Mao's political opponents inside the party. In reality, however, it resulted in a broad-based power struggle. Mao encouraged the common people to rise up and denounce not only Liu Shaoqi and followers, but also local capitalist sympathizers, thus expanding a higher-level power feud to the grassroots.

Universities were shut down during these years. Factory workers and farmers were encouraged to read Mao's *Little Red Book*, leaving their regular work aside. Red Guards destroyed historical relics to get rid of the old culture. Intellectuals were, once again, the target of investigation. On the other hand, many people, particularly the youth in their high teens and early twenties were thrilled with the exciting anarchism. They finally stopped suffering from schoolwork that often came in a great abundance, since teachers had been sent home. They joined the Red Guards, convinced of their cause of safeguarding Chairman Mao. They were encouraged to use force against those labeled "capitalist roaders." They devastated historical relics, because those ancient statues and temples represented the past China that had to be overthrown. One example of the rampant irrationality was the change of the traffic signal system. The green light became the sign for "stop" and the red light became the sign for "go." This was simply because that the red color represented the revolution, the national flag ... and all those sacred symbols. Therefore, the red color must not stand for "stop."

In the political arena, Mao's opponents within the party were expelled from their government positions one by one, starting with State Chairman Liu Shaoqi and the party secretary Deng Xiaoping. Ironically, the last enemy that Mao wiped out was Lin Biao, Mao's handpicked successor, the Defense Minister, and the one who built up a personality cult of Mao by inventing the *Little Red Book*.

Mao disbanded the Red Guards in July 1968 and sent them to support the border regions. From then on, high school graduates had to spend at least three years in rural areas to live among peasants. The purpose of this practice was to train a new generation of intellectuals who would truly represent the working class. The young people who answered Mao's call of "Going up to the mountains and going down to the rural regions" later categorized themselves as "the lost generation."

The devastation of the GCR continued until Mao's death in October 1976. With an abysmal economy and chaos befalling the country, China was apparently ready for a drastic change. Mao's third wife, Jiang Qing and her three aids were arrested and charged with anti-people and anti-revolutionary crimes. They were sentenced to death with delayed executions, the Chinese version of "life in prison." However, Mao's handpicked successor Hua Guofeng was determined to continue with Mao's legacy. Hua put forward the slogan of what was known as the "two whatevers" referring to "obey to whatever Mao had said and continue with whatever Mao had decided." Hua's hardline policy proved to be unpopular. The power base of the deceased chairman had shrunken, and Hua lacked support from the military. On the other hand, people had suffered from decades of political struggles to a point that they could no longer put up with it. Under such circumstances, China had only one choice left: Reform.

Economic Reform

Deng Xiaoping, the former party general secretary who was ousted during the Great Cultural Revolution, returned to the political arena in 1977. Deng was elected the Second Deputy Party Chairman. Once in power, Deng worked effectively to discredit Hua Guofeng. Deng was clearly aware that without demystifying Mao's God-like image, people's minds would remain chained as before, and China would return to the old track. Contrary to Hua's "two whatevers," Deng argued that any truth must be tested against the reality. The same would be true to Marxism, Leninism, and Mao's thought. These once sacred communist theories must be re-examined against China's new reality. Deng admitted that Marxism was a valid revolutionary theory, but indicated that Marxism was a centenarian theory, some of which may no longer fit. Deng reminded people that even Mao himself had admitted that he was seventy percent correct and thirty percent wrong. In other words, Mao was a man rather than the God.

Without delay, Deng launched the debate "Seeking Truth from Facts" which was intended to free people's minds from the rigid Maoist framework. Similar to the "Hundred Flowers" debate of 1957 whereby Mao invited criticisms against the CPC, Deng encouraged people to question the communist theory from the angle of China's reality. It did not take a rocket scientist to figure out that China's reality was poverty. The part of communism that failed to meet this reality was obviously one that encouraged the nation to denounce capitalism and to be content with being poor but communist. And, obviously, there was no compelling reason for the post-Mao China to plunge into such fanaticism. The time had changed.

Deng encouraged people to be creative in making money. "Getting rich is glorious," Deng told the nation during his tour to the south in 1992, because "China has been poor long enough." For that reason, Deng is remembered as a pragmatic reformer. Deng was known for his "cat theory" which held that a good cat would be the one capable of catching the mice. The color of the cat would be of no relevance. Deng's allegory was taken to mean that reviving the economy was essential; to achieve this goal, any effective measure would be good. The Truth-from-Facts debate brought about a general confidence in pursuing individualism, profit, as well as a variety of individual rights that had never been accessible to the common people.

In December 1978, the Third Plenum of the Eleventh Party Central Committee of the CPC was held in Beijing. The meeting is considered a turning point of communist China and the hallmark of the Deng Era. Modernizing industry, agriculture, science and technology, and national defense, better known as the "four modernizations" was adopted as the party's new goal. The new agricultural policy encouraged peasants to engage in side occupations, such as growing cash crops to improve family income. The "Responsibility System" assigned equitable plots to rural households allowing them to keep for themselves whatever was beyond the dues to the government. Perfecting the legal system and decentralizing state control on the economy were on the agenda. In 1979, in light of the "Open Door Policy," four coastal cities — Shenzhen, Xiamen, Zhuhai, and Shantou were open to foreign investment under the title of Special Economic Zones (SEZ). In the same year, the Sino-U.S. diplomatic relationship was resumed. Coca

Cola and Boeing became as the first American companies to invest in China. In 1981, Hua Guofeng was removed from all positions. Two vanguard reformers, Zhao Ziyang and Hu Yaobang, assumed the positions of Premier and General Secretary of the Party. Deng himself assumed the positions of Chairman of the CPC and Chairman of Military Commission. A "socialist market economy" was underway.

Anti-spiritual-pollution Campaigns

While Deng Xiaoping was the determined driving force of the reform, he was clearly equally firm on maintaining the socialist system. In 1979, Deng laid down the "Four Cardinal Principles" which included the socialist road, the proletarian dictatorship, the party's leadership, and the dominance of Marxism-Leninism and Mao's thought. Unfavorable as these cardinal principles were to the reform, they reflected Deng's priority of maintaining a stable system.

Clashes between the "Four Cardinal Principles" and a runaway market economy were incessant. Corruptions, bureaucracy, and the lack of an effective legal environment raised tremendous barriers to the reforming economy. The influence of Western democracy posed tremendous challenge to the struggling system. Deng admitted that engaging in reform was similar to crossing the river by feeling the rocks under the water. The danger of getting drowned was eminent. During the 1980s, several anti-spiritual-pollution campaigns were launched against radical reformist tendencies. Procedures included cleaning up pornographic readers that flooded the night markets and promoting communist values, most of which were drawn from the "three-threes" of the early 1960s. When the wide-scaled student democratic demonstrations broke out during May and June of 1989 in Tiananmen Square, Deng did not hesitate to send in military forces to put down the demonstrations. For Deng, stability was above all. Three years after the crackdown, Deng reaffirmed to the nation that the reform would continue.

Deng was a paramount reformer, however, he would not tolerate any radicalism that would jeopardize stability and the party's control. Deng dismissed Premier Zhao Ziyang for supporting the 1989 student movement. And, Zhao's dismissal happened shortly after the General

Party Secretary Hu Yaobang, a radical reformer, fell out of political favor and died. Deng wanted the reform to happen orderly, and it did.

Stepping up to the top party leadership position in 1992 was Jiang Zemin, former mayor of Shanghai. Jiang skillfully pacified student demonstrations in Shanghai in June 1989 at the time when Tiananmen Square was out of control. Jiang's comrade-in-arms, Zhu Rongji, who once succeeded him as mayor of Shanghai was promoted to be the Deputy Premier in 1991, and later, the Premier, in 1998. After Deng passed away in 1997, Jiang followed Deng's guidance by diligently continuing with the economic reform.

Jiang Zemin yet had to launch multiple "Anti-corruption Campaigns" during his reign as a means of purging such opponents as Chen Xitong, former member of the Politburo and former Secretary of the CPC Beijing Municipal Committee. Jiang skillfully demoted several higher officials who engaged in smuggling and gambling. Meanwhile, he launched an ambitious drive to privatize China's massive, debt-ridden state sector from 1997 onward. This led to a significant rise in foreign investment and paved the way to China's WTO entry in late 1999. Under Jiang Zemin's leadership and Premier Zhu's effective control over an over-heated economy in late 1990s, China successfully weathered the Asian Financial Crisis that started in 1998 and played an important role in stabilizing the falling Asian economy.

On the ideological front, Jiang Zemin's theory of the "Three Representations" that stands for the representation of the broad masses of the people, the representation of the most advanced productivity, and the representation of the foremost culture, triggered heated debates. While some praise Jiang's theory as a bold step beyond Deng's finish line, his critics are concerned that the new direction of the CPC would eventually amount to abandoning the proletariat, embracing social-democratic norms, and eventually changing the party's color. Apparently, President Hu Jintao who succeeded Jiang Zemin in 2002 is not only a believer of the economic reform, but also a political reformist. Hu insisted that the CPC must constantly improve itself in order to stay ahead of the great leaps of the economy. As for how the CPC transforms itself, it remains to be seen.

[1] Patricia Buckly Ebrey, *Cambridge Illustrated History — China* (Cambridge University Press, 1996): 10-37. See also, John K. Fairbank et al., *East Asia* (Boston: Houghton Mifflin Company): 17-33.

[2] Robert L. Thorp and Richard Ellis Vinograd, *Chinese Art and Culture* (NJ: Prentice Hall, 2001): 27-49.

[3] Ibid.

[4] More of the primitive myths can be found in Mao Dun, *A Study of Mythology [shenhua yanjiu]* (Tianjin, China: Baihuawenyi Publishing Company 1981).

[5] Spencer Wells, *The Journey of Man, a Genetic Oddyssey* (NJ: Princeton University Press, 2002): 156.

[6] Ibid., 151.

[7] Ibid., 159.

[8] Hippolyte Taine, *Lectures on Art,* translated by John Durand (New York: Holt, 1971).

[9] CIA, *The World Fact Book: China*, 18 December 2003, <www.cia.gov/cia/publications/factbook/geos/ch.html> (1 January 2004).

[10] Cyril Birch and Donald Keene, eds., *Anthology of Chinese Literature — from Early Times to the Fourteenth Century* (New York: Grove Press inc., 1965): 7.

[11] Ibid., 11.

[12] Ebrey, *Cambridge Illustrated History — China*, 25.

[13] *Exhibition of Posthumous Script of Shang Tombs*, National Palace Museum (Taiwan: 2001).

[14] Paul Rincon, "Earliest Writing Found in China," 17 April 2003 <news.bbc.co.uk/2/hi/science/nature/2956925.stm> (3 January 2004).

[15] Ebrey, 25-27.

[16] Ibid., 26

[17] Robert L. Thorp and Richard Ellis Vinograd, *Chinese Art and Culture*, 67.

[18] Ibid., 56-117.

[19] Ibid., 63.

[20] Arthur Cotterell, *China: A Cultural History* (New Meridian Library, 1988): 13-33.

[21] Yuanfang Cai, *Records of Eastern Zhou States [dongzhou lieguo zhi]* (Beijing: Writers' Publication, 1957).

[22] Jianshi Shen, *History of China's Examination System [zhongguo kaoshi zhidu shi]* (Taiwan: the Commercial Press [shangwu yin shu guan, 1995]): 5.

[23] Ibid., 9.

[24] "Mystery of Qin Shi Huang Mausoleum Revealed" (Xinhua News Agency: August 26, 2002).

[25] Lao Tsu, *Tao Te Ching*, translated by Gia-Fu Feng and Jane English (New York: Vintage Books, 1972): Seventy-Four.

[26] Jianshi Shen, *History of China's Examination System*, 25.

[27] *Historical Population Data*, China Popin, <cpirc.org.cn/popnum.htm> (15 August 2003)

[28] Gavin Menzies, *1421 The Year China Discovered America* (Great Britain: Transworld Publishers, 2002).

[29] Xiaokang Su, *River Elegy,* CCTV, 1988.

[30] Marianne Bray, "China mega-book gets new life" (Hong Kong: CNN, 18 April 2002) <edition.cnn.com/2002/WORLD/asiapcf/east/04/18/china.book/> (16 August 2003).

[31] Yangming Wang, *The Philosophical Letters,* translated and annotated by Julia Ching (South Carolina: University of South Carolina Press, 1972): 29-30.

[32] Ebrey, 235.

[33] Jonathan Spence, *The Search for Modern China,* 2nd ed. (New York, London: W.W. Norton and Company & Company Ltd., 1999): 130.

[34] *Chinese Repository*, Vol. 8 (February 1840), pp. 497-503; reprinted in William H. McNeil and Mitsuko Iriye, eds., *Modern Asia and Africa*, Readings in World History Vol. 9, (New York: Oxford University Press, 1971), pp. 111-118.

[35] John T. Meskill, *An Introduction to Chinese Civilization* (D.C. Heath and Company, 1973): 197-202. See also: Patricia Ebrey, *Cambridge Illustrated History: China*; and Jonathan Spence *The Search for Modern China.*

[36] Spence, 217-219.

[37] Claire Lee Chennault, *Way of a Fighter* (New York: G.P. Putnam's Sons, 1949): 212-123.

[38] Claire Lee Chennault, *Way of a Fighter,* 174.

[39] Chennault, 40-41.

[40] Spence, 505.

3
Ideological Heritage

The classical Chinese thoughts flourished during a period of two and a half centuries before the founding of the Qin Empire (221 B.C.). Because this was a time of incessant wars among more than seventy states that broke free from the Zhou House, the historical period is known as the "Warring States"(475-221 B.C.). The fact that a variety of philosophies emerged during such a time of chaos was by no means coincidental. Political pluralism, quest for strategies of survival, and urge for conquering constituted an environment of ideological freedom. Any ideological eccentricity was regarded as creativeness and earnestly sought after. The prosperity of the classical thoughts vanished as soon as the country was reunited under the great Qin Empire. Under the Qin dictatorship liberal thinking was forbidden, thinkers were persecuted, and ideological creativity died out.

Overall, the classical Chinese philosophies are pragmatic in nature, stressing the here and the now more than the faraway or the world beyond. Obviously, the warring time imposed its selection. The demand for practical strategies to deal with brow-burning situations was obviously higher than the quest for profound spiritual cultivation. On the other hand, as mentioned in the previous chapter, the Chinese ideology started with an atheist penchant for historical reasons. Hence, instead of creating religions, philosophers at the time wrote down their practical thoughts in plain language and delivered them to kings and lords. For these reasons, the classical Chinese philosophies are also referred to as "codes of behavior." The works of Confucius, *The Analects*, serves as a good example in this regard as a guidebook for the virtuous conduct. Similarly, *Han Feizi* of Master Han Fei offers an effective roadmap for a dictator to build his empire. This does not mean, however, that every philosophy of the era reads like an industrial handbook. In fact, some are written in a quite suggestive style, particularly earlier philosophical works, resorting to allegories to convey abstract concepts. *Dao De Jing* of Lao Zi and the works of Zhuang Zi represents the tendency.

Time of Wars, Time of Thoughts

Historian Liu Xin (46 B.C. - A.D. 23) of the Han Dynasty recorded ten schools of thought. His categorization was later included by Ban Gu (A.D. 32 - 92) in his *History of the Former Han,* under "Treatise on Literature." According to Liu Xin, most of the ten schools of thought actually originated from the teachings of the government officials in the early time of the Zhou Dynasty, approximately from the 11th to the 5th century B.C. Because ministries were dedicated to specific functions, officials were able to formulate their theories based on their experience in executing their functions. For these officials, sharing their thoughts with the masses was not only a voluntary effort, but also an implied duty. During the Zhou time, education was an integral part of the duty of any government official. Ministers also assumed teaching duties at the Royal University.[1] With the disintegration of the Zhou House, its officials lost their positions and merged into the broader society. They disseminated their visions of the world for one reason or another, thus creating systems of thoughts based on their learning. Liu Xin's ten schools are listed below.[2]

1. The School of "Ru" (the literati) was represented by Confucian scholars. Its members were mostly officials of the Ministry of Education. Ethics and behavior were the subjects of study.

2. The Daoist School was represented by Lao Zi. Members of this school were officials of the Ministry of History. The primary goal was to enlighten the world with lessons learned from history.

3. The School of the Yin and the Yang reflected the thoughts of royal astronomers. Interpreting signs of the constellation constituted the main concern.

4. Scholars of The Legalist School belonged to the Ministry of Justice. These scholars focused their studies on the rule of law.

5. The School of Names represented views of officials serving in the Ministry of Ceremonies. They were primarily linguists studying ways of accurately naming things according to their realities.

6. The theory of the Moist School originated from the Guardians of Temples. Moism stressed the worship of God, the practicality of actions, and the meaning of equality.

7. The Diplomatist School represented theories from the Ministry of Embassies. The art of diplomacy was the core of the studies.

8. The Eclectic School represented theories of counselors. Most ideas were derived from other schools of thoughts. The scholars believed that a successful government must rely on a broad range of strategies.

9. The Agricultural School had its origin in the Ministry of Soil and Grain. Members concerned themselves with such issues as planting and food supply.

10. The School of Story Tellers had its origin in the Petty Offices. These offices were responsible for relating street talks that revealed the mentality of the masses.

Liu Xin's efforts in tracing the origins of the classical thoughts represent a typical intellectual endeavor of traditional scholars. However, such classification is likely to be insufficient due to the fact there were more schools of thoughts than the number of ministries. Hence, much must have been left out. Moreover, within each school, theoretical mutations may have distorted the original trend completely. One example on hand is Daoism. The Daoism of Lao Zi and the Daoism as a religion are opposite theories. Lao Zi stresses the sacredness of the Nature. In Lao Zi's view, the proper behavior of man is "non-action," because only when man gives up his endeavor can he be at one with the Dao. Therefore, whatever is simple and natural is good. Daoism as religion, on the contrary, defies the law of the Nature by seeking immortality. Longevity constitutes the ultimate target of pursuit. To prevent the body from ageing, many Daoists became the world's first chemists through concocting longevity medicines.

Similarly, the Confucianism of Confucius and the Neo-Confucianism of the Song Dynasty are drastically different theories. The classical Confucianism is aimed at providing moral and behavioral guidance to men, while Neo-Confucianism offers guidance to introspection. Hence, it is important to examine a theory on its own merit.

Confucianism

Confucius (551-479 B.C.) was born in a small state by the name of *Lu*, located in today's Shandong Province. Mostly self-taught, he was able to acquire a great wisdom and subsequently establish a system of moral values and ethical behavior. A great educator as he was, Confucius did not profusely publish. His thoughts were recorded in the book *The Analects* which was put together by those attentive note-takers among his disciples.

Confucianism has obviously been the most influential school of thought throughout the history. Confucius and his follower, Mencius (370-300 B.C.), laid down a moral system that was not only taught to kings and lords, but also to commoners. The system gained the status of state philosophy during the Han Dynasty. Since then, Confucianism had been viewed as the most authoritative source of wisdom and stability by almost every dynasty.

The status of Confucianism has, however, gone through many changes. Since the May 4th Movement of 1919, the once state philosophy has been faced with challenges coming from science and democracy. After 1949, Confucianism virtually vanished from the ideological arena until the start of the reform in 1978. Today, as China is dashing toward an industrialized society, there seems to be a reviving interest in Confucianism. Despite many outdated details, Confucianism contributes to the modern life by bringing about peace, unity, and the family bonding. Premier Wen Jiabao summarized the modern value of Confucianism in his speech delivered at Harvard University, 12 December 2003, as follows:

> From Confucius to Dr. Sun Yat-sen, the traditional Chinese culture
> presents many precious ideas and qualities, which are essentially

populist and democratic. For example, they lay stress on the importance of kindness and love in human relations, on the interest of the community, on seeking harmony without uniformity and on the idea that the world is for all. Especially, patriotism as embodied in the saying, "everybody is responsible for the rise or fall of the country;" the populist ideas that, people are the foundation of the country and that people are more important than the monarch; the code of conduct of, don't do to others what you don't want others to do to you; and the traditional virtues taught from generation to generation: long suffering and hard working diligence and frugality in household management, and respecting teachers and valuing education. All these have played a great role in binding and regulating the family, the country and the society.[3]

Indeed, the Confucian system, as a whole, conveys an unwavering conviction that the nature of man is primarily good, and that the goal of the mankind is to pursue happiness. The sure way of pursuing happiness is in self-improvement, according to the theory, and through education. For that reason, Confucius is commemorated more as an educator than a philosopher. To establish a system as such, however, Confucius had to break many new grounds. In fact, the concepts of "equality" and "gentleman" were not only revolutionary at his time, but remain to be the goal of human progress today.

Gentleman

For Confucius, the concept of "gentleman" is not one that refers to the social stratum or the good birth of a person, but rather one that represents the person's moral standing and his capability of serving the country. As such, what matters are the qualities acquired through education, rather than any title that is inherited from ancestral lineage.

Confucius' lecture hall must have presented a scene of what we call in modern terms "cultural diversity." There were the rich, the poor, the brilliant, and the mediocre. At any rate, Confucius put everyone on the same ground or the moral virtue. For instance, Confucius showed admiration of Yu, a student who "wearing a shabby hemp-quilted robe" was able to hold his chin high among those "dressed in badger and fox."[4] What transcends from this example is a further depth of the Confucianism: in addition to acquiring knowledge, a gentleman must give up prejudice. Confucius insists that a person who cannot give up prejudice "is not yet worthy to be discoursed with."[5] Confucius' emphasis on equality and his courage in breaking the social stratification might have been related to his own humble background. Indeed, in multiple occasions Confucius voiced his despise for people who were well fed but good for nothing. Nevertheless, the status of wealth has no footing in his system.

If equality was a revolutionary concept at the time, it was because the title of "gentleman" was one of nobility; no one could be a gentleman without a compatible birth status. Confucius changed this title to one of qualification with respect to moral standards. Lineage is irrelevant, since only when a man is in possession of sound moral values and the capability of ethical behavior does he deserve the title. Moreover, a gentleman is entitled to serve in the government, whereas those who do not meet the moral standards must not be trusted with leadership. For Confucius, the ruler governs by moral excellence, "He who governs by his moral excellence may be compared to the pole-star, which abides in its place, while all the stars bow towards it."[6] It is obvious that moral principles are not only what Confucius intends to teach, but also the foundation on which his theoretical system stands.

Equality

While human nature is of primary concern to most philosophers, for Confucius equality is of greater importance. Without declaring openly that man's nature is good, as his follower Mencius did, Confucius is a believer in man's good penchant. Moreover, the predisposition for being good is equal to all men of all strata. Thus, everyone is entitled to education, the rich and the poor alike, and everyone can be a gentleman to either serve the state or be model citizens. This would further imply that an honest administrative system is one that assigns positions according to the competence and the moral standing, which was a revolutionary concept at the time when the privilege of the legacy was the norm.

Confucius particularly encouraged his students to seek positions in the court, because it is in the court that the gentleman finds the most leverage. He expected his students to study and be good at it, so as to ultimately serve the state. He further urged them to be outspoken in front of lords and kings, because they would be in the court for many reasons and blind loyalty must not be one of them.[7]

It remains to be pointed out, though, that the Confucian equality does not exclude hierarchy. However, in the Confucian system, the hierarchical inequality must reflect differences in individual achievement rather than those of personal backgrounds. This was an admirably advanced thought at the time. The Confucian system does have historical limitations as well as system weaknesses. As one may have noticed that the right to equality, in particular, is not extended to women. In fact, while Confucius himself did not establish a system of social confinement for women, his theory obviously paved the way to a male dominant society.

Values

Confucius considers kindness, justice, respect, and filial piety to be the essential values that a gentleman must acquire, as these are fundamental to a harmonious society. The extent to which Confucius stresses the importance of filial piety may appear radical; from a practical angle, however, filial piety played an important role in stabilizing the society at a time when resources were scarce. The duty of caring for the elderly held the family together. Hence, the system was the equivalent of the modern social security system. Confucius even goes further to state that only when a son is capable of maintaining his father's ways for three years after the farther dies, can he qualify to be filial.[8] Obviously, Confucius extended filial piety to the level of safeguarding the *status quo*, which may well be his higher intention, given the fact that social order was being lost, respect was vanishing, and the era of the Warring States was looming. In an admonition to the youth, Confucius has this to say:

> When a youth is at home let him be filial, when abroad respectful to his elders; let him be circumspect and truthful and while exhibiting a comprehensive love for all men, let him ally himself with the good. Having so acted, if he have energy to spare, let him employ it in polite studies.[9]

Confucius believes that general happiness is achievable through mutual respect, and that it is respect that brings about order and peace. In his teachings, Confucius urges people to care for others for the same reasons that they do for themselves. When asked what would be the lifelong rule of one's conduct, Confucius replied, "Is not sympathy the word? Do not do to others what you would not like yourself." [10]

In the Confucian framework, self-cultivation and a well-regulated family constitute the first level of perfection. In the classic text entitle *The Great Learning* (from *Li Ji* or *Book of Rites*) ascribed to Zeng Can, a student of Confucius, the procedure for scholarly cultivation follows the order of perfecting the self, regulating the family, bringing peace and order to the country, and expanding peace and to the mankind. In fact, probably few scholars were able to clarify the family-government relationship better than Confucius. When a high official of Qi consulted on principles of governing, Confucius answered: "Let the prince be prince, the minister be minister, the father be father, and the son be son." [11]

Rule of Virtue

Confucius is an idealist. In the Confucian framework, social justice should be achieved through the implementation of moral virtues. Therefore, a government is worth respect only when its officials are upright. A ruler must rule by virtue, but not by authority alone. Confucius believes in the power of the role model. If a ruler is himself upright, Confucius indicates, his people will do their duty without orders; "but if himself be not upright, although he may order they will not obey." [12]

In addition to valuing the rule of virtue, does Confucius equally promote the rule of law? The answer is "no." Confucius considers rule of law unreliable without the backing of a good set of moral values. Laws and regulations would ultimately become infinitely complicated, he assumes, and yet perpetrators would unfailingly outsmart the rules. Hence, moral cultivation must come first; rule of law will follow. In Confucius' view, it is only after the people have acquired a sense of shame, can they become law-abiding citizens. Confucius argues:

> If you govern the people by laws, and keep them in order by penalties, they will avoid the penalties, yet lose their sense of shame. But if you govern them by your moral excellence, and keep them in

order by your dutiful conduct, they will retain their sense of shame, and also live up to this standard.[13]

Therefore, Confucius concludes that it would be better off if the government does not have to resort to reward and punishment. This does not mean that he ignores the fact that the "sense of shame" is insufficient to induce order by itself, which may explain why Confucius, while promoting moral cultivation whole-heartedly, does not discard the law. In contrast, Lao Zi, the founder of Daoism does.

Learning

In the Confucian framework, learning is the utmost thing to do for all men. It is through learning that one acquires lofty ideals. Moreover, it is not high positions that one should primarily be concerned with; it is rather about gaining the qualities that make one deserving.

The Analects is an inspiring set of admonitions that Confucius provides to his students. His recommendations encompass not only issues of virtues, but also learning methodology. Confucius stresses the importance of modesty. He argues that a modest attitude is the most important premise for learning. A good learner needs to have a broad mind so that he could draw knowledge even from the mediocre. "When walking in a party of three," said Confucius, "my teachers are always present. I can select the good qualities of the one and copy them, and the unsatisfactory qualities of the other and correct them in myself."[14]

In addition to providing general guidance, Confucius does not miss small issues such as manners. Once when he saw a student talking to him while maintaining a squatting posture, he went up and hit his shank with his staff, "When young being mannerless, when grown up doing nothing worthy of mention, when old not dying, this is being a rogue!"[15]

Then, there is the premise to modesty: Sincerity and altruism, according to Confucius, are qualities that a serious scholar must have. The pursuit of the truth, or the Dao, must be the primary goal in one's life: "He who heard the truth in the morning might die content in the evening."[16]

In teaching, Confucius stresses patience. Instead of constructing a fantastic metaphysical framework, Confucius rather presented a step-by-step guidance to the righteous conduct, a code of behavior, so to speak, something that ordinary people can easily follow. In learning methodology, Confucius is a strong advocate for critical thinking. He urges his students to think as they read, because if a learner does not question what he reads, he is only accumulating stagnant and useless knowledge. This detailed approach, however, has not limited the generality of the Confucian theory. In fact, while the Chinese society has tremendously modernized, Confucianism continues to be an under current that marks the behavioral pattern of the Chinese people.

The multiple facets of Confucianism put together converge to a theory that emanates from the trust of the human nature and relies on education to both maintain and enrich its quality. Confucius believes in man's capability in improving the human conditions and trusts man to be able to do good. For that reason, Confucianism is said to be a philosophy of "human heartedness and righteousness." [17] When compared with Daoism and Legalism, one realizes that this is indeed the hallmark of Confucianism.

Close-up: The Analects

When Zigong asked what were the essentials of government, the Master replied: "Sufficient food, sufficient forces, and confidence of the people." "Suppose," rejoined Zigong, "I were compelled to dispense with one, which of these three should I forgo first?" "Forgo the forces," was the reply. "Suppose," said Zigong, "I were compelled to eliminate another, which of the other two should I forgo?" "The food," was the reply; "for from the old death has been the lot of all men, but a people without faith cannot stand." [18]

The Master said: "In teaching there should be no class distinctions" [19] (Chinese text on the right).

Confucius said: "There are three ways of pleasure-seeking that are beneficial, and there are three that are harmful. To seek pleasure in the refinements of manners and music, to seek pleasure in discussing the excellences of others, to seek pleasure in making many worthy friends — these are beneficial. To seek pleasure in unbridled enjoyment, to seek pleasure in looseness and gadding, to seek pleasure in conviviality — these are harmful." [20]

The Master said: "Yu, have you ever heard of the six good words and the six things that obscure them?" "Never," was the reply. "Sit down then, and I will tell you." "Love of kindness, without a love to learn, finds itself obscured by foolishness. Love of knowledge, without a love to learn, finds itself obscured by loose speculation. Love of honesty, without a love to learn, finds itself obscured by harmful candor. Love of straightforwardness, without a love to learn, finds itself obscured by misdirected judgment. Love of daring, without a love to learn, finds itself obscured by insubordination. And love for strength of character, without a love to learn, finds itself obscured by intractability." [21]

The Master said: "By nature men nearly resemble each other; in practice they grow wide apart." [22]

Mencius (370 - 330 B.C.)

The philosophy of Mencius is recorded in the book that bears his name.[23] *Mencius* is a lengthy book with more than thirty-five thousand Chinese characters, which is much more voluminous compared to *The Analects* of Confucius and *Dao De Jing* of Lao Zi combined. In terms of writing style, *Mencius* represents an interesting change from the brisk and sketchy style in which the Confucian and the Daoist texts were written. The writings of Mencius are more articulate in language use and better structured in presentation.

Similar in a way to most Confucian scholars, Mencius sought governmental positions. He traveled from court to court, lecturing kings and lords. As much as he was revered as a master of profound learning, he never received a commensurate position. The failure in "job search" was probably due to his straightforward personality that he had no intention to hide. On the other hand, Mencius kept a safe distance from the murky politics. As he put it, "A gentleman delights in three things and being the ruler over the Empire is not amongst them."[24]

Benevolence Above All

Mencius trusts human nature to be good and endowed with heavenly qualities.[25] He believes that the truth of the universe dwells inside the human nature and enables man to know right from wrong. Man's senses may be deviated by his surroundings, as some may be rich while others poor; Mencius insists, however, that everyone is entitled to pursue happiness and all men deserve benevolent treatment.

Benevolence, as Mencius argues, is in the human nature. This is because every human being wishes to be treated well and, therefore, would naturally be willing to respect others. In governing, Mencius stresses benevolence above all. In his view, the ruler is in a crucial position to exercise benevolence, and must take people's well-being as his primary concern. History has shown that without benevolence, the ruler loses his people, while with it, he gains people's support. Therefore, the best government is one that puts people to work, enabling them to raise their families.

One example is the conversation with the King Hui of Liang. When the King inquired about the reason why his people were running away from his state despite his sensible care for them, Mencius pointed out that his majesty was too fond of warfare and vanity. He explained that there would be no difference between killing a man with a knife and letting him die under a misruled regime. The neighboring king might be cruel to his people, but getting people killed in battlefields, the kind of actions that King Hui was fond of, was simply worse. Therefore, a successful ruler should rather win by exercising benevolence, thereby attracting people from other states to his side, than by expanding the territory through wars.[26] Mencius stated:

> A territory of a hundred *li* square is sufficient to enable its ruler to become a true king. If your majesty practices benevolent government towards the people, reduces punishment and taxation, gets the people to plough deeply and weed promptly, and if the able-bodied men learn, in their spare time, to be good sons and good younger brothers, loyal to their prince and true to their word so that they will in the family serve their fathers and elder brothers, and outside the family serve their elders and superiors, then they can be made to inflict defeat on the strong armor and sharp weapons of Qin and Chu armed with nothing but staves.[27]

On Human Nature

By trusting human nature to be good, Mencius further accepts that the goodness is bestowed by Heaven, one that includes "benevolence, dutifulness, conscientiousness, truthfulness to one's words, unflagging delight in what is good."[28] Moreover, for Mencius, the heart of compassion is possessed by all men alike. Likewise, the heart of shame, the heart of respect, and the heart of right and wrong are pre-existing qualities that man is born with. The fact that some people turn bad, Mencius argues, is "only because there are people who fail to make the best of their naïve endowment."[29] According to Mencius, a great man is simply the product of the guidance of greater interests. Because men are not exposed to the same circumstances, they may be drastically different.

The difference between the Mencian theory and that of Confucius lies in their perceptions on learning. Confucius believes that all of the qualities that Mencius endorses need to be learned through conscious efforts. Hence, self-cultivation is a diligent process that must not be left out. The sense of shame, for example, is a derivative of the great moral values acquired. This is what differentiates inherited nobility from the moral standing of a gentleman. Thus, Confucius does not openly confirm human nature to be good. Instead, he rather stresses learning. Mencius, on the contrary, makes every effort to justify the point that the best way to know Heaven is by understanding one's own nature to the fullest. Furthermore, it is by introspection that one reaches the truth, as Mencius argues, because human nature is bestowed with perfection, and learning is only supplemental. Here is how he argues for the source of benevolence:

> All the ten thousand things are there in me. There is no greater joy for me than to find, on self-examination, that I am true to myself. Try your best to treat others as you would wish to be treated yourself, and you will find that this is the shortest way to benevolence.[30]

In spite of his trust on human nature, Mencius does not ignore the impact of material well-being on spiritual perfection. The Mencian economic theory stresses the concept of storing the nation's wealth in people's homes rather than in the royal warehouse. In fact, Mencius insists that without a sufficient living, the good nature couldn't be expected to fully develop. Similarly, benevolence or the "kingly way" (wang dao) would hardly be feasible in a poverty and starvation-stricken state. Mencius states:

> The common people cannot live without water and fire, yet one never meets with a refusal when knocking on another's door in the evening to beg for water or fire. This is because these are in such abundance. In governing the Empire, the sage tries to make food as plentiful as water and fire. When that happens, how can there be any amongst his people who are not benevolent? [31]

In retrospect, it is a fact that throughout the history, rulers routinely failed to heed Mencius' admonition to put people's livelihood ahead. Consequently, instability in the government, failing economies, and social conflicts have been typical causes of the downfall of every dynasty. On the other hand, however, Mencian theory has generated heated debates over the kingly way ruling. Could an unbridled human nature be trusted? Would an anarchic state of the society lead to stability and a plentiful life? Would the Mencian theory have, in effect, discouraged the quest for the rule of law and, hence, contributed to a long-lasting authoritarian legacy?

In any case, it may well be reminded that what Mencius offers to us is only one of the many dimensions of thought in history. To achieve a better understanding, one may benefit from examining some opposite theories.

Lao Zi and Zhuang Zi

The Daoist bible *Dao De Jing,* or "the Way and Its Spirituality," was accredited to Lao Zi who is assumed to be living in the 5th century B.C. Lao Zi may have been a contemporary of Confucius and may have encountered Confucius one way or another. This is only a speculation based on the fact that there are multiple commentaries in *Dao De Jing* on such concepts as "virtue" and "filial piety" that are essential components of Confucianism. However, little is known about Lao Zi's identity. Even the name itself is a mystery: "Lao" means "old and venerable," and "Zi" means "master." Given his great learning, Lao Zi is believed to be an archivist working for the royal library of Zhou House.

A legend goes that as Lao Zi had reached his old age, he decided one day to ride off to the desert and die there. At the gate of the desert, he was greeted by the gatekeeper of the desert by the name of Yin Xi. The latter convinced Lao Zi to leave his enlightening words to the world, upon which Lao Zi wrote down the 5,000 characters in rhymed verses.

Dao De Jing is recognized by many as the necessary opposite of Confucianism, that is, without the Daoist contrarian view, much of Confucianism would hardly have been as meaningful as it is. The opposite is also true. In terms of its volume, *Dao De Jing* is equivalent to an average journal article today. In terms of its contribution to the Chinese civilization, however, the 5,000 characters have left an astounding impact.

The human nature is irrelevant within the framework of Daoism, because Lao Zi argues that man must be at one with the Dao in order to be powerful. Moreover, the best action is non-action. The most power is achieved when human beings give up their striving and let the Dao take care of all. These concepts constitute a sharp contrast with the Confucian human-heartedness and righteousness and what appears to be an unpractical idea, if not completely nonsense, one may say.

The attractiveness of Daoism lies in that it offers a dimension of thinking that is often ignored, one that argues in favor of the negative rather than against it. Maspero appropriately commented that Daoism is such a mystical philosophy that it may seem nonsense to a point; however when one goes out to the nature to enjoy the view of the trees, the mountains and the fury of the thunderstorms, everything Lao Zi says would seem possessing of a very touching truth.[32] In fact, in exploring the Daoist bible, one may be surprised to realize that there are so many connections between the seemingly absurd theory and the life experiences of the modern day. Below is a story that serves as an illustration on where the concept of non-action may continue to fit in modern life.

> A casually dressed fisherman was fishing on the Hudson River when a Wall Street stockbroker strolled over to have his lunch. Sympathizing with the fisherman's worn out gear, he whispered, "Well, you should do stocks, like me." "Why?" asked the fisherman. "Well, here is the plan for you: You'll make big money trading stocks; then, with that money you'll set up your own company, say a telecom firm. Then, you make a public offering and people will buy your stocks like crazy, so you make tons of money in no time." "Then what?" asked the fisherman in a flickering voice. The stockbroker laughed out loud, "Then what? Then you will finally be able to sit down fishing, happy, content and without worries!" "Money is what I don't have, but I surely am happy catching fish." the fisherman murmured.

The Dao

For Confucius, Dao represents the truth that can be gained through learning. For Lao Zi, the Dao means the absolute, the source that generated the tens of thousands of things. It is "nameless" and "eternal"; it is the beginning of heaven and earth.[33]

Non-action

As previously mentioned, Daoism is a theory of the reversal, one that counters the positive thinking typically represented by Confucianism.

While Confucianism and many other schools of thought approve one way or another of human progress, Daoism would rather despise it. "Returning is the motion of the Dao," [34] as Lao Zi put it; every human achievement is of no significance, if not counterproductive. For that reason, Daoism has been labeled "skepticism" by some, and "pessimism" by others.

For the Daoist, the best action is non-action. The ultimate power comes from non-striving. The less man strives, the better the Nature runs its course. Therefore, only when man is at one with the Dao, can he be the most powerful. "Non-action" and "non-striving," however, are not intended to mean that man should give up all cravings and actions. What it means is to be content with the simple, to do less, and to avoid the unnecessary. Maintaining simplicity to the utmost is the recommendation. To explain this, Lao Zi has the following verses:

> Do you think you can take over the universe and improve it?
> I do not believe it can be done.
> The universe is sacred.
> You cannot improve it.
> If you try to change it, you will ruin it.
> If you try to hold it, you will lose it.
> ...
> Therefore, the sage avoids extremes, excesses, and complacency.[35]

If striving is unbeneficial, then, such effort would more likely hurt the natural course and ultimately man himself. Therefore, from the Daoist perspective, when man abides in non-action, nothing is left undone, and everything would be in order.[36]

Daoist Way of Governing

Being concerned with the fact that man is essentially a creature constantly striving for the more and the better, Lao Zi dedicates a significant portion of his book to dissuade the human endeavor. In addition, the Daoist master laid out perspectives about how things should be managed in order to be beneficial. The laissez-faire way of governing is one of such plans.

In light of Daoism, things that are typically positive within the Confucian framework yield negative relationships. Thus, striving for a better material life leads to poverty. Intelligence gives rise to cunningness and pretentiousness. Thieves and robbers are borne by laws and regulations. If the Confucian ideals have never been achieved, why not give the Daoist way of governing a chance? But this proves to be practically inconvenient. As expected, the best way to govern, according to Lao Zi, is not to govern, because what gives rise to wars and chaos is exactly human interference. Lao Zi states:

> The more laws and restrictions there are,
> The poorer people become.
> The sharper men's weapons,
> The more trouble in the land.
> The more ingenious and clever men are,
> The more strange things happen.
> The more rules and regulations,
> The more thieves and robbers.[37]

Therefore, when the ruler takes no action, people are reformed all by themselves. When the ruler has no desires, people return to the good and simple life. Lao Zi is aware, however, that a country needs to be governed, and that anarchy cannot be the chosen policy. At least, from the point of view of practicality, government is needed, as people must be guided into the right direction. How would the Daoist sage govern a country? Here is Lao Zi's recommendation (The Chinese text follows.):

> Not exalting the gifted prevents quarreling.
> Not collecting treasures prevents stealing.
> Not seeing desirable things prevents confusion of the heart.
> The wises therefore rule by emptying hearts and stuffing bellies,
> by weakening ambitions and strengthening bones.
> If people lack knowledge and desire,
> Then intellectuals will not try to interfere.
> If nothing is done, then all will be well.[38]

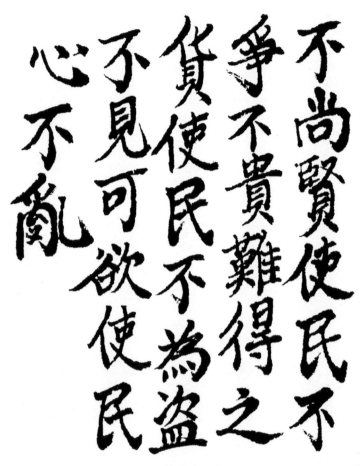

不尚賢使民不爭不貴難得之貨使民不為盜不見可欲使民心不亂

As one may realize through reading these verses that it is, in effect, incomplete to assume that the Daoist framework is anti-government. On the contrary, Daoists trust the "wise" and the sage king to build the ideal society. As for how the Daoist government functions, Lao Zi does not elaborate. It is obvious, however, that depriving the will of action is the first step.

Daoism and Legalism share a common ground here. Legalists stress that the sage king, instead of trusting men to be able to do good, makes sure that no one dares to do bad. The difference is, while Daoists intend to achieve non-action by depriving the will of action, legalists strive to mold people's action. Hence, legalism has been directly applicable, while Daoism has not. If there is a connecting point between the two theories, than, it is in absolute control.

Daoist View on Learning

Daoism and Confucianism have opposite views on learning. Confucius believes that man must first perfect himself through personal cultivation before he can do any good to the world. From the Daoist perspective, learning is unnecessary. Knowledge can be confusing. When knowledge is mingled with desires, it makes man pretentious and counterproductive. Thus, Daoism despises learning, and promotes simplicity and innocence as virtuous ways of life. In this regard, Lao Zi has the following to say:

> I am a fool. Oh yes! I am confused.
> Other men are clear and bright,
> But I alone am dim and weak.
> Other men are sharp and clever.
> But I alone am dull and stupid.
> . . .
> I am different.
> I am nourished by the great mother.[39]

What is implied here is that intelligence is counterproductive preventing man from receiving enlightenment from the Dao or the "great mother." Furthermore, Lao Zi complained in multiple occasions that people had lost their original innocence and, hence, their strengths, because they had gained too many desires and too much knowledge. Therefore, if man's endless pursuit of satisfaction makes him miserable and distant from the Dao, the following is what man should do:

> Give up sainthood, renounce wisdom,
> And it will be a hundred times better for everyone.
>
> Give up kindness, renounce morality,
> And men will rediscover filial piety and love.

> Give up ingenuity, renounce profit,
> And bandits and thieves will disappear.[40]

On Virtue

Unlike Confucius who dedicatedly constructs a moral system for man, Lao Zi rejects such efforts. For the Daoist sage, the utmost and only virtue is "knowing harmony,"[41] because only when man understands the significance of being in harmony with the natural course, can he truly be an enlightened being. Therefore, Lao Zi maintains, "All things arise from Dao. They are nourished by virtue." And furthermore, "the greatest Virtue is to follow Dao and Dao alone."[42]

What is the Daoist opinion on Confucian virtues, then, such as kindness, justice, respect, and loyalty? In Lao Zi's view, the fact that these qualities were raised to the level of duties signifies that they are lost already. If morality is enforced, that is because the Dao has fallen into oblivion. If filial piety becomes the primary duty of the youth, that is because there is no peace within the family. Similarly, if loyalty is valued, that is because loyalty is diminishing.[43] Lao Zi states:

> Therefore, when Dao is lost, there is goodness.
> When goodness is lost, there is kindness.
> When kindness is lost, there is justice.
> When justice is lost, there is ritual.
> Now ritual is the husk of faith and loyalty, the beginning of confusion.
> Knowledge of the future is only a flowery trapping of Dao.
> It is the beginning of folly.[44]

Lao Zi does not deny the Confucian values. In fact, he is all for them. However, from the Daoist point of view, introducing these values to the mankind through education is like putting the donkey behind the cart. The right way, then, would be to return to a state of simplicity and non-striving, in which case filial piety and kindness would be the norm.

Daoist Advice on Human Behavior

Similar to Confucius, Lao Zi demonstrates an unabated patience in elaborating his concepts. Although Confucianism and Daoism are drastically different philosophies, one may find many points of connection. For example, both Confucius and Lao Zi stress modesty in attitude, although the intention of Confucius is to encourage learning, while that of Lao Zi is to urge people to be content. The following are a few recommendations by Lao Zi:

1. Be content. "He who knows he has enough is rich." "He who is attached to things will suffer much. He who saves will suffer heavy loss. A contented man is never disappointed. He who knows when to stop does not find himself in trouble. He will forever stay safe." [45]

2. Be modest. "Those who know do not talk. Those who talk do not know." "Achieve results, But never glory in them. Achieve results, but never boast. Achieve results, but never be proud. Achieve results, because this is the natural way. Achieve results, but not through violence. ... That which goes against the Dao comes to an early end."[46]

3. Be truthful and focused. "In dwelling, be close to the land. In meditation, go deep in the heart. In dealing with others, be gentle and kind. In speech, be true. In ruling, be just. In business, be competent. In action, watch the timing."[47]

4. Be moderate. "Better stop short than fill to the brim. Over sharpen the blade, and the edge will soon blunt. Amass a store of gold and jade, and no one can protect it. Claim wealth and titles, and disaster will follow. Retire when the work is done. This is the way of heaven."[48]

5. Be flexible. "Yield and overcome; bend and be straight; empty and be full; wear out and be new; have little and gain; have much and be confused." "The softest thing in the universe overcomes the hardest thing in the universe. That without substance can enter where there is no room. Hence I know the value of non-action."[49]

Daoism and Confucianism seem to be two banners marking the ends of the ideological racetrack in which other philosophers compete. They are different, yet complementary. As Creel appropriately puts it,

"...paradoxically this philosophy [Daoism], so anti-Confucian, so anti-governmental, and in some ways so anti-democratic, has in fact collaborated with Confucianism to produce the very considerable amount of social and political democracy that China has known."[50] On the other hand, however, it is only fair to say that both Confucianism and Daoism contributed the authoritarian system, making it long lasting and at times prosperous.

Zhuang Zi's Search for Human Happiness

Zhuang Zi (369-286 B.C.) is among the first Daoist philosophers to ponder such concepts as freedom and happiness. Zhuang Zi's philosophy is recorded in his writings entitled *Zhuang Zi*. With respect to the style of presentation, Zhuang Zi breaks the traditional way of philosophical reasoning. His arguments are supported with the liveliest and boldest allegories and anecdotes, often leaving the reader with an experience of the wildest freedom.

Zhuang Zi searches into the meaning of happiness, freedom, as well as that of life and death, as these concepts are often related. In *Happy Excursion*, Zhuang Zi tells the story of a giant bird and a small bird: The giant bird flies high and far while the small bird barely flies from tree to tree. Yet, the difference in size does not seem to bother them a bit, as they are equally happy and proud, because both perform "the best kind of flying anyway."[51] Hence, happiness depends on the individual.

In another chapter, Zhuang Zi gives the example of ducks and cranes. Ducks' legs are short and cranes' are long. If one lengthens ducks' legs or shortens cranes' to make them look happier, one would definitely end up killing them. Therefore, whatever is natural and spontaneous is essential to happiness; whatever man imposes on the Nature leads to failure. In politics, Zhuang Zi opposes the way of governing by law and by implementing reward/punishment, which he considers the same as lengthening ducks' legs and shortening those of cranes.

If happiness depends on the self, then, it must be the same for unhappiness. Therefore, the source of both happiness and unhappiness is the self. Again, in *Happy Excursion*, Zhuang Zi suggests that the absolute happiness can indeed be obtained by denying the self. Zhuang

Zi asserts that a perfect man has no self; the spiritual man has no achievement; and the true sage has no name. Unpractical, indeed, would it be for a man who seeks happiness to forget himself, the beneficiary, in the first place. Zhuang Zi tells us that forgetting the self is indeed the way to happiness. Here is a story of Zhuang Zi dealing with the death of his wife:

> When Zhuang Zi's wife died, Hui Zi went to condole with him, and finding him squatting on the ground, drumming on the basin, and singing, said to him "When a wife has lived with her husband, and brought up children, and then dies in her old age, not to wail for her is enough. When you go on to drum on this basin and sing, is it not an excessive (and strange) demonstration?" Zhuang Zi replied, "It is not so. When she first died, was it possible for me to be singular and not affected by the event? But I reflected on the commencement of her being; when she had not yet been born to life, not only had she no life, but she had no bodily form; not only had she no bodily form, but she had no breath. During the intermingling of the waste and dark chaos, there ensured a change, and there was breath; another change, and there was the bodily form; another change, and there came birth and life. There is now a change again, and she is dead. The relation between these things is like the procession of the four seasons from spring to autumn, from winter to summer. There now she lies with her face up, sleeping in the Great Chamber; and if I were to fall sobbing and going on to wail for her, I should think that I did not understand what was appointed (for all). I therefore restrained myself.[52]

Zhuang Zi's witty writings, indeed, have never failed to entertain and inspire. Particularly, Zhuang Zi contributed to making an otherwise profound but obscure theory, Daoism, one of the most popular philosophies enjoyed by ordinary people. It was under Zhuang Zi's pen brush that Daoism found its way into people's daily life. Even in modern life, Zhuang Zi's writings continue to offer the much needed relief to the broad masses who are faced with an intensely competitive living environment, making people realize how rewarding it is to be appreciative of what one already owns.

There is, however, another dimension where Daoism found its best application: The world of military strategies. The military theory of

Master Sun Zi is in essence a successful implementation of the Daoist concept of relativity.

Legalism

Xun Zi (310-220 B.C.) and his student Han Feizi (d. 233 B.C.) are representative theoreticians of the Legalist school of thought. Their books entitled *Xun Zi* and *Han Feizi*, provided effective guidance to rulers on a rule-based administration throughout the Chinese history. The promise of Legalism is best summarized by Han Feizi, "No state is forever strong or forever weak. If those who uphold the law are strong, the state will be strong; if they are weak, the state will be weak." [53]

Xun Zi and Han Feizi lived in the "Warring States" era. According to the tradition at the time, the nobles were bound by *li* or the rituals, but not by the laws. Laws and regulations were used on commoners. As the saying goes, "the *li* does not reach down to the commoners, the law does not punish court officials." Clearly, the "above-the-law" privilege granted to the nobles leads to inertia. This situation must be changed, as the survival of the states became more and more of a challenge. It was under these circumstances that Legalism emerged as an appealing thought.

The goal of legalism is to bring everyone, rich or poor, to an equal footing in front of the same set of laws and regulations. The king would govern only by the laws, rather then relying on kinship and favors. Xun Zi stresses employing men solely based on their merit instead of noble backgrounds. He urges rulers to swiftly appoint competent people to critical positions without waiting for their turn to come up. Similarly, incompetent officials must be dismissed without hesitation. Xun Zi states, "No man of virtue shall be left unhonored; no man of ability shall be left unemployed; no man or merit shall be left unrewarded; no man of guilt shall be left unpunished." [54] Although the legalist ideal was never literally implemented as the masters intended, it brought about a revolution at the time.

On Human Nature

A distinct difference between Legalism and the Confucianism lies in their perceptions of the human nature. Contrary to Mencius' conviction that human nature is good, legalists hold that human beings are born vicious. The proof for this judgment is derived from general tendencies of man, such as profit seeking, selfishness, and the insatiable pursuit of sensual pleasures. Xun Zi argued that such tendencies, if let develop unbridled, would result in strife, wrangling, hate and jealousy.[55]

Contrary to Mencius' belief that courtesy and moral values are endowed to man, Xun Zi argues that qualities had been created by sages to save man. And man has to learn these qualities in order to be saved. As further justification, Xun Zi cites the words allegedly said by the ancient wise ruler Shun,

> Once a man acquires a wife and children, he no longer treats his parents as a filial son should. Once he succeeds in satisfying his cravings and desires, he neglects his duty to his friends. Once he has won a high position and a good stipend, he ceases to serve his sovereign with a loyal heart.[56]

Hence, the legalist definition of man's nature is pessimistic, "... a man's nature is evil and that his goodness is the result of conscious activity."[57] Based on such understanding, the king's duty is to make man improve by forcing them to follow laws and rituals. Without enforced training, a man that is "wanton, reckless, and disobedient, vicious, evil, and lacking brotherly feeling"[58] is ill-omened, and wouldn't arouse sympathy if he falls into the hands of the law.

On the other hand, however, Xun Zi was aware of the fundamental flaw of legalism. When challenged on why only sages are able to create moral guidance while the rest are not, Xun Zi simply indicates that the sages perform "conscious activities" that are not part of the human nature.[59]

"Equality is Based on Inequality"

As aforementioned, legalism pursues equality on the basis the law. This, however, does not contradict with the essence of a seemingly conflicting view that men must be hierarchically divided. What legalists intend is primarily a matter of accountability.

Hierarchy must be reinforced, as legalists argue, before there could be peace and order. In fact, Xun Zi holds it that equality is a bad thing, simply because human beings are kind of creatures that prefer forming societies and hierarchies to maintaining equality. In places without hierarchical division, people would quarrel among themselves, and disorder will result: "When power is equally distributed, there will be lack of unity; where there is equality among the masses it will be impossible to employ them."[60] Therefore, Xun Zi places his hopes on the sage king, one who is enlightened and capable of governing in the light of the principle of higher and lower. He embraces the concept that equality is based on inequality, and calls it a rule from Heaven and Earth.[61]

The Trainer King

In terms of the techniques of governing, Xun Zi recommends that the king's duty be to lay out clear boundaries and to enforce responsibility through reward and punishment. This is all that a king needs to do. As long as the rules are clear, people will be happy to serve without hiding their talent. A king needs not worry about details, because they are taken care of by his subjects.

Legalism stresses the role of the king as the absolute dictator, not without being aware of the king's human limitations. In fact, the theory does emphasize that the king must be a skillful dictator. In this aspect, Han Feizi is a resourceful contributor to the theory. His book is a detailed manual on governing skills. Han Feizi proposes, for example, that punishment and rewards must go hand in hand. "The ruler never delays in handing out rewards, nor be merciful in administering punishments."[62]

On the issue of strengthening government control, Han Feizi strongly favors ideological uniformity that lines up with the law:

> ... in the state of an enlightened ruler there are no books written on bamboo slips; law supplies the only instruction. There are no sermons on the former kings; the officials serve as the only teachers. There are no fierce feuds of private swordsmen; cutting off the heads

of the enemy is the only deed of valor. Hence, when the people of such a state make a speech, they say nothing that is in contradiction with the law; when they act, it is in some way that will bring useful results; and when they do deeds, they do them in the army.[63]

If man is born with an urge for the gain, as Legalists contend, and if profit leads to the loss of moral values and, furthermore, to wrangling and strife, then, blocking the channels to profit must be the best cure. Han Feizi says:

An enlightened ruler will administer his state in such a way as to decrease the number of merchants, artisans, and other men who make their living by wandering from place to place, and will see to it that such men are looked down upon.[64]

With all these concepts established, an authoritarian regime is on its feet. The task of such a regime is to carry out absolute control; the way of implementation is through building a police society. Han Feizi summarizes the Legalist way of ruling as follows:

When a sage rules the state, he does not depend on people's doing good of themselves; he sees to it that they are not allowed to do what is bad... But if he sees to it that they are not allowed to do what is bad, then the whole state can be brought to a uniform level of order. Those who rule must apply measures that will be effective with the majority and discard those that will be effective with only a few. Therefore, they devote themselves not to virtue but to law.[65]

Comparing the Confucian virtue-based administration with its Legalist counterpart, one is tempted to place these theories in opposite camps. They are, indeed, very different theories particularly with regard to human nature. However, a deeper observation reveals their complementary aspect. In fact, the struggle between Legalists and Confucians was a never-ending one in history. While a pronounced difference exists between these theories, isn't it a fact that the Chinese empires were able to sustain their patterns for thousands of years by relying on both? A point of connection is that both theories serve to strengthen the authoritarian regime. Confucianism may well promote benevolence; however, to characterize Legalism as "a philosophy of counterrevolution seeking to defend the authority of the ruler against the increasing insistence that government exists for the people, not for the ruler"[66] is obviously an unfair judgment in favor of Confucianism.

The Art of War

Authored around the 6th century B.C., *The Art of War* of Master Sun remains a valuable resource for military as well as business strategists today. The author of the book, Sun Zi, or Master Sun, was probably a contemporary of Confucius (551-479 B.C.). Little is known, however, of his life. The popular belief is that he was a native of Wu, a small state at the time in southern China, and he dwelled away from civilization, so that he could avoid having to use his military talent to serve kings and lords. Eventually, however, Sun Zi made his theory known to the world; and more likely than not, he might have served the court in person.

One story of Master Sun's life is recorded in *Records of the Grand Historian* by Sima Qian (145-86 B.C.) of the Han Dynasty. The story goes that Master Sun was summoned to the court of Wu, for the King would like to test his military talent. As a challenge, the King let him train 300 women from the inner court, to which Master Sun agreed. He appointed two of the King's beloved concubines as company commanders. He then ordered the women to wear helmets and armor, and carry swords and shields. He proceeded to giving them instructions and orders to form battle formations. The master's sternness or maybe the drum beats might have been amusing to the ladies. They covered their mouth with their hands and laughed. After three orders and five instructions, the women laughed even louder. Upon this, Master Sun called in the Master of the Laws and executioners. The Master of the Laws read out the punishment for violation of the discipline: "Decapitation." Master Sun ordered to have the company commanders beheaded. The King descended from the viewing stand and pleaded for the lives of the two women saying that without them the food would be tasteless. Master Sun replied sternly that a general in command of the army may reject the king's orders. He indeed had the women beheaded.

When Master Sun again beat the drum, the women followed the orders faithfully. Master Sun then turned to the King, "Your majesty, the army is ready for the battlefield. Your majesty might send them into fire and water, and they will obey his orders. Use them to conquer all nations under Heaven."

The Art of War consists of thirteen chapters, each dealing with a specific aspect of warfare. Over the centuries, commentators have contributed a tremendous wealth of interpretations and illustrations. The fundamental concepts of Master Sun have proved to be a never-exhausting source of inspiration. A brief explanation of the principles is presented in the next section.

Warfare Must Not Be Taken up Lightly

Throughout the thirteen chapters, probably the most emphasized principle is prudence. Because wars determine the life and death of a nation, they must be planned most carefully. Moreover, wars must only be fought as the last resort. Therefore, the necessity of war must be thoroughly examined in terms of advantages and disadvantages. This includes assessing the enemy's strength in terms of terrain, effectiveness of command, discipline, and logistics. If the situation is not advantageous and the chance of victory is slim, then, one should not choose to fight. Neither the king nor the general should mobilize the troops out of anger. This is because, "Anger can revert to happiness, annoyance can revert to joy, but a vanquished state cannot be revived, the dead cannot be brought back to life."[67]

Winning with the Least Fighting

An evident and yet often ignored truth that is stated in *The Art of War* is that the goal of any armed struggle is winning but not persistence. Winning without fighting is better than winning by engaging in battles. For the attacker, a prolonged war is seldom beneficial, because it could easily exhaust the economy and result in the nation's own defeat. Therefore, according to Master Sun, long-term warfare should be avoided. The best strategy would be to win a war without bloodshed at all. That is why Master Sun argues that subjugating the enemy without fighting would value more than winning a hundred battles.[68]

If battles have to be fought, then, the best would be to attack the enemy at their planning stage; next would be to attack the troops; and the lowest would be to besiege a city or butcher a town.

Use Psychological Strategies

Master Sun considers psychological maneuvering a fundamental military strategy. He indicates that a military strategist must take into account the use of deception, and warfare is primarily based on deception. Therefore, the good warrior pretends to be incapable, though capable; pretends to be inactive, though active; and pretends to attack far away, though attacking nearby. On the other hand, a skillful general is able to seize or induce weaknesses on the opponent. In light of this principle, Master Sun gives the following strategies:

> Display profits to entice them. Create disorder in their forces and take them. If they are angry, perturb them; be deferential to foster their arrogance. If they are rested, force them to exert themselves. If they are united, cause them to be separated. Attack where they are unprepared. Go forth where they will not expect it.[69]

Military Decisions Must Not Be Disturbed

Countless historical examples show that when the ruler interferes with military decisions, the army could hardly be expected to win the war. This is simply because the civilian ruler, from his non-military perspective, would more likely issue wrong commands to confuse the army. Many classical military failures are known to have been caused by the civilian ruler who ordered the army to advance when it shouldn't, or to retreat when it shouldn't. Master Sun indicates, "the army whose general is capable and is not interfered by the ruler will be victorious."[70]

Emptiness and Fullness

It is common knowledge that an army that is fatigued and unprepared would more likely lose to the one that is rested and ready. Without a doubt, the effectiveness of military actions depends to a great extent on the army's readiness. This is why Master Sun has the following admonition: "With the near await the distant; with the rested await the fatigued; with the sated await the hungry. This is the way to control strength."[71] Therefore, one should not rely on the enemy not attacking, but rather depend on having an unassailable position.[72]

According to Master Sun, emptiness and fullness is a dynamic pair of concept. Fullness in oneself and emptiness in the enemy can be creatively induced. In application, this would involve striking the weak points of the enemy's defense line, or causing the enemy to come to you. To be always on the side of "fullness," however, requires that one maintain a sophisticated subtlety. By being subtle, "one can be the enemy's Master of Fate."[73]

Leadership

A general's ability to command an army can be judged through his relationship with soldiers, according to Master Sun. An effective general loves his soldiers and yet avoids spoiling them. Master Sun contends that when the general regards his troops as his beloved children, they will be willing to die with him. On the other hand, a general must be competent in implementing a strict discipline and have in place a clearly defined reward/punishment system. Without such a system, soldiers are spoiled and useless.[74]

Using Espionage

Master Sun stresses, once again, the importance of fighting a prepared war to avoid heavy losses. He is possibly one of the earliest military strategists who believes in information war. Master Sun agues that before mobilizing troops, the general must obtain accurate intelligence information on the enemy. Such knowledge cannot be gained by praying for the help from ghosts. It is gained by using spies. Master Sun lists five kinds of spies. They are the local spies who know the region, the internal spies who reside inside the enemy, the double agents who are spies of the enemy, the expandable spies who spread rumor to the enemy camp to cause split, and the living spies who bring back reports.[75] On the one hand, without using spies one could hardly gather some of the most valuable intelligence; on the other hand,

Master Sun indicates that unless the general has the utmost intelligence, he cannot deploy spies.

Buddhism and Its Impact

The introduction of Buddhism dates back to the Han Dynasty (206 B.C. - A.D. 220). The popular belief is that Buddhism made its way into China from the northwest by crossing the Kashmir region and over the Karakoram Mountains during the first century. The decline of the Western Han Dynasty opened an ideological window, allowing Buddhism to contend with the state philosophy Confucianism.

In fact, from the time of its introduction, Buddhism blended seamlessly with Chinese thoughts and expanded rapidly. From emperors to ordinary people, seekers of spirituality found a home in Buddhist teachings. The promise of *nirvana* (the cessation of rebirth and the cessation of sufferings) answered a pursuit that did not get fulfilled in Chinese philosophies. Buddhism, hence, was not regarded as a completely foreign injection, but rather as a continuation from where the classical Chinese thoughts ended.

Chinese thoughts, Daoism in particular, had already prepared an ideological foundation for the incoming of Buddhism. The Daoist concepts of non-striving, simplicity, and contentment found their counterparts in Buddhist teachings. As such, Buddhism became a natural extension of Daoism with an added section of afterlife. To some scholars, the *Soutras* (sacred texts), are simply a "foreign variant" of Lao Zi's *Dao De Jing*.[76] The saying goes that Buddhism was born in India and grew up in China.

The word "Buddha" means the "enlightened one." According to one tradition, a prince was born in 623 B.C. in Lumbini Park at Kapilavatthu, a border town between India and Nepal. He was named Siddhattha (wish fulfilled) and his family name was Gotama. He had a happy childhood and got married at the age of sixteen. After thirteen years of marriage and luxury life in the palace, he set out to look for the truth of life. The view of the poor, the sick, the aged, and the dead became the source of his awakening. At the age of thirty-five, while sitting under the Bodhi tree, the prince was enlightened and became the Buddha.

While there are many schools of thoughts under the umbrella of Buddhism, there are a number of concepts that are at the foundation of every theory. According to Buddhism, *Karma* or the sum of "volition" and "deed" propels all human endeavors. If *Karma* is the cause, then, the effect is the human life filled with desires. Ambitions need to be fulfilled; desires need to be satisfied; the cost that comes along is endless disappointment and sufferings. It is Karma that generates craving and cleaving. In Daoism these concepts belong to "striving." Both Buddhism and Daoism try to convince people that in order to be saved or to live in happiness, one must strive to be freed from such urge. Buddhism holds that life is *cyclical.* What one is today, being a human or a non-human, is a result of *Karma* of previous existence, the process of which is called *reincarnation.* Human is considered a higher form of life in Buddhism. Being a human, one has the option of accumulating good deeds and kind volition, which will be redeemed for a better next life.

Nonetheless, life on the wheel of *Rebirth* is a haunting worry. To be relieved from such worries, one needs to seek the permanent emancipation or *Nirvana,* a term that refers to the cessation of the cycles. Apparently, to be emancipated, one must cut off the source of sufferings by giving up *Karma.* The first step is to acquire the awareness that craving and cleaving are results of ignorance, and that everything material, such as wealth and fame, is *empty* at best. Realizing this means realizing that all striving eventually leads to deeper sufferings.

While everyone can achieve enlightenment and eventually gain salvation, one must first be committed to the Buddhist process of self-cultivation that entails the acceptance of the *Four Noble Truths* which includes the truth of suffering, the truth of origin of suffering, the truth of cessation of suffering, and the truth of the way to the cessation of suffering. In practice, on must follow the *Noble Eightfold Path* in all aspects of life. The *Eightfold Path* includes the right view of understanding, the right thoughts of intentions, the right speech, the right action, the right livelihood, the right effort, the right mindfulness and the right concentration. In principle, this means that one must strive to be benevolent, simple, and selfless. The minimum practice, particularly designed for the layman, involves refraining from killing, dealing in weapons and arms, using intoxicants, or dealing in poisons. For the dedicated practitioner, practicing celibacy is a further assurance for completion. Austerities are considered an empowering force to one's wisdom and perception.[77]

Until the Christian era, *Hinayana Buddhism* had been the dominant theory whereby the believer dedicates himself or herself to the pursuit of salvation. For the believer, salvation is a reward to the individual's effort. Therefore, helping others acquire enlightenment is not high on the agenda. *Mahayana Buddhism* was a development at a later stage based on a broader and deeper understanding of salvation. According to *Mahayana Buddhism*, one cannot be finally saved until all human beings are saved. Therefore, Mahayana Buddhists strive to work for the enlightenment of others. The broad acceptance of Buddhism in China is largely attributable to the universal spirit of *Mahayana Buddhism* and its practice.

In addition to bringing the gospel of salvation to the broad masses, Buddhism connects seamlessly to the traditional Chinese moral cultivation. In particular, the Confucian ideals of the "middle path," "respect," "benevolence," and "filial piety" are also found at the core of Buddhist teachings. Many monographs by Chinese literati believers offer a clear account of how their moral cultivation draw from Daoism, Confucianism, and Buddhism. The following narrative is an example of how Buddhism is used to extend Mencius theory on fate. The excerpt comes from *Liao Fan Si Xun*, a book of family admonitions written by Liao Fan who was a scholar-official during the Ming Dynasty and a Buddhist:

> I asked (to Yun Gu, a Buddhist monk): "Mencius said, 'if one's pursuit is fruitful, that is because one searches in his heart.' Therefore, virtues and kindness can be acquired through dedicated pursuit. As for wealth and fame, can one expect to acquire these through an ardent pursuit as well?" Master Yun Gu replied: "Mencius is not wrong, your understanding is. You may have forgotten what master Kumarajiva once said: all lands of wealth are close to the heart. As long as one searches in one's heart, one will find. The reward comes because of one's dedicated pursuit; virtues and kindness can be acquired along with wealth and fame. The reward is dual, both from within and from without. It is one's truthful pursuit that makes it so.[78]

Wealth and fame *per se*, as much as these are dreamed of, are ranked low and deemed misleading by almost every school of the classical Chinese philosophy. Profit is the source of evil and fame that of disasters, as the Chinese saying goes. This is where Buddhism introduces the much-needed balance: Buddhism attributes wealth and fame as a reward to the pursuit of moral virtues and kindness. Wealth and moral cultivation are thus connected.

Because Liao Fan diligently corrected every bit of his inappropriate behavior and accumulated thousands of deeds of benevolence in the meantime, he was able to reverse his fate that had been revealed to him by a Daoist monk. He had been destined to die at the age of fifty-three, and his best achievement would have been to succeed in a provincial test and to be rewarded the position of a county level official. Until he received Buddhist wisdom, every bit of his fate had panned out just as what the Daoist fortune-teller had predicted. Liao Fan related that he had been living an inactive life, without motivation to pursue anything beyond the daily routine, since all was predestined. It was Buddhism that brought him a new perspective of life, making him believe that one's fate can be changed. Not only one can choose the next life, but one can also make changes to this life, as long as one is committed to the Buddhist cultivation.

As a result, Liao Fan not only enjoyed a long life of over eighty years, but also acquired a prominent administrative position in the Capital, and a doctorate degree granted by the Palace. Clearly, it is in Buddhism that the Chinese more confidence and relief, because if good deeds lead to a next life that one prays for, they might as well be practically beneficial in this life. With the blessings of Buddha, everything is possible.

Another anecdote is that of Bodhidarma, a famous Indian monk who established Mahayana Buddhism in China. The story goes that Bodhidarma was once sitting in a hunter's hut when he learned that hunters were torching the mountain. After a deep meditation, he said, "Fire does not get ignited by itself; it is born from the heart. My heart is not burning, therefore, it gives rise to no fire." As he was saying these words, the mountain fire went extinguished. The moral of the story is, to the Buddhist, as long as one seeks, one will find. Moreover, the barrier between the natural and the supernatural does not exist.

Chinese Buddhists found rich resources in the Chinese culture to enrich Buddhism. One well-known example is the story of Yan Zhu, a hermit of the Warring States time. The story goes that the King of Qi learned that Yan Zhu was a person of tremendous learning and wanted to assign him to a high administrative position that would assure him wealth and fame. Yan Zhu refused, "My late meals are as tasty as meat; walking on foot is as comfortable as riding a pompous horse cart; having nothing to do with criminal offenses is the honor that I seek." Buddhists believe that the story best represents the spirit of content that underpins the true wealth.

Since Buddhism offers promises to the gentile and to the poor alike, the religion was widely accepted by the Chinese masses. Unlike the studies of traditional Chinese philosophies that impose a prerequisite on intellect and knowledge, thus reducing the enlightened to the very few, anyone can practice Buddhism in hope for salvation. Bodhisattva is a powerful god who is ready to lend a hand to anyone calling for his help, and all are entitled to redeem good deeds for a better next life.[79]

Zen Buddhism

Among the early schools of the religion, Zen Buddhism, or Zenism, is probably the most popular branch. The theory could be traced back to the 5th century of the Christian era. Zenism stresses "comprehension" or "awakening." The word "Zen" in Sanskrit means meditation. According to one tradition, an Indian monk by the name of Bodhidarma, known to the Chinese as Da Mo, introduced a Mahayana sect of Buddhism to China, which was later known as Zenism.

The most important contribution to the Zenist school is credited to Monk Hui-neng (638-713) who is believed to be of Guangdong origin. In a way, Hui-neng's theory moved Buddhism a step closer to Daoism. This is probably why Zenism means a lot more to the Chinese followers than other Buddhist theories. Chinese paintings and poetry are notoriously influenced by Zenism. An eminent feature of these art forms is their emphasis on the natural sceneries, the quietude, and the nonchalance of human figures.

Zenism builds on the concept of *wu* which means "non-existence" or "emptiness." As one recalls, non-existence and non-striving constitute the core of Daoism. In fact, in the *Soutras*, the word "non-action" is frequently used. The *Diamond Soutra* says, for example,

"The reason why sages are different is because they abide by non-action,"[80] which echoes the Daoist belief.

Zenism, however, is more thorough and more systematic in its practice of the *wu*. As one may remember, Buddhism recommends to its followers to perceive the "four noble truths" and to adhere to the noble "eightfold paths." Accumulating good deeds is even the most practical way for one to invest in a good next life. Buddhist believers often keep a detailed documentation of the good deeds accumulated. The previously mentioned Ming scholar Liao Fan was one of them. However, the dilemma is that the action of seeking salvation, in itself, is nevertheless a human "striving." Isn't the accumulation of good deeds a selfish act, given the fact that the practitioner has an agenda for himself? Early Buddhism was willing to accept such striving as an acceptable action. But Zenism picked up this detail and made it unacceptable: If emptiness is true, then no material gain can be a legitimate part of the truth, whether such gain is material or spiritual, benevolent or otherwise. The denial of striving has to be complete; making exceptions simply upsets the integrity of the system.

Without accepting part of the human striving as acceptable, wouldn't the religion be impossible to implement? How would one preach Zenism, for example, if speech is considered an unnecessary action? In fact, Zenism believes that the truth of Buddhism is inexpressible. Thus, the process of attaining spiritual enlightenment is through meditation, but not through learning from books or by taking lessons. It is said that Bodhidarma was enlightened after sitting faced to the wall for nine years.

Zenism does not trust words, because the net of words belongs to the material world and thus may well trap the truth and distort it. Therefore, if one inquires about enlightenment, the Zenist master would answer by saying things that are completely irrelevant. One story about keeping silence goes that Monk Hui-chung (d.775) was to debate another fellow monk. Instead of debating, he remained silent. Upon request, Hui-chung said, "I have already proposed my thesis, and I know, it is beyond your understanding." What Zenism stresses in this story is comprehension instead of learning.[81]

Following the same logic, Zenism does not value an important practice that is commonly promoted by other sects of Buddhism: Accumulation of good deeds in life. Good deeds are similar to bad ones, in light of Zenism, in the way that they all belong to the wheel of life and death powered by karma. Good deeds are not permanent; they are purposeful and moral-oriented. Good deeds are thus irrelevant in light of the truth of non-existence. Therefore, spiritual cultivation is primarily one of non-striving. As long as one avoids doing things purposefully, one is distancing the self from karma day by day. When eventually all current actions are free from the old karma, then, one is on the right path to attaining Nirvana.

Spiritual cultivation is not equivalent to enlightenment, according to Zenism, because enlightenment is attained through *sudden awakening* or the *dun wu* in Chinese. Self-cultivation is of no use, unless it eventually leads to one's awakening. Hence, an illiterate farmer is saved if he perceives the truth through witnessing the growth of the crops; a learned scholar may engage in life-long studies but remains in the darkness. As a Zen master once explained, a bad mistake is to look for ass while one is riding one. An even worse mistake, however, is to ride an ass and to be unwilling to dismount. These are both of deluded state of mind, because the search and the clinging are what tie the soul to the wheel of life and death. [82] However, the Zenist way of getting off the horse is indeed one of the most unpractical ways to follow in life.

Just as in implementing almost every principle in life, there are those who adopt the fundamentalist approach, while most tend to be more moderate. In Buddhism, there is a wide range of options to choose from the practitioner to quench the spiritual thirst. Even within the Zenist circle, not all practitioners follow Monk Hui-chung's approach. For the majority, the coming of Buddhism bridged the worlds of believers and non-believers, such that there is a perspective of the other shore in each. This explains why it is a trend today for many atheist business entrepreneurs to invest much of their hard-earned fortunes in sponsoring Buddhist temples. Meanwhile, Buddhist temples constantly come out with creative ways to meet the demand.

Close-up: Conversations of Shen-hui

[Shen-hui was a Zenist master of the 8th century. His lively debates shed light on important Buddhist principles. The following is a dialog on *birth* and *destruction*.]

The Master Shen-tsu asked Shen-hui: "You say that our Original Nature has the characteristics of the Absolute. In that case it has no colour, blue, yellow or the like, that the eye can see. How then can one perceive one's Original Nature?" Shen-hui answered, "Our Original Nature is void and still. If we have not experienced Enlightenment, erroneous ideas arise. But if we awaken to the erroneous nature of these ideas both the Awakening and the wrong ideal simultaneously vanish. That is what I mean by perceiving one's Original Nature." Shen-tsu again asked: "Despite the light that comes from the Awakening, one is still on the plane of Birth and Destruction. Tell me by what method one can get clear of Birth and Destruction?" Shen-hui answered, "It is only because you put into play the ideas of Birth and Destruction that Birth and Destruction arise. Rid yourself of these ideas and there will be no substance to which you can even distantly apply these names. When the light that comes from the Awakening is quenched, we pass automatically into Non-being, and there is no question of Birth or Destruction." [83]

---

[1] Jianshi Shen, *History of the Chinese Examination Systems [zhongguo kaoshi zhidu shi]* (Taipei: Taiwan ShangWu Publishing, Inc., 1995): 11.

[2] Yu-Lan Feng, *A Short History of Chinese Philosophy*, edited by Derk Bodde (New York: The Free Press, 1948): 36-37.

[3] Jiabao Wen, "Turning Your Eyes to China — Full Text of Premier Wen's Speech at Harvard University," 11 December 2003, <www1.chinadaily.com.cn/en/doc/2003-12/11/content_289494.htm> (14 January 2004).

[4] Confucius, *The Analects,* translated by William Edward Soothill (Originally published by Oliphant, Anderson, & Ferrier, Edinburg, 1910. Reprinted by Dover Publications, Inc., 1995): 51.

[5] Confucius, *The Analects*, 18.

[6] Ibid., 5.

[7] Ibid., 96.

[8] Ibid., 20.

[9] Ibid., 2.

[10] Ibid., 95.

[11] Ibid., 69.

[12] Ibid., 74.

[13] Ibid., 5.

[14] Ibid., 36.

[15] Ibid., 90.

[16] Ibid., 18.

[17] Yulan Feng, *A Short History of Chinese Philosophy*, 42.

[18] Confucius, 98.

[19] Ibid., 97.

[20] Ibid., 101.

[21] Ibid., 107.

[22] Ibid., 105.

[23] Mencius, *Mencius*, translated by D.C. Lau (England: Penguin Books, 1970).

[24] Ibid., 185.

[25] Ibid., 163-164.

[26] Ibid., 52.

[27] Ibid., 53.

[28] Ibid., 169.

[29] Ibid., 163.

[30] Ibid., 182.

[31] Ibid., 187.

[32] Henri Maspero, *Le Taoisme* (Paris, 1950): 227.

[33] Lao Zi, *Tao Te Ching*, translated by Gia-fu Feng and Jane English (New York: Vintage Books, 1972): One.

[34] Ibid., Forty.

[35] Ibid., Twenty-nine.

[36] Ibid., Thirty-seven.

[37] Ibid., Fifty-seven.

[38] Ibid., Three.

[39] Ibid., Twenty.

[40] Ibid., Nineteen.

[41] Ibid., Fifty-five.

[42] Ibid., Fifty-one, Twenty-one.

[43] Ibid., Eighteen.

[44] Ibid., Thirty-eight.

[45] Ibid., Thirty-three, Forty-four.

[46] Ibid., Fifty-Six, Thirty.

[47] Ibid., Eight.

[48] Ibid., Nine.

[49] Ibid., Twenty-two, Forty-three.

[50] H.G. Creel, *Chinese Thought from Confucius to Mao Tze-tung* (New York: The New American Library of World Literature, Inc., 1960): 97.

[51] Zhuang Zi, *Zhuang Zi*, translated by Burton Watson (New York and London: Columbia University Press, 1968): 31.

[52] *The Sacred Books of China — The Texts of Taois*, translated by James Legge (England: Oxford University Press, first print, 1891; India: reprinted by Motilal Banarsidass, 1968): 4.

[53] *Basic Writings of Mo Tzu, Xun Tzu, and Han Fei Tzu*, translated by Burton Watson (New York and London: Columbia University Press, 1967): Han Feizi, 21.

[54] *Basic Writings of Mo Tzu, Xun Tzu, and Han Fei Tzu*: Xun Zi, 42.

[55] Ibid., 157.

[56] Ibid., 168.

[57] Ibid, 157.

[58] Ibid., 30.

[59] Ibid., 160.

[60] Ibid., 36.

[61] Ibid.

[62] *Basic Writings of Mo Tzu, Xun Tzu, and Han Fei Tzu*: Han Feizi, 104.

[63] Ibid., 111.

[64] Ibid., 116.

[65] Ibid., 125.

[66] Creel, H.G. *Chinese Thought from Confucius to Mao Tze-tung,* 141.

[67] Sun Tzu & Sun Pin, *The Complete Art of War,* translated by Ralph D. Sawyer (Colorado: WestviewPress, 1996): 150.

[68] Ibid., 50.

[69] Ibid., 42.

[70] Ibid.,52.

[71] Ibid., 78.

[72] Ibid., 84.

[73] Ibid., 68.

[74] Ibid., 98.

[75] Ibid., 119.

[76] Feng, 241.

[77] Venerable Dr. Balangoda Ananda Maitreya Mahanayaka Thera Aggamaha Pandita, Dlit Dlit and Jayasili (Jacquetta Gomes BA DipLib MLS FRAS ALA), *Introducing Buddhism*, (Taipei: 1993).

[78] Liaofan Yuan (Ming Dynasty), *A Four-part Family Admonition (Liao Fan Si Xun) with Vernacular Annotation* (Taipei: Foundation of Buddhism Education, 1992): 23.

[79] Creel, 161.

[80] *A Course in Diamond Soutra* [Jin Gang Jing Jiang Yi] (Texas: Dallas Buddhist Association, 1993): 128.

[81] Feng, 258.

[82] Ibid., 263.

[83] *Buddhist Texts through the Ages*, Edward Gongze, ed. (New York: Philosophical Library, 1954): 299.

4
China in Transition

The Changing Communist Ideology

Mao Zedong Thought

Despite his destructive political campaigns, Mao Zedong (1893-1976) is recognized as a charismatic communist leader who brought about the most profound changes to China in the 20th Century. Unlike many of his contemporary revolutionaries who learned Marxism from the book and practiced it in a bookish way, Mao creatively integrated the theory with China's reality. Such integration gave rise to a revolution under the leadership of the CPC that defeated Jiang Jieshi's American-backed Nationalist forces, and gained China's independence in 1949. It was the same force, however, that led the new China into abysmal dark periods of the 1950s and 1960s when millions of lives were lost to senseless political struggles.

A variety of opinions exist on Mao's impact. Mao's communist revolution is typically blamed for interrupting the Chinese heritage. Mao's denial of traditional Confucian values is typically condemned as causing devastations to the Chinese culture in general. The trouble with this view is that it shifts the responsibility to one person, ignoring the fact that Maoism is also deeply rooted in the tradition. On the other hand, a contrarian view holds that thanks to Mao's drastic revolution, a new path is finally opened. The devastations of the 1960s-1970s forced China to break away from the traditional conservatism. The violence-dominated police society finally resulted in its own denial. These two factors are believed to be the underpinnings of the current economic reform. As Deng Xiaoping admitted in an interview with *CBS 60 Minutes* in 1986, Mao's failures inspired the choice of a new way for China.[1] It is only fair to say, however, that the full impact of Mao's legacy is yet to pan out as China forges ahead with its economic transition.

A Farmer's Son

What is known as "Mao Zedong Thought" is inseparable from the unique background of its founder. Mao Zedong was born in Shaoshan, a village forty miles away from Changsha, the capital city of the Hunan Province. Mao's father, a well-to-do farmer, was able to afford his elementary education at a village school. At age fifteen, to run away from a marriage arranged for him with a local girl who was five years his senior, Mao left home to attend a middle school and lived on a meager support from his father. Mao recounted later in his autobiography that he never lived with the girl and completely ignored the marriage.[2]

From 1913 to 1918, Mao went to Changsha to attend the First Normal School of Hunan. Being bored by teacher training, he read Adam Smith's *The Wealth of Nations* and Charles Darwin's *The Origin of Species*. These books had a great impact on him and raised his interest in Western philosophies.[3] By this time, important changes had taken place in China. Sun Zhongshan's republican revolution had failed. However, the Russian Bolshevik Revolution had succeeded, and the first socialist country had been founded.

After graduating from the First Normal, Mao went to Peking and accepted a job at the library of Peking National University, the predecessor of today's Beijing University. Under the influence of the head librarian Li Dazhao, Mao soon became a fervent communist. On 1 July 1921, Mao was one of the original founders of the CPC to attend the party's first conference. He soon proved to be the unrivaled mastermind of the communist movement. He demonstrated superior capability in interpreting and implementing communist principles. He was particularly a fine military strategist who saved the Red Army from peril on multiple occasions. Mao's leadership as the Chairman of the CPC was established in 1935 during the Long March. He guided the revolution through the toughest times, expanded the military forces during the Anti-Japanese War, and eventually defeated the Nationalist forces during the Civil War. Mao's unsurpassed leadership cast a glowing aura, such that a personality cult was conveniently developed during the 1960s by his handpicked successor Lin Biao. Mao maintained the highest positions until his death in 1976.

Military Ingenuity

Mao's rise to the leadership position was first attributable to his brilliant military ingenuity. Much it was drawn from Master Sun's *Art of War*, one of his favorite classics of all time. Back in 1947, Mao summarized the military experience of the Red Army into ten military principles. These principles are:

1) Attack the dispersed, isolated enemy first; attack the concentrated, reinforced enemy later.

2) Occupy the smaller cities and the vast rural areas first; attack the bigger cities later.

3) Wiping out the enemy's combat forces must be the main objective. Occupying territories is secondary.

4) In every battle, concentrate an absolutely superior force, surround the enemy, and assure a complete victory.

5) Never fight a battle that is unprepared for; never fight a battle that is unsure of victory.

6) Give full play to the Red Army's own style of fighting which highlights persistence and fearlessness.

7) Attack while the enemy is on the move. Be tactful in attacking enemy's fortified points and cities.

8) Attack weakly defended cities and fortified points; avoid attacking well-defended cities; wait till conditions are ripe.

9) Feed off the enemy's goods and supply; reinforce the troops with captured personnel.

10) Rest the troupes without giving the enemy the time to breath. [4]

The ten military principles effectively integrated China's reality with sound military strategies. At the foundation of these principles is the insightful master plan of enclosing cities from the countryside. This strategy assured the mobilization of the broad masses of the poor in supporting the communist cause. The result was eminent: the Nationalist forces residing in large cities were isolated. The flow of supply was tightened each day directly threatening the existence of the Nationalist bases. Meanwhile, the communist forces were as free as "fish swimming in the river," in Mao's words.

"Never Forget Class Struggle"

From the Marxist point of view, the victory of the proletariat over the exploiting classes is inevitable. Class struggle is the propelling force of all social changes in the history. Mao believes that class struggle, as a form of rebellion of the exploited classes, is reflected in all fronts. Domestically, class struggle manifests itself in the form of conflicts between poor peasants and landowners, between capitalists and factory workers, between Nationalists and Communists, and so on. This is determined by the reality of the economic discrepancy between the broad masses of the poor and the minority of the exploiting classes. Internationally, conflicts among countries ultimately boil down to class struggle as well, because imperialism is nothing but a form of exploitation. Mao argues: "in class society everyone lives as a member of a particular class, and every kind of thinking, without exception, is stamped with the brand of a class." [5]

Recurring peasant rebellions were the main cause of regime changes throughout the Chinese history. The pattern shows that polarization between the wealthy and the poor tends to intensify at significant economic downturns. Coming from the farmer's background and armed with the theory of class struggle, Mao was aware that the key to a successful revolution in China was in mobilizing the poor. Mao was further aware that while the goal of a communist revolution was to eliminate private ownership altogether, this goal must not be realized over night. As the first step, land must be equalized. Without satisfying the dream of ownership, the masses would not be willing to participate.

The Land Reform Movement launched during the Civil War (1946-1949) achieved the first goal. The nature of Land Reform was to redistribute ownership; the procedure was to confiscate landlords' property and distribute it equitably among the poor. In return, the poor farmers replenished the People's Liberation Army with the much-needed manpower. Through Land Reform, the CPC not only acquired soldiers, but also affected the morale of enemy combatants most of whom were drafted farmers wishing to own their share of land. Deserters from the Nationalist forces were not in the small numbers; immediately, the Nationalist troops that were "armed to the teeth" found themselves isolated in city strongholds. Their failure was only a matter of time. Meanwhile, Mao's military strategy of "enclosing cities from the countryside" brilliantly took advantage of the China's geographical and demographical situations, making the vast rural China a favorable battlefield.   There was little surprise that by 1 October 1949, the Nationalists had to abandon their footing in China and escape to Taiwan.

The second goal of the communist revolution, which is to eliminate private ownership completely, was achieved by 1958 through the movement of the People's Communes. Given that the power was assured in the hands of the CPC, the process of having farmers give up their land and work in communes was a relatively easy process. In urban areas, a similar process of de-privatization was launched whereby the state transformed private industries through state purchasing or simply through confiscations.

Bridging the West and the East

The success of the Russian Bolshevik Revolution brought inspirations to Chinese revolutionaries. However, for a Western theory to be adapted to the Chinese reality, much work needed to be done. As a totalitarian system, Marxism found its partner in Legalism. Mao perceived the connection, and from there developed his Chinese version of the communist theory.

A self-declared worshipper of the Qin Emperor, Mao was a firm believer in Legalism. Similarities between Communism and Legalism are abundant, indeed. From the Legalist view point, man is born selfish and greedy, therefore, must not be trusted to be able to do good. Instead, man must be forced to abide by the rules. In the communist framework, selfishness and greed are believed to give rise to economic inequality that necessarily results in exploitation. Consequently, the control of human nature is high on the agenda. Lin Biao, Mao's handpicked successor made it clear, "The entire communist theory can be summarized as doing away with selfishness and working for the public good.   While there are many theories of communism, the fundamental principle remains the same which is to uphold the public interest and to do away with selfishness."[6]

Mao raises the issue of control to a higher and more general level, the level of "class struggle." He argues that conflicts between the oppressors and the oppressed are inevitable; moreover, such conflicts tend to be violent, because "the enemy will not perish of himself."[7] In Mao's vivid description, class enemies are like dust that must be swept into the dustpan. In fact, Mao never hesitates to use cruelty on his class enemy. He eloquently elaborates: "A revolution is not a dinner party, or writing an essay, or painting a picture, or doing embroidery; it cannot be so refined, so leisurely and gentle, so temperate, kind, courteous, restrained and magnanimous. A revolution is an insurrection, an act of violence by which one class overthrows another." [8]

In fact, even the Legalist social control procedure proves to be directly applicable to the communist society. The practice of neighborhood watch, for example, dates back to the Qin Dynasty (221 - 210 BC). For thousands of years, the implementation of a police state had been helpful to the government in repressing dissidence. The Legalist policy of reward and punishment is, once again, the typical way of control during the 1960s and the early 1970s. In the Legalist framework, the role of the "trainer" is played by the sage king, while in communism it is the "people's democratic dictatorship" that assumes the control. In reality, the communist dictatorship is more under the control of one man than under the working class. It is obvious that while the terminology varies, the one-class-rule proves to be no different from the one-man-rule or Mao's rule.

The similarities may even go into the details. Under the Qin Dynasty, books are burned and intellectuals persecuted. Similarly, under the communist regime, Mao urges arts and literature to serve the communist goals. Those who fail to follow often find themselves punished one way or another. In Mao's system, intellectuals are ranked the lowest in social strata, after landlords, rich peasants, counter-revolutionaries, bad elements, rightists, renegades, enemy agents and capitalist roaders, all of whom are targets of the socialist dictatorship. In his speech delivered on 3 May 1975 to members of the Political Bureau, Mao quoted a line from a well known Revolutionary Peking Opera *Attacking the Tiger Mountain with Strategy*: "We can't do without the Number Nine." The comment was taken by some to mean a positive re-evaluation of intellectuals after years of political suppression. It is only fair to indicate that while intellectuals as a class are targets of the socialist revolution, Mao earnestly deploys scientists who were trained in the U.S. and Europe to take on key projects such as the first atomic bomb.

Friends and Enemies

Safeguarding the newly founded socialist country is Mao Zedong's top priority. He constantly re-evaluates the challenges and redraws the line between friends and enemies. Mao's criterion is simple and straightforward: "Whoever sides with the revolutionary people is a revolutionary. Whoever sides with imperialism, feudalism and bureaucratic capitalism, is a counter-revolutionary."[9] Mao constantly reminds his countrymen that the ruling party is faced with two types of contradictions – one between the people and the enemy, and the other within the people themselves. Conflicts between the people and the enemies and those within the people must be handled differently. "To put it briefly," Mao said, "the former are a matter of drawing a clear line between friends and enemy, and the latter a matter of drawing a clear distinction between right and wrong."[10]

Mao's methodology proves to be crude and indiscriminative. Take the handling of criticisms as an example, it is never easy, if not impossible, to tell whether a criticism comes from a constructive or a destructive motivation. Often times, much of the screening is left to the wildest interpretation, resulting in violent feud among innocent people. Even Mao himself realizes the complexity. "Within the ranks of the people," he admits, "the contradictions among the working people are non-antagonistic, while those between the exploited and the exploiting classes have a non-antagonistic aspect in addition to an antagonistic aspect."[11] In reality, however, the line between friends and foe is rather one drawn on the sand. The ever-changing Party policies render the task of "class categorization" even more difficult. The consequence is endless political campaigns and innocent people be persecuted.

But Mao is ready to carry on his crusade against potential enemies. He warns the Party, "After the enemies with guns have been wiped out, there will still be enemies without guns; they are bound to struggle desperately against us, and we must never regard these enemies lightly."[12] Through political movements, Mao aims at ridding the Party and the society of "bad" or "potentially bad" elements. The Anti Counter-revolutionary Campaign, the Anti-rightist Campaign both launched in the 1950s and the Great Cultural Revolution (GCR) launched in the 1960s are examples in this regard. Investigations are conducted at every level and everyone lived in fear.

Destruction and Construction

In addition to physically eliminating class enemies, Mao is forceful in utilizing the state propaganda machine to reinforce the communist ideology. The propaganda campaigns invariably encourage people to be loyal to the communist cause and to give up their selfishness. Such effort intensified after the failure of the Great Leap Forward that resulted in the Great Famine.

Known as the Campaign of Socialist Education (1964), the brainwashing campaign included educating people to put collectivism, patriotism, and socialism ahead of their own interests. Every citizen was urged to guard against capitalist, feudal, and extravagant life styles. Ironically, even three meals a day could hardly be guaranteed at the time; yet, people were called upon to guard against extravagance. This seemingly absurd maneuver, however, has a valid logic built-in: Reducing people's will of pursuing material wealth and letting everyone be content with the survival level are essential to the regime.

Mao was an idealist communist revolutionary in his early career. Coming from a farmer's background, he saw a solution to China's problems in communism and in the support from the broad masses. Mao genuinely worked for the founding of an equality-based state. However, he eventually found himself entangled in power struggles. From a revolutionary, he turned into a fanatic dictator in his later career, becoming a guardian of the traditional totalitarian regime that he had fought against until 1949.

As an idealist, Mao was convinced that the changeover from private ownership to public ownership would eventually eradicate exploitation and "bring about a tremendous liberation of the productive forces."[13] The socialist revolution that he envisioned would replace the prevalent family-based handicraft industry with the large-scale modern machine production.[14] The Great Leap Forward of 1958, though irrational at best, demonstrated Mao's resolve.

The lack of motivation to work soon proved to be pandemic throughout the state-owned enterprises (SOEs). The cause of inefficiency was two fold: On the one hand, the workers' self-interests were excluded from their work; on the other hand, the nervous regime viewed political loyalty more important than improving the economy. Workers were urged to be "red and expert" during the years of the Cultural Revolution. The slogan implied that one's expertise in doing one's work must come after the correct political affiliation or "loyalty." Without loyalty, expertise would be useless or even dangerous. Hence, political studies took away valuable work time. Consequently, the economy was on the brink of collapse.

Mao was torn between the challenges of building a fanatic communist empire and the need to revive the economy. Without the latter, the communist cause would be doomed. To heighten the morale, Mao had no other choices but to do even better in elevating the communist conscience, such as the spirit of selfless contribution. Mao constantly urged members of the Party to dedicate themselves to the construction of "a socialist state with modern industry, modern agriculture, and modern science and culture."[15] The reality, however, repeatedly proved that Mao's communist crusade was deadlocked in power struggle, and that developing the economy was simply not an integral part of the system.

"Bad things may turn into good things," as Mao's successor Deng Xiaoping put it. It was only after paying a heavy price that the nation finally came to realize that Mao's system was wrong. Seeking a great economy by practicing Maoism, as some say, was as wrong as trying to harvest fish from a tree. However, not everything was lost. Construction results from destruction, as Daoism preaches. Through Mao's failure, China found its future. By the time Mao died, a general enlightenment had been acquired: It was time for a reform.

Deng Xiaoping's Reformism

By the time Mao's widow Jiang Qing was arrested in 1976, it was obvious that a landslide was underway. Mao's failed reign was a stop sign for future leaders, forcing them to drastically modify Maoist legacy. A new way had to be opened for China. The struggle for a change is commonly known as "the reform."

However, while most CPC officials came to the understanding that China must engage in a different path, they needed guidance. In general, it was the consensus that China did not need a revolution, given the political chaos that had lasted for more than two decades. It was also commonly perceived, however, that communist countries were not doing nearly as well as their capitalist counterparts in improving people's living conditions. Hence, the superiority of the market economy and the Western democratic system were readily accepted. But if China were to engage in a market orientation, much explanation would need to be made, because people were ideologically unprepared for engaging in what they had been brainwashed against for more than half a century. Furthermore, it was not even in the tradition to openly and proudly seek material wealth and happiness.

Questions such as whether market economy, rule of law, democratic elections, the rise of the middle class, and whether all these put together would ultimately challenge CPC's leadership, remain to be immediately answered. More of a concern, however, would be consequences from a drastic rise of expectations among the common people, if the changes happened too fast. Unemployment, for example, was an eminent concern and viewed as a hanging sword. If the over staffed, inefficient, and debt ridden SOEs were to lose in competition with private companies, what would the tens of millions of urban workers do for a living? If cheap foreign agricultural products defeated China's labor-intensive agriculture, how would the tens of millions of peasants be taken care of? To make things even worse, the Third Census of 1982 revealed that the population had passed the one billion mark. Under such circumstances, any social instability would yield serious consequences.

Obviously what China needed was a "transition," one that must be conducted under a determined and yet experienced guidance. The critical historical moment called for an experienced leader; and Deng Xiaoping stepped forward to meet the challenges. Deng insightfully analyzed the situation and indicated that stability must be maintained at all costs:

> Without a political environment that is based on security and solidarity, economic construction is impossible; let alone implementing the policy of reform and open up; none as such could ever happen. Open up is by no means simple; reform is even more difficult; things must proceed orderly.

"Orderly" means both boldness and prudence; it means timely summarizing experiences and proceeding at a steady pace. If social order is lost, then, we will encounter interference of all sorts, and we will use up our energy in dealing with these things rather than in carrying out the reform. [16]

Rise and Fall

Deng Xiaoping (1904–97) was born in Guang An of the Sichuan province. At age sixteen, taking advantage of a government grant, he left home to study in France. There, he joined the Communist Youth League in 1922, and the CPC in 1924. He then went to the Soviet Union in 1926 to continue with his studies before finally returning to China to lead the communist revolution. A veteran of the Long March, Deng joined the Party Central Committee in 1945.

Called to Beijing as deputy premier in 1952, he rose rapidly to the Politburo Standing Committee in 1956. He worked with Liu Shaoqi, Chairman of the PRC, after the Great Leap Forward to restore the economy. During the Great Cultural Revolution he was attacked as the "Number Two Capitalist Roader" after Liu. Purged, he was sent to work in a tractor factory in 1966. Reinstated as Deputy Premier in 1973 by Premier Zhou Enlai who was suffering from cancer, he took over the administration. He enthusiastically implemented Zhou's "Four Modernizations." After Premier Zhou died in 1976, Deng was again purged from all party and government positions.

Mao's death in 1976 seemed to finally clear the way. In 1977 Deng again became Deputy Premier, as well as Vice Chairman of the CPC. In 1979, he visited the United States after the diplomatic relationship was resumed. For most of the 1980s Deng served as head of the Party, Chairman of the Central Military Commissions, and Chairman of the newly created CPC Central Advisory Commission. Without holding any of the high-ranking posts for the long term, Deng was the de facto most powerful leader since Mao Zedong. In 1981 Deng strengthened his position by replacing Mao's handpicked successor, Hua Guofeng, as the chairman of the CPC. He resigned from his last party post in 1989, designating Jiang Zemin his successor, thus, setting an example to hundreds of non-performing or low-performing veteran leaders who followed suit. By the time Deng died in 1997 at the age of ninety-three, Deng had assured a stable social environment and a rapid economic revival for his successors to take on further challenges, such as the in-depth reforms of the SOEs launched under the Ex-President Jiang Zemin, and the opening of government by the current President Hu Jintao.

Deng's Blueprint

If Mao is remembered as the founder of the PRC, then, Deng is remembered for starting the reform. In simple terms, reform means shifting from stressing ideological control and "class struggle" to putting the improvement of the people's lives on the top of the party's agenda.

According to the economic blueprint Deng laid out in 1987, China would modernize itself through three stages: Sufficiency, relative comfort, and reaching the living standard of medium-level developed country.[17] In terms of income figures, the first step was to reach a per capita GNP[*] of $500 by 1990, doubling the 1980 figure of $250. The second step was to reach a per capita GNP of $1,000, achieving "relative comfort" by the turn of the century. The third step was to quadruple the $1,000 figure of the year 2000 within thirty to fifty years. That will mean a per capita GNP of roughly $4,000 or the living standard of a medium-level developed country.[18]

Recent figures confirmed the plan to be on schedule. According to the report of the National Bureau of Statistics,[19] in 2002 the gross domestic product topped ten trillion Yuan, standing at 10,239.8 billion Yuan, which converts to about 1.3 trillion U.S. dollars. In the report of the *Work of the Government* delivered on 5 March 2003, Premier Zhu Rongji declared that China had reached the goal of achieving the "relatively affluence."[20]

---

[*] Gross National Product (GNP) consists of the total output produced by land, labor, capital, and entrepreneurial talent supplied by Chinese citizens, whether these resources are located in China or abroad.

Truth from Facts

A steady economic recovery depends primarily on favorable government policies. Improvement of production output requires motivation, hard work, effective administration, and in particular, a market where trade could be conducted freely. None of these would have existed, however, without reforming the state-controlled economic structure. But, to touch the state-controlled economy, one has to reform the ideological structure first. Hence, the very first step out under Deng's leadership was an ideological campaign aimed at liberating people's minds from the hard-line communist mentality. The campaign was launched in the form of a debate entitled "seeking the truth from facts" whereby people were encouraged to question Marxism and Mao Zedong thought from the perspective of China's reality.

China's reality was easy to identify: the country had a population passing the billion mark; years of political campaigns had destroyed the economy and had reduced people's life to the survival level. All these consequences, without a doubt, resulted from the mismanagement during the Mao era. Without revising the governing communist theory, China would have to repeat the past mistakes. "Our people's living conditions are so hard," stated Deng, "that if we do not make every effort to develop the economy, how could we demonstrate the superiority of socialism? The 'Gang of Four' lauded 'poor socialism' and 'poor communism.' They distorted communism by saying that it is primarily spiritual. This is purely nonsense!"[21]

Indeed, Deng made every effort to educate people with the concept that the reality is the only criterion for judging whether a theory represents the truth. For Deng, the truth is in the reality rather than in some ephemeras dreams. Likewise, Deng stressed that Marxism was a century-old theory imported from the West. To expect Marxism to reflect China's reality in the 20th century would simply be unrealistic. Deng put up his own defense for the market economy: Marxism defines the market economy as the source of exploitation; Deng insisted that there is no contradiction between market economy and socialism, because the market system is simply an economic tool that may serve any ideological cause, including the socialist cause.[22] Deng's challenge to what had been the sacred principles opened up people's views, installed confidence, and gave rise to a broad-based economic recovery.

The debate of "seeking the truth from facts," however, proved to be a challenging endeavor. People remembered vividly what happened to them during the "Hundred Flowers Campaign" of the 1950s and the ensuing "Anti-rightist Campaign" when they did speak out. On the other hand, one year after Mao died, Mao's handpicked successor Hua Guofeng urged the nation to resolutely uphold whatever policies and decisions Mao made, and to unswervingly follow whatever instructions Mao had given. Hua's instruction is known as the "two whatevers." Hua's hard-line communist position posed a tremendous threat to the reform. To this, Deng rebutted by indicating that Mao himself had admitted to his own mistakes, and that none of the prominent communist leaders including Marx, Lenin, and Stalin had ever claimed that their words would be forever and universally true. Deng stressed that Mao's thought must be taken as a comprehensive system, therefore, must be understood in its entirety. Hence, the "two whatevers" represented dogmatism that was at best an effort of distortion.[23]

Black Cat and White Cat

Deng's legacy is one of pragmatism. Deng put economic development before anything else. To the end of reviving the economy, it does not matter what means is adopted. As long as the strategy works, every way leads to success. Deng is remembered for elaborating his theory by using the allegory of cat: It is not essential whether a cat is black or white; as long as it is capable of catching mice, it is a good cat. Deng is the first communist leader to encourage people to get rich. "In rural and urban areas alike," he states, "some people must be allowed to get rich ahead of others. Getting rich through hard work is perfectly legitimate... In a word, our work is aimed at building a socialist country with Chinese characteristics; and we must be evaluated according to how much we facilitate people's happiness, their material well being, and how much we contribute to the nation's prosperity."[24] With his economic recovery plan and with his slogan "To be rich is glorious," Deng won people's support. Hua Guofeng was dismissed from all positions at a Political Bureau meeting in 1980, replaced by Deng Xiaoping and his handpicked reformers.

In Deng's system, Marxism and Mao Zedong thought became "means" to support the reform, rather than "ends" that the party had to abide by. Under Deng's influence, the Third Plenum of the Eleventh Central Committee held in 1978 endorsed the "Four Modernizations" as the party's primary goal in the new era. At this meeting, however, the CPC also spelled out the "four cardinal principles" that include keeping to the socialist road, upholding the people's democratic dictatorship, sticking to the leadership by the Chinese Communist Party, and adhering to Marxism-Leninism and Mao Zedong Thought.

These cardinal principles were established essentially for the purpose of ensuring the party's control. It was Deng's firm belief, as he argued in an article published in 1987 that while China must keep its door open to the world, the party must be in control. Deng insisted on making two points clear: 1) China must only take the socialist road; 2) without political stability, it would be impossible to modernize.[25] Deng was ready to maintain a stable environment by all measures.

To achieve a fast economic development and to maintain a socialist system at the same time poses many serious challenges. Creatively and courageously meeting these challenges is the hallmark of the Deng Xiaoping theory. Deng introduced capitalist management into China by establishing the "special economic zones" (SEZ) as early as 1979. He later expanded the experience into a rapidly spreading market economy infiltrating both urban and rural areas. A rough estimate is that the share of private ownership has mounted up to thirty percent to thirty-five percent of the economy as of today and has become the leading force of productivity. A direct outcome of this change is that the private sector is pushing the state-owned sector to reform. For the SOEs, they must either shake off the inertia or disintegrate into privately owned companies.

Market Economy Fits Socialism

Would a market economy lead to capitalism or, to word it differently, to the change of color of the CPC? Deng does not believe that socialism and the CPC are incompatible with the market economy. The socialist system is ultimately superior, in Deng's opinion, to capitalism.

Deng provided a versatile answered by resorting to a Marxist terminology: Both planning economy and market economy are ways to "liberate the productivity."[26] In a speech given in February 1987 to high-level officials, Deng pointed out that both planning and market mechanisms are instruments to serve the economic growth, "if they serve socialism they are socialist; if they serve capitalism, they are capitalist." Moving a step further, Deng said, "At one time we copied the Soviet model of economic development and had a planned economy. Later we said that in a socialist economy planning must occupy the dominant position. We should not say that any longer."[27]

The concept of "socialist market economy" dates back to 1979. During an interview with Frank B. Gibney of *Encyclopedia Britannica*, Deng assured the world that China will develop a market economy under socialism. He emphasized that China does not want capitalism, but neither do people want to be poor under socialism. What China needs, in Deng's words, is "socialism in which the productive forces are developed and the country is prosperous and powerful."[28] In an interview with *CBS 60 Minutes*, when confronted with the question on the relationship between profit making and socialism, Deng explained that unlike the capitalist society where individualism prevails, the socialist market economy leads to common prosperity. Although some individuals or regions get rich ahead of others, Deng pointed out, this would not lead to polarization, because the socialist system has the strength of working effectively for the common prosperity. It is absurd to prefer the communist poverty over the capitalist material wealth, in Deng's opinion, because communism is defined from the beginning to be a system whereby a tremendous prosperity of people's lives is finally achieved.[29]

The political structure must be compatible with the economic reform. It must be a propulsive force instead of a dragging force. Deng's reform had a tremendous impact on the political structure, resulting in many changes. The party's authority on administrative affairs was significantly reduced. At the grass roots level, for example, while both the party's leadership and the managerial system widely co-exist, it is the production manager who has more say in decision making today. The reform also resulted in the elimination of the life-long tenure of government functionaries. As aforementioned, Deng successfully consolidated the administrative structure by encouraging senior leaders to retire. Being deeply aware of the inertia of state planning, Deng implemented a series of measures aimed at decentralizing the government, thus allocating more responsibility to local management.

The patriarchic style used to be the hallmark of the management. In a speech given in 1986 entitled "On the Reform of the Political Structure," Deng laid out three objectives: 1) leading cadres must be young, preferably in their 30s and 40s; 2) bureaucracy as well as overstaffed units must be eliminated; and 3) the initiatives generated by the grass roots levels must be encouraged; they must be trusted with the power of decision-making in production.[30] In rank promotion, the traditional practice used to be following the "ladder" or the seniority-based system that often resulted in the suppression of creativity. Deng had the system replaced with civil service examinations, which was cheered as a tremendous progress in direction of fairness and efficiency.

Collision, Clash, …

The reform brought about impressive changes. A few comparisons suffice to illustrate the differences. First, the crisis of food shortage was solved. From the 1950s to the 1970s, food was rationed. Ration stamps were used in parallel to the cash. Today, people are more concerned with the healthiness of their diet rather than with sufficiency of food; food ration has become the past. Second, work attitude has changed. Before the reform, farmers lacked motivation in farming the public land, while workers employed by SOEs typically chatted their work time away. There was no reward for the hard worker, and no one would ever worry about losing the job. Jobs were guaranteed, hence, known as "iron rice bowls." Today, diligence is seen in every work place, and competition routinely leads to layoffs. Productivity has tremendously improved. Third, people's attitude towards one another has changed. Before the reform, tension was felt everywhere as people were extremely mindful of their speech. While the spirit of selflessly helping others was promoted, there was little Samaritan spirit in reality. Today, people are becoming friendly neighbors and helpers, not only because friendship generates opportunities, but also because Mao's police society is gone.

While much progress has been made, people eye on more and speedier changes. The truth is, with the advent of the economic prosperity arose further challenges to the CPC's political system. Conflicts intensify as the private sector gains more grounds. In fact, from day one of the reform, conflicts were born. Radical reformers insisted on a top-down style of change, one that would include replacing the communist government with a multiparty system modeling the U.S. government. Without realizing the "5th Modernization," which refers to democracy, as a leading critic Wei Jingsheng argued in 1979, the "Four Modernizations" would ultimately fail. Other intellectuals denounced corrupted high-level cadres as "monsters" (Liu Bingyan) and blamed the CPC for safeguarding its bureaucratic political structure (Fang Lizhi). The malaise culminated in June 1989 when Golbachev, renowned for initiating the Soviet's top-down style reform, the hero in the eyes of the Chinese students, paid an official visit to Beijing. Hunger strike persisted in Tiananmen Square. Students' ardent pursuit of democracy aroused the deepest sympathy from Beijing residents. Taxi drivers transported demonstrators free of charge, households delivered food to students, military units were reported to defy orders of using force. On 4 June 1989 the government bloodily suppressed the peaceful student demonstration.

For Deng himself, he may have made it clear from the very beginning that the reform was not meant to be a revolution. Many, however, had indeed taken the reform as a revolution and could not wait for a thorough change to happen right away. Students learned a cruel lesson.

Deng, on the contrary, was particularly keen on maintaining stability that he believed to be the premise for economic development. Probably, having experienced too much political turmoil in his life, Deng was stubbornly convinced that China could only be saved through an economic revival, that the economy could only be revived in stability, that only the CPC could guarantee a stable environment, and that everything else would be a waste of time. Deng expressed his thoughts in a speech entitled "We are Revitalizing the Chinese Nation" delivered in 1990, one year after the crackdown of the Tiananmen Demonstrations: "Unless we modernize, China will never attain its rightful position in the international community. But the modernization we are working for is socialist modernization. Only socialism can bind the people together, help them overcome their difficulties, prevent polarization and bring about common prosperity."[31]

In retrospect, Deng's legacy is one of breaking the Marxist and Maoist chains and leading China onto the path of economic prosperity. Deng's political reform changed the CPC from being Chairman Mao's loyal political executive system to a system with an economic dimension. Finally, Deng's introduction of the market economy under socialism is clearly a modern revision of the classic communism. One may be very much tempted to speculate that sooner or later the Chinese Communist Party might as well recruit business entrepreneurs as its members. Indeed, without it being actually declared by Deng's successor, Jiang Zemin, the speculation would have been no more than just a speculation. How could it be possible for a communist party to represent the broad masses including property owners? The goal of mass representation has, indeed, already been written into the CPC's Constitution at the 16th Party Congress of 2003.

In fact, Deng's reform has made such nomenclature as "democratic dictatorship," "socialist market economy," and "one country, two systems" more acceptable than questionable. More like terms might yet be coming, as China continues to engage in transition.

Close-up: Quotations from Deng Xiaoping

Instead of behaving like a woman with bound feet, we must be more aggressive in carrying out the economic reform and in implementing the policy of openness. Once we are determined to achieve our goal, we must boldly launch new trials and boldly forge ahead. The Shenzhen experience is one of daring to take risks. Without taking risks one can never open up a good road or a new road, let alone engaging in any new cause. [We must not] be free from the fear of taking risks and from the attitude of engaging only in projects that are one hundred percent guaranteed successful. In fact, is there anyone who could boast to know a sure way to success? From the very beginning I have never believed myself to be one hundred percent correct. Such belief would be ridiculous. Every year the administration must re-evaluate its work, maintain whatever was done correctly, discard any mistakes without delay, and deal with new problems promptly. It is possible that we need thirty more years before we could establish an all round, more mature, and stable system. Such a system is expected to produce better policies and tactics. We are currently building our socialism with Chinese characteristics and our experience has been accumulating day by day. New strategies with local characteristics are constantly reported in local newspapers and reports. This is excellent. Creativeness is what we need.

All conservativeness in conducting reform and experimentations, as a matter of fact, results from the fear of running capitalism and engaging in the capitalist road. In essence, people are afraid of being labeled capitalist instead of socialist. The criterion, however, must be one's contribution to the development of the socialist productivity, or whether the personal conduct enhances the socialist nation's comprehensive strength, and whether it improves people's lives. Some people had reservations for building the Special Economic Zones (SEZ) out of the concern that we would be doing capitalism. The success of Shenzhen now addresses such concerns effectively. The SEZs belong to socialism, not to capitalism. In the scenario of Shenzhen, the public ownership is predominant with foreign investment counting for only one fourth of the total. Even out of the foreign capital we have derived benefits in such areas as tax collection, employment, and so on. Please set up more tri-capital enterprises* and discard your worries. As long as we keep a clear mind, we should not be afraid. We have advantages, we have our state-run large and medium-size enterprises, we have county-level enterprises, and particularly, we have the political power in our hands. Some argue that every additional foreign investment contributes to more capitalism, and that more "tri-capital enterprises" would mean more capitalism or more sponsorship for capitalism. People with such opinions lack the basic knowledge. The current policy certainly allows foreign investors to make money. However, we collects taxes, our workers get paid, and in particular, we acquire technology, management skills, and information. Hence, "tri-capital" enterprises operate within the constraint of our country's global

---

* "Tri-capital enterprises" (san zi qi ye) refers to three types of companies that are funded with domestic capital, foreign and domestic joint capital, or foreign capital only.

political and economic conditions. They are complementary to the socialist economy, and they benefit socialism after all.

("Speech Given in Wuchang, Shenzhen, Zhuhai and Shanghai," 18 January 1992) [32]

Jiang Zemin's Populism

Maintaining stability, staying the course of Deng Xiaoping, and achieving a fast economic growth are among the major deeds of Jiang Zemin who was Chairman of the CPC for thirteen years and President of the PRC for ten years. Jiang's theory, known as "The Three Represents," is applauded as a breakthrough in modern Chinese communism.

Rising from the Ground-level

Jiang Zemin's political career was one of a rapid ascension. In March 1993, Jiang Zemin was elected President of the PRC and Chairman of the Central Military Commission. Five years later, in March 1998, he was reelected President of the PRC. He was also twice elected Chairman of the CPC in 1992 and 1997. On 15 March 2003, Jiang Zemin finished serving his second term as Chairman and President, but was reelected Chairman of the Central Military Commission of the PRC. President Hu Jintao succeeded him in other major functions.

Born on 17 August 1926 in an literati family in Yangzhou, a culturally famous city in east China's Jiangsu Province, Jiang received a good education. Both his grandfather and father were noted local scholars. He received higher education at the prestigious Shanghai Jiaotong University where he majored in electrical engineering. During his college years, Jiang participated in the CPC-led students movements and joined the CPC in 1946. After the founding of the PRC, Jiang worked his way up the ladder. He started as an associate engineer. In 1955, He went to the then Soviet Union and worked in the Stalin Automobile Works as a trainee for one year. After returning, he served as deputy division head, deputy chief power engineer, director of a branch factory, and director of factories and research institutes in

Changchun, Shanghai and Wuhan. In the ensuing years, Jiang served as director of the foreign affairs department of the No. 1 Ministry of Machine-Building Industry. Jiang speaks well English, Russian, and Romanian, and has limited reading knowledge in Japanese and French. Before he became Mayor of Shanghai in 1985, Jiang had accumulated much management experience through his service as the Minister of the Ministry of the Electronics Industry.

Three Representations

Jiang Zemin's unique career experiences enabled him to observe and solve problems with international perspectives in mind. Jiang was dispatched by Deng Xiaoping to construct Shenzhen, the first SEZ established in 1979. Soon afterward, Jiang was appointed mayor of Shanghai 1985, where he initiated a series of infrastructure improvement projects to take advantage of overseas capitals. The city raised 3.2 billion U.S. dollars from international capital markets, of which 1.4 billion dollars were used on such key projects as the city's subway, Nanpu Bridge, polluted water treatment, airport expansion, and program-controlled telephone exchanges. These projects were immediately beneficial to improving the standard of living and therefore highly appreciated by the Shanghai people.

Jiang Zemin's communist theory is represented by his speech delivered on 1 July 2001, during the celebration of the CPC's 80th Anniversary, later known as the "three represents."[33] While "Jiang Zemin thought" is not yet part of the official terminology as of this writing, Jiang's theory, however, represents a significant development along the line of Deng Xiaoping's reformist ideology. On the one hand, Jiang remains a loyal guardian of the "Four Cardinal Principles;" on the other hand, he expands the party's representation to a level unseen before. Clearly, Jiang's system reflects a sharpened picture of the classic dilemma of a market economy under the CPC's control.

If the CPC were to remain the helmsman of the market economy, the most important thing to do to qualify for such a role of leadership is to maintain an open-minded approach. The "three represents" offers a more liberal guidance to the CPC's leadership, compared to Deng Xiaoping's admonition of strictly observing the "Four Cardinal Principles." The system includes representing 1) the development trend of China's advanced productive forces, 2) the orientation of China's advanced culture, and 3) the fundamental interests of the overwhelming majority of the people.[34]

The term "advanced productive forces" used to refer to the proletariat or factory workers primarily. Because science and technology are the primary productive forces and represents a hallmark of the advanced productive forces today, Jiang's system includes intellectuals as an essential part of the "advanced productive forces." With respect to the composition of the working class, the classic fence line that separates the working class from the "other laboring people" is erased. The purity of the "working class" is no longer maintainable, because "some workers have changed their jobs" and become materially affluent. Jiang insists, however, "this has not changed the status of Chinese working class."[35]

"China's advanced culture" may be the hardest concept to define. While stressing the importance of adhering to the communist cardinal principles, Jiang encourages the development of "healthy, progressive, rich and colorful socialist culture with Chinese styles and characteristics."[36] He calls upon the nation to continue to behold the "lofty ideals, moral integrity, a better education, and a good sense of discipline," all of which is copied form Mao's revolutionary theory. To these Jiang added "self reliance, competition, efficiency, democracy, rule of law, as well as pioneering and innovative spirit"[37] to create a new paradigm that meets the demand of the new economy. Here, following the classic pattern, the definition from the positive angle is coupled with its counterpart. Jiang urged to "clean up" the old decadent and dying culture, such as superstition, ignorance and vulgarity. Warnings against material gains and money remain an essential component.[38]

Welcome to Capitalists

Representing the fundamental interests of the "overwhelming majority" of the people is a new kind of task that Jiang assigns to the CPC for the new era. The theory of broadening representation is obviously the hallmark of Jiang's theory. Instead of representing the working class and the laboring people in exercising the proletarian dictatorship, often in detriment to other social strata, the Party will work for the well being of all people. To achieve this goal, Jiang made a step further to revise the party membership requirement which is now based on whether a person works whole-heartedly for the cause of the country, and this factor alone in place of other backgrounds. Since Marxism needs to adapt to China's new economic and social reality, it is "not advisable to judge a person's political integrity simply by whether one owns property and how much property he or she owns."[39] Clearly, if private property ownership is no longer an adversary factor in the definition of communist revolution, then, the nature of communism has to be redefined. The 16th CPC Congress held in 2003 has practically so amended the Party's constitution with respect to its membership. Jiang's theory represents a breakthrough of the redefinition process.

Reform in Literature

Literature has always been a barometer for the political weather. Back in the Han Dynasty, the Music Bureau was dedicated to detecting the mood of the people through collecting and studying folk songs. The ups and downs of the Chinese literature since 1949 indeed vividly reflect the transition in people's mentality.

The nature of the literary transition is one of the literary creativity being gradually liberated from its assigned function of serving the Party and socialism. After the founding of the PRC, two fundamental principles had dominated literary creation until the start of the reform. The first principle "literature and arts must serve the workers, peasants, and soldiers" was adopted at the First National Art Conference held in July 1949, in the eve of the founding of the new China. The second principle "Literature and arts must serve the people and socialism" was declared in 1978 at the Third Plenum of the Eleventh National Conference of the CPC. On the surface, there is hardly any discernable difference between the two principles. In reality, however, the second one where "workers, peasants and soldiers" is replaced with "the people and socialism" marked the beginning of a profound literary reform.

From One Literature to Another

The literary transformation is customarily divided into three phases: The first phase, known as the period of the "17-years," refers to the period from 1949 to 1966. The second phase, known as "ten years of cultural revolution," refers to the period from 1966 to 1976. The third phase, known as "post-revolutionary literature," refers to 1977 to present.

The "Literature of the 17-years" is characterized by its tendency of supporting the new government. These works sing praise of the socialist transformation and serve almost as manuals to government policies. Writers who had been part of Mao's democratic revolution were the major contributors. Their works reminisce the revolutionary struggles since the early 1920s when the CPC had been newly founded. Good representatives are He Qifang's poem *Our Greatest Festival*[40] and Hu Feng's poem *The Time Starts — The Ode of Joy*[41] which retrace the revolutionary background and describes the pompous celebration of the founding of the PRC. Another major theme at this time was reflective of the on-going de-privatization campaigns in rural China in the 1950s. Novels of this trend depict the transitional mentality of the Chinese peasants, workers, and bourgeoisie. Without exception, in every story the communist ideology prevails, while all "selfishness" is labeled "backward." In these novels, people with low communist consciousness are unfailingly transformed into staunch revolutionary followers. *The Morning of Shanghai*[42] by Zhou Erfu, for example, vividly depicts the transformation of urban industries in the 1950s, reflecting the process whereby Shanghai business owners accept the socialist reality and bid goodbye to their factories. *Records of the New Cause*[43] by Liu Qing reflects the rural collectivization movements in which the peasants adapted to a new life after giving up the land that was allocated to them during the Land Reform Movement in the late 1940s.

Under the influence of the Soviet literature, the dominant literary trend at this time was realism. The hallmark of realism is its political tendency and the stress on loyally mirroring the reality. Most literary works reflect the political agenda of the government. Furthermore, to show support to the Party's cause, literary works were often hero-centered. A very small percentage of literary works were purposefully written to support the political campaigns, serving as tools for disseminating political instructions. The majority of the literary works nevertheless truthfully reflect the mentality of a people enthusiastically embracing a new life in the freshly independent China. However, from time to time, writers reveal their confusions about the on-going campaigns. In *Records of the New Cause* for example, author Liu Qing shows suspicion on the Anti-rightist Campaign and the Great Leap Forward frenzy.

As political struggles intensified, particularly during the GCR (1966-1976), literature finally became the Party's propaganda machine. Literary works were molded according to the principle of the "three prominences" put forward by Mao's wife Jiang Qing: To create "positive characters," to build "revolutionary heroes," and to sing praise of "revolutionary dedication." Because such stereotypical figures are fabricated, the stories are lifeless political lectures at best. At this time, real artistic creativity, one that was distant from Mao's political agenda, not only had minimal place in literature, but was also criticized often for its bourgeois tendencies. Writers who inserted romantic episodes in their writings, such as expressions of feeling and emotion, would be looked at with a suspicious eye, as such "bourgeois" weaknesses would not belong to brave revolutionaries. Moreover, Mao had clearly instructed that the revolution must not be a dinner party, but a rather bloody struggle.

The most popular literary works at the time that exemplify the principle of the "three prominences" are the eight "Revolutionary Model Operas" created under Jiang Qing's direct supervision. The themes of these operas are derived from the CPC's revolutionary history. These operas are a successful blend of the traditional Peking Opera with the communist content. The roles of emperors and kings are replaced with revolutionary heroes and heroines. The slogan-filled lyrics as well as the dynamic performance transformed the traditional art form into a modern day entertainment. The practical function of these operas was two-fold: To glorify the party's leadership in winning China's independence and, in particular, to strengthen the personality cult of Mao as the leader of the nation. Heroes and heroines in these operas, typically with big round eyes and heavy eyebrows, all demonstrate dedication, wisdom, and the spirit of self-sacrifice for the revolutionary cause.

The Red Lantern, for example, tells the story of a family of three who dedicate themselves to the cause of driving the Japanese occupiers out of China. Li Yuhe, the father, is a railroad worker and an undercover agent of the CPC. After being captured by the Japanese, he refuses to surrender the secret radio communication codes to the Japanese. He is tortured and finally executed by the Japanese. Li's mother and daughter are determined to carry on his cause.

It is a common feature to the model operas that the revolutionary heroes and heroines live in celibacy, either husbands or wives having died for the revolution. "Revolutionary emotion" is an enigmatic concept that is not stressed on the stage. Heroes must live a puritanical way of life, because a thorough revolutionary is one who has nothing to lose.

Wounded Generation, Wounded Literature

The decade-long Great Cultural Revolution suppressed artistic creativity by putting every literary work under political magnifying glass. The suppression, in a sense, prepared for a dynamic reverse once the turmoil was over. The post-revolutionary period is represented by several literary trends showing an increasing depth of introspection and analysis. The "literature of the wound," for example, represents the initial stage of the post-revolutionary period. Novels such as *The Wound*[44] by Lu Xinhua, *Memories*[45] by Zhang Xuan, and *A Chinese Winter's Tale*[46] by Yu Luojin were part of a healing process of a whole generation. In these works, writers dig into the chaotic decade that made them lose the best years of life to the absurd political movements. The authors condemn the dark time when people were led to mistreat one another under the urge of demonstrating loyalty to the communist cause. The authors relive the sufferings by staging traumatizing moments of their lives. Some also express a deep remorse in contributing to their own sufferings by actively answering to Mao's calls. Wei Junyi in the novel *Bathing Ceremony* created a hero who, in deep remorse, regrets his support to the Great Cultural Revolution, a nightmare that ended up alienating himself.

The "Literature of the Wound" soon gave rise to what is later called "Literature of the Wound," one that examines the reality at a theoretical height. Writers belonging to this trend believe that blaming

Mao alone is not enough, because China's problems are more deeply rooted in its cultural tradition and Mao is only a figure of representation. *My Remote Qingping Bay*[47] by Shi Tiesheng, *There will Be Storm Tonight,*[48] *This is a Miracle Land,*[49] and *The Ancient Boat*[50] by Zhang Wei are representative works. Unlike their predecessors, these novels dedicate much less volume to blaming and weeping over the past, but give the utmost attention to analyzing the history, the cultural tradition, and the people. *The Ancient Boat* by Zhang Wei, for example, reveals the traditional mentality of Chinese peasants who are typically bound to the land for generations. The farming tradition results in closed and stagnant communities that become hotbeds for internal feud. Members of such communities would outdo one another in safeguarding their selfish interests, which often ends up dragging entire villages into conflicts. They cultivate relationships with higher-level officials and channel wealth and opportunities into the hands of their friends and relatives. The majority of the peasants invariably fall victims of a society where there is no law but only rules of the authority. To these peasants, parents are gods at home, and party officials are gods outside of the home. A good life would only be in the dream or something that comes out of sheer luck. Independence and individual development would be out of question. Such mentality is also reflected in *Li Shunda Building His House*[51] by Gao Xiaosheng where the hero, Li Shunda, is unable to build his house for thirty years, as he has been robbed one way or another by officials.

In addition to putting the Chinese tradition under scrutiny, literature of reflection examines a broad range of current social issues. *The Story of Factory Manager Qiao*[52] by Jiang Zilong and *Garden Street Number Five*[53] by Li Guowen dissect the traditional social barriers that obstruct the reform. The writers denounce the deep-rooted bureaucratic system that generates an infinitely complex social network involving kinship as well as corrupt officials. If any progress were to be made, the authors warn, the first step is to destroy the backward yet persistent bureaucratic system.

The traditional ethical system came under fire as well. The concepts of country, nation, home, patriotism, and filial piety used to constitute the core of the Chinese value system. Individual interest must not be put ahead of that of the broader community. One may have to go through the most unbearable political persecutions, but violating any part of the system would mean moral conviction. As such, crossing the country's border to escape from political persecution would be morally wrong. The perpetrator would be looked down upon as a weakling and a traitor. On the contrary, remaining in the country to endure mistreatment of all sorts would be laudable. In *Snow Falling Quietly on the Yellow River* by Cong Weixi, two prisoners who fall in love are able to forgive each other for any crimes that the other has committed, but have to terminate their relationship under the moral shame of treason when one of them decides to escape into a foreign country. The tragedy puts the old value system under the spotlight.

Reflectionist writers believe that the unconditional loyalty to the traditional value system is deeply rooted in the agrarian way of life and the closed environment that comes with it. In *The Old Well*[54] by Zheng Yi, the hero, a young peasant, dreams of running away from the village with his lover as soon as he finishes digging the well. He is bound by the obligation of finishing the project left by his ancestors. He soon finds himself a victim of flaming by his surroundings for simply harboring the dream of leaving the village. He suffers, more than anything else, from his own moral obligation. Eventually, crushed between the sense of guilt and a strong longing for freedom, the young peasant finally turns into a piece of well stone, stuck to the land forever.

With the traditional values and the communist principles being questioned came the crisis of belief. As Mao's communist dream dissipated, the people were left in a spiritual vacuum. The loss of hope generated a growing depression that prompted writers to ponder deeply over the meaning of life. Li Ping's *When Evening Clouds Dissipated* published in late 1980s in the literary journal *Dang-Dai*, is written in the form of a conversation between a pilgrim visitor and a Daoist master over the meaning of life. Although both Western religions and traditional Chinese beliefs appear to be convenient spiritual shelters, decades of materialist education has branded religious beliefs as superstition and "spiritual opium." In a way, the past brainwashing has immunized people against the spiritual dimension. The author recognizes that breaking the spiritual barrier is a challenge. Hence, what the beautiful sunset leaves behind, as implied in the title, is uncertainty and darkness.

Experimentalist Literature

"Experimental literature" became a significant trend in the late 1980s and early 1990s. The experimentalist writers are greatly influenced by Western Avant-Gard literature and by the philosophies such as existentialism. Ma Yuan and Gao Xingjian are among the representative writers of this school. Ma Yuan's novels are marked by a non-traditional narrative style often with multiple timelines crisscrossing. Playwright Gao Xingjian reaches the audience by resorting to special stage effects and through manipulation of the logical sequence of conversations. He was awarded the Nobel Prize for Literature in the year 2000. The comments from the Swedish Academy praise his works as "œuvre of universal validity, bitter insights and linguistic ingenuity, which has opened new paths for the Chinese novel and drama."[55]

A typical feature of experimental works is that the stories do not have to be "meaningful" in the traditional sense, nor do they need to be logical or chronological. Content-wise, some stories appear to be rather absurd, yet their impact on the reader is often peculiarly strong. Ma Yuan's literary approach, for example, is typical for its multidimensional narration in which the author is not only one of the narrators, but also in the story. As such, the novel effectively combines the life of the author with those of other characters in the story, creating an authentic feel of the reality. Using this approach, in *Up and Down the Road Is Flat and Wide*,[56] Ma Yuan effectively conveys his fatalistic view of life. The author announces at the beginning of each story that the individual in the story has died, which is contrary to the traditional romantic or realistic approaches that tend to hide the hero's fate until the end. Furthermore, because the characters are also best friends of the narrator/author, the reminiscences invoke a profound sense of cruelty of fate, as intended.

Gao Xingjian's representative play *The Other Shore*[57] was first published in 1986. One of the unique features of this play is its utilization of unconventional stage effects to involve the audience. With respect to the theme, a lover of traditional literature would be disappointed: Other than showing a group of men and women crossing a river, the play has little "story" to tell. The conversations are almost meaningless, incoherent, and even unconnected. However, taken as a whole, the play conveys a deeply embedded message: While everyone dreams of an "other shore" that is free from the troubles of this world, such "other shore" is non-existent. At the end of the play, the actors and actresses remind the audience that they have just staged an absurd game, and they have go home now and get ready for the next day's work. Using a stage procedure like this, the author skillfully erases the line between the audience and the actors on the stage. Hence, the line dividing the chores of the real life and stage acting, as implied, does not exist. The author really achieves his goal of convincing his audience that they should not expect to escape from the real life, that whether it is on the stage or in the work place, the reality remains unchanged. The ending of *The Other Shore* is recognized as an impressive segment:

> (The sound of a car engine starting.) How are you going to get back? It's so bad, what kind of stupid play is this anyway? Are you doing anything tomorrow? Shall we have dinner together? (Sounds of a baby crying, a car engine starting and running bicycle bells and the trickle of running water from a tap, and in the distance, the siren of an ambulance.)[58]

Close-up: Ma Yuan's Works

Preface

When he (a friend) reminded me of this, I felt like waking up. Indeed, why do the girls in my stories all die in their flower age? In real life, I have never come across such coincidence. Was this originated from a dark corner in my heart? Searching my memories, I remember that I was thirty-four years old when I wrote this book. That was already thirteen years after the traumatizing experience of my life. Has my memory gone awry, or has my mental health really declined? Similarly, written into the book *The Temptations of Gangdisi* (completed in 1984), but the real event happened afterward, was a young girl by the name of Yingjin. She died in an accident in her best years of life. Was this all coincidental?

In reality, the most fascinating part of this story is its fatalism. Fatalism has seeped into my heart long ago, which is probably the primary reason why I became a writer. The old couple that both died on the same day inspired my true feeling of destination. On that day,

I happened to have just moved to the countryside from the city. Right next door to my residence was the retirement home of the village. To a city boy, everything was fascinating, including this miraculous event that could only happen in legends. The saying goes, "though born on different dates, to die on the same day is our wish." Such coincidence indeed could be real, and I witnessed one with my own eyes. I helped with the funeral ceremony; I saw Mother Earth taking this aged couple back into her arms like caring for infants. Later on, many of my views on life and on the world in general were very much inspired by this experience, whether it is about value, significance, ideology at the spiritual level, or about eating, sex, ageing, and death at the material level. From that day on, I learned to watch weather patterns, to discern facial expressions, and to tell precursors of events. I also learned to deal with all sorts of harshness in life.

In a word, this book is about trivial things in life dished out in a somewhat mysterious atmosphere, with a little bit of supernaturalism, a certain taste of fatalism, and a tiny dose of primitive urge. While writing this book, I forgot my sufferings, ignored the poetic fragrance of life, and even felt relieved from youth and love. I erased the sorrows and scars of a whole generation, replacing them with a cup of icy Coke, one that I like to chug down after a soccer match. How about I'll stop here?

(Ma Yuan, *Up and Down the Road Is Flat and Wide*)[59]

Economic Reform

China's economy has gone through a sea change since 1949. Changes in economic policies have been even more remarkable. From the Civil War (1946-1949) to 1952, the Land Reform Movement in rural China completely transferred land ownership to the poor farmhands. Later on, due to the incompatibility of property ownership within a communist society, a second de-privatization movement — the People's Commune, took place around 1958. The movement went through several intermediate stages, such as from "mutual-aid groups" of a few households to "preliminary stage communes" composed of hundreds of households, gradually grouping farmers into larger production units. By 1962, family-owned land was completely converted to commune property. Meanwhile, urban industries went through a similar but tougher process. Owners of factories were given the choice of selling their businesses at government's price tags or facing the confiscation. Once private ownership was eliminated, the planning economy was underway. The first five-year plan (1953-1957) put heavy industry ahead of improving people's living conditions. The Great Leap Forward of 1958 demonstrated a devastating incapability of the new regime in managing the economy, which led to the famine of 1960 that killed millions of people.

The economic failure during the first ten years of the PRC put the government and the CPC on the defensive. To consolidate the control, the next two decades were dedicated to ideological education, enforcement of rules and regulations, and mass campaigns aimed at purging dissidents. During those years, the economy was a forbidden zone. Economists were condemned, unless they would support Mao's principle of "revolution first, production second." As such, the decade-long Great Cultural Revolution resulted in the collapse of the economy.

Opportunities for opting a different track finally arrived with Mao's death in 1976. The Third Plenum of the Eleventh National Conference of the CPC in 1978 refocused the Party's goal from ideological control to the "four modernizations." Meanwhile, to ramp up agricultural output, a series of new policies led to a vibrant rural economic recovery. In rural areas, land was returned to families in the form of land lease. Following the new responsibility system of 1979, peasants were allowed to keep the portion beyond the submission quota. Motivation in farming was high, and so was the yield. In urban industries, transformation of SOEs was underway along with the process of privatization. The "Open Door" policy of 1979 introduced capitalist management, first in the Special Economic Zones (SEZ), followed by the rest of the country. The incoming of foreign capital in the forms of "direct foreign investment" (FDI) and "foreign invested enterprises" (FIE) significantly contributed to the rise of private companies and to the disintegration of the SOEs as well. From 1978 to 2002, foreign trade skyrocketed from a mere $20 billion or less than ten percent of the GDP to $620 billion or fifty percent of the GDP. In 2001, China became a WTO member. By 2002, from a completely closed country, China had become the largest FDI hosting country in the world, with $52.7 billion for the year and $446 billion investment cumulated.[60]

The "Open Door" policy marked the beginning of a series of chain reactions, such that an administrative reform became unavoidable. Decentralization and rule of law gradually challenged the absolute control by the party. The traditional central management started to loosen up. This situation led to broadened latitude of individual freedom, which generated tremendous enthusiasm and creativity. Given the favorable conditions the economy took off at an impressive velocity.

Agricultural Reform

Rural China is where over eighty percent of the population resides. Back in the time of the democratic revolution, Mao relied on poor peasants to gain the control of China. After the founding of the PRC, however, peasants' well-being was largely ignored. Changes finally happened after 1979 when farmlands were redistributed to individual families. By the early 1980s, the People's Communes had disintegrated, and farmers, once again, were in touch with their land.

The "Household Production Responsibility System" of 1979 allowed individual families to lease public land and repay the rent in the form of production quota. The family was allowed to keep the surplus and dispose of it the way it sees fit. When farmers began to trade their surplus products for the badly needed cash, a preliminary market system was opened up. The rural markets, in turn, gave rise to markets in other sectors of the economy. This was how the private sector took off.

In addition to a rising grain output, the Responsibility System led to a better redistribution of labor, as well as a flourishing variety of township and village enterprises. Most of these enterprises specialized in crafts, clothing, and simple value-added processing of industrial products. These entities were generally collectively owned. They contracted primarily with SOEs, although some were more independent and had their own distribution channels. In the mid-1990s, township and village enterprises contributed one-third of rural per capita incomes and employed some 130 million workers or about half of China's surplus rural laborers. In 1998, they contributed twenty-eight percent of the nation's GDP.[61] By 2000, township and village enterprises contributed about one third of the GDP, nearly fifty percent of country's industrial growth, and more than sixty percent of the rural economy. Moreover, these enterprises employed 127 million rural labors that year.[62]

The flip side of the rural industrial boom was the diversion of farmland to non-farming purposes, often at the detriment of agriculture in the long run. Moreover, farmers tended to migrate into urban areas whenever industrial or service opportunities became available, putting pressure on urban employment. To deal with the situation, the government promulgated regulations in early 1990s to restrict the usage of farmland, and meanwhile extended the standard land lease term from the previous fifteen years to thirty years. On the same time, the PRC Law of Township and Village Enterprises of 1997 recognized village enterprises as the mainstay in rural economy and legalized their development by way of joint venture, annexation, and so on.

As a transitional phenomenon, a dual pricing market was born when farmers were allowed to dispose of their surplus products. Since the 1950s, most agricultural products were procured by the state and consumers purchased their rations of food with ration tickets. A mild competition has arisen since the early 1980s when farmers started to sell their agricultural products at fluctuating market prices against the government's fixed prices. This led to the elimination of the ration system by 1993. Today, state supply continues to be an important source of food in the market. People have access to fresher products, though at slightly higher prices, from farmers. The competition has not forced the government out of the market, as government grains indeed have been playing a stabilizing role in a constantly fluctuating and sometimes chaotic new market system

Privatization of Urban Industries

Before 1949, the private industrial sector produced more than seventy percent of the Gross Value of the Industrial Output (GVIO) and state-run industries accounted for twenty-six percent. In the mid 1950s, however, after urban industries were de-privatized through the movement of "transforming proprietors towards socialism," the situation was reversed. By 1978, SOEs produced seventy-seven percent and collective-owned (COE) 22.4 percent of the GVIO. Since the start of the reform in 1978, the tide was turned once again, with privately owned enterprises (POE) on the rise and SOEs on the decline. By the end of 2001, 12.8 million urban and 11.39 million rural, or a total of 24.07 million people were employed by POEs. The total number of POE-employment reached 30 million by June 2002. Employment by all non-state enterprises, both urban and rural, reached eighty-eight percent nationwide. The number of POEs in Beijing, for example, was 150,873, in addition to 312,932 sole proprietors, representing 21.54 percent and 20.77 percent growth from 1998 to 2002. POEs' contribution, less than one-fourth of the GDP in 1998, reached one-third by 2002.[63]

There are several explanations about why private enterprises grew at a lightening speed. The most important one is that the POEs are "burden free," in the sense that they do not have hundreds or thousands of state employees on the payroll. Moreover, the POEs are market oriented, fast in seizing market opportunities, and efficient in adapting to the market.

On the contrary, SOEs are plagued with inefficiency and overstaffing. This is determined by the way SOEs conduct their businesses traditionally. Since the beginning, the government contracts orders to SOEs and takes charge of the distribution. The government does the transaction on predetermined fixed prices. In a typical SOE entity, the worker's performance is not tied to his/her performance. There is no need to worry about losing the job or to seek opportunities to get rich. Raises are given on the basis of seniority instead of performance. An SOE typically has its own kindergartens, partner hospitals, and housing compounds. The *danwei*, or the "work unit," a popular synonym of SOE, is a comprehensive system covering every aspect of the worker's daily life, and sometimes, the employment of the worker's family members as well. A popular nickname given to SOE is "iron rice bowl," because once one acquires a job, one can relax, as the "iron rice bow" will never break. For many decades, SOE has been the home of a huge urban population. The non-competitive nature of SOEs has taken its toll on the nation's productivity, which has become an increasing concern since the reform started.

Ever since 1978, reformists have placed SOE at the bull's eye. During the early stage of SOE reform, the stress was put on nurturing the motivation of workers and enterprises by providing incentive programs. One of such programs was the "two-track system" that, similar to the rural responsibility system, lets SOEs submit contracted orders to the government at fixed prices. The enterprises were allowed to market the surplus and keep the profit. As the reform deepened, the market mechanism seeped into pricing and distribution. The price fixing power, a typical government monopoly, for example, soon found itself fallen to the mercy of the market. Lack of competitiveness, shares of SOE in the economy has eroded rapidly. The "iron rice bow" is no longer safe. By 2000, over eighty percent of SOEs had restructured somehow through mergers and regroupings. Foreign capitals have been introduced into new SOEs, making some of these enterprises multinational entities.

As the economic reform moved forward in the late 1980s, the planning and decision on hiring was permitted to individual enterprises. Life-long employment was being replaced with a contract system whereby the worker signed contract with the employer for a limited term. The contract would be renewable primarily based on the employee's performance. In 1992, the state stopped issuing labor recruitment plans, and the job contractual system was eventually legalized in the *Labor Law* of 1994[64] that gave enterprises the right to layoff workers. On the other hand, housing and medical provisions gradually separated from the traditional features of the state enterprise and transformed into independent businesses.

During the economic restructuring, particularly during the economy cool-down period from 1999 to 2001, a large number of SOE workers lost their jobs and registered themselves as "unemployed." The unemployment Insurance Act launched in 1999 required both the worker and the employer to contribute to the insurance that provides unemployment benefits for up to two years. By September 2002, the number of people shielded by unemployment insurance had totaled 101 million, an increase of 36 million over 1989's figure. The unemployment rate, according to the government's claim, has been kept below four percent as of November 2002.[65]

The transformation of SOEs has been conducted cautiously since the very beginning. The government's strategy has been one of gradually phasing out SOEs, rather than letting the disintegration happen too fast. To achieve a gradual and peaceful exit, the government's policy is currently "grasping the big and letting go the small," meaning, the biggest SOEs remain under the control of the government while smaller ones are open for privatization. Most of the large-size SOEs are located in the northeast heavy industrial bases such as Shenyang, Harbin, as well as some central regions such as Chongqing and Wuhan. In fact, most of the companies in remote regions are predominantly SOEs. However, with China's entry into the WTO, many traditionally government-monopolized sectors are opened up for competition, making the effort of sustention costly.[66] Eventually, under fierce competition, SOEs will likely disappear, in which case the solution to securing unemployment benefits will rely on an improved social security system.

The CPC has so far willingly "watered down" the theoretical dilemma of privatization under a communist system. Creative minds have always found ways to bypass the nature of the issue. Deng Xiaoping's framework of "socialist market economy," for instance, justifies that the market economy is only an instrument that may serve capitalism as well as socialism. Hence, China's color has not changed; the CPC remains in control.

The political status of private entrepreneurs has been improving. The Ex-CPC Chairman Jiang Zemin's theory argues that the CPC membership must be granted primarily on the basis of a person's political tendency rather than on such background as property ownership. The 16th Party Congress held in 2002 carried out Jiang's theory in amending the Party's constitution to enroll private entrepreneurs.

Urbanization and Migration

The economic reform has brought about many changes. The weight of agriculture has been decreasing while that of construction, manufacturing, and service has been on the rise. Agriculture used to count for 50.5 percent of the GDP back in the 1950s. It has shrunken down to fifteen percent by 2001. On the other hand, construction and manufacturing, which contributed only 20.9 percent of the GDP back then, stood for 51.2 percent in 2001. The service industry made rapid progress, reaching one-third of the GDP due to the fact that the number of cities grew from 450 in 1989 to 663 in 2000, and urban population increased from 17.92 percent in 1978 to 37.66 percent in 2001. The number of towns increased from 2,176 in 1978 to 20,374 in 2001.[67]

Urbanization provides solutions to surplus rural labor by creating non-farming jobs. With the progress of farming technology, the need for labor is reduced. The expansion of urban areas has resulted in the reduction of farmlands, which has translated into more surplus population. For many people, getting rich through farming is not only an unpopular concept, but also an unrealistic one, given the rising prices for agricultural products. They are eager to migrate into large cities and enjoy city life.[68]

Migrant population was estimated to be between 100,000 to 150,000 in 2001. Accommodating the huge influx poses an unprecedented challenge to existing cities and towns. One solution, probably the highest on the government's current agenda, is to open up the "Great West." The term is used by official media to refer to remote regions in western China that includes Chongqing, Sichuan, Guizhou, Yunnan, Tibet, Shaanxi, Gansu, Qinghai, Ningxia and Xinjiang.

The western part of China has fallen behind the coastal regions in economic development ever since 1978. The ten western regions, combined cover 56.8 percent of the total territory and have only one fourth of the total population. By investing in the economic infrastructure and applying incentive policies, the government is expecting to attract a great number of the surplus population from the east. Actually, the migration plan has been implemented since the early 1950s, though mostly for political reasons and in relatively small scales.

There may be two barriers, however, to the migration project. The first one is possible conflicts between the Han and local ethnic groups. Take Tibet for example, from 1952 to 1998 the population increased from 1.15 million to 2.51 million. A significant portion of the increase came from government personnel sent in to secure the "stability and democratization process" of the region. The migration rate picked up after 1987 when the government granted permission for people from inland to open businesses in Tibet. Currently, in Lhasa City, according to local Tibetan residents' estimate, only 40 percent are Tibetans, the rest are Han people from inland provinces. In July 2001, the government gave the go-ahead to the Qinghai-Tibet railroad project.[69] It is estimated that the project will be completed by 2007. The railway is expected to boost the pace of urbanization in Tibet.

The convenience of transportation is a double-edged sword that assures both material well-being and changes to the traditional Tibetan style of life. *The People's Daily*, for example, reported lately that private car ownership in Lhasa steadily rose to 70,000 by the end of 2003, averaging one car per hundred households.[70] With monastery students riding motorcycles and engaging in lucrative business dealings, it may not take long for further modernization to take place. There is concern that the influx of more and more better educated Han Chinese people, local Tibetans may only hold on to their traditional skills for a couple of years, and will gradually be marginalized.[71]

The second barrier to migration is the structural inflexibility. In fact, out of the fourteen SOE-concentrated industrial bases, except Beijing and Liaoning Province, the remaining twelve are all in the west. Presumably, the bureaucratic provincial governments share many interests with the rigid SOE system. Overcoming bureaucratic barriers may well be a long-term and up-the-hill battle. From the perspective of migrant workers, for now, at least, the Great West is not as attractive as Shanghai. Most of them will not line up their wagons until a clearer picture for individual's development pans out.[72]

Close-up: Reform of the Hukou System

The *hukou* system was installed back in the 1950s. In the form of an identification booklet, the document was issued to identify the carrier as belonging to a particular administrative entity. Residential regions were responsible for providing food rations, as well as social services such as education to its own *hukou* holders. The *hukou* system had other functions, one of which was migration control. During the 1960s and 1970s, migrant individuals could be arrested and even jailed if found without proper *hukou* status.

With the reform, the economic scenario has changed. In the 1980s and 1990s, the economic demand prompted most urban areas to relax barriers to travelers, resulting in influx of rural migrants. Until today, the *hukou* system continues to be a migration population control mechanism, although its functionality has been significantly reduced as more and more cities have eliminated the system.

The *hukou* reform is primarily about granting urban registration to those rural migrant individuals who have found stable jobs. The concept of "stable job" is defined as at least a one-year of hiring. This requirement was written into Document No. 11 (a CPC Central Committee circular) of November 2000. Completely eliminating the *hukou* system is a major objective of China's urbanization strategy for the Tenth Five-Year Plan (2001-05). Currently, college students of rural origins as well as rural entrepreneurs acquire their urban registrations automatically.

Since mid-2001, Document No. 11 and State Council Circular No. 6 of March 2001 both mandate that, starting from 1 October 2001, all small cities (those with populations of less than 100,000) must grant urban *hukou* to residents with fixed jobs and urban dwellings. The reform now encompasses all towns and small cities in Anhui, Guangdong, Hebei, Jiangsu, Shandong, Sichuan, and Zhejiang provinces. The changes have extended to several large municipalities, including Beijing, Chongqing, and Shanghai. The Guangdong province has reportedly eliminated the urban-rural distinction altogether and no longer stamps *hukou* as "urban" or "rural." Nevertheless, rural residents still try to obtain a Guangzhou *hukou* in order to obtain full access to the city's social services.[73] It is estimated that more than 180 million rural Chinese will move to urban areas by 2010.

Multiple factors lead to the fast-paced migration. The most significant factor is the surplus population caused by higher productivity. Analysts estimate that the number of surplus labor is under 180 to 200 million. Clearly, influx requires an urgent solution. Even for farmers who make a comfortable living in rural areas, the imbalance of living, educational, and health care conditions still make urban environment attractive. It is estimated that seventy percent of the growth of industrial output in the mid-1990s was contributed by migrant laborers.[74] As a recent move, the Beijing Municipality issued a policy on 1 April 2003 that allows newborns of the city's suburbs to register for urban *hukou*. In fact, creative measures are being deployed to facilitate migration and yet to maintain an effective control over influx.

Family in Transition

The family planning policy, or better known as the "one-child policy," has been in place since the late 1970s. The goal of the policy is to avert the threat of a population explosion. Back in the 1950s, the government urged mothers to provide more soldiers for the nation and purged economists who warned of looming danger of an oversized population. The issue of family planning was brought up again in the 1970s when large cities started to urge population control. The policy was only forcefully implemented after the National People's Congress of 1980 called for the inclusion of family planning into China's long-term development strategy. In the same year, the *Marriage Law* was revised to restrict the minimum age of marriage to twenty-two for men and twenty for women. The Law also encourages late marriage and late childbearing. The 1982 census revealed that the population had crossed the one billion mark. Until then, the Chinese government had rejected "population explosion" as a real and significant threat to the economy. Later on, Article 25 of the *Constitution* of 1982 was formulated to state, "The state promotes family planning so that population growth may fit the plans for economic and social development."[75]

The family planning policy restricts urban families to one child and families in rural and pastoral areas to a maximum of two children. A government report released earlier in 2001 claimed that the policy had effectively curbed the rapidly growing population. According to government data, without the one-child policy, China would have added 330 million people by 2001, more than the U.S. population. Benefits of family planning, according to the government, include better quality of life, liberation of women from frequent births, and the availability of more educational opportunities.[76]

Since the implementation of family planning, the average fertility rate has dropped from six children per family in the 1970s to about two per family by the beginning of the year 2000, according to the data of the Fifth National Census.[77] In addition to regulatory measures, financial punishment has been forceful as well. Violators pay a heavy fine equivalent to $300 in some areas and lose all benefits.[78]

The one-child policy met tremendous resistance, especially in the early 1980s during its beginning phase of implementation. The traditional concept of having a son to carry on the family name is deeply rooted. Rural people still harbor the traditional concept of family happiness: The more children the better. From time to time, violent protests often broke out in rural areas. Because the policy was never formalized into law, local officials had wide latitudes in carrying out the policy, resorting to brutal force at times.

As the market reform gains momentum, and as population ageing is becoming a real pressure in the late 1990s, the government has started to reform the stiff population pragmatism. In fact, it has been written into the law to legalize the right of a single-child couple to having two children.[79] Some cities allow couples to have two children, as long as the births are five years apart. In rural areas, some villages abolished birth permits (a quota system) allowing couples to decide on their own when to have a baby. The government also encourages local officials to initiate and fund their own pilot projects on family planning, expecting to achieve both population reduction and stability.[80]

A noticeable change is in the market of birth control devices. Since 2000, a variety of birth control pills and devices have been put on the market as alternatives to IUDs. For some people, the forbidden area of family planning has transformed from a simple arena of law enforcement to an attractive market of business opportunities. The prospect of profitability is attracting both state-owned and private enterprises. It is not rare for newspapers, electronic media and educational materials prepared by government agencies to include graphical instructions. Analysts suspect, however, that the policy change may actually reflect recent governmental effort in dealing with consequences caused by the overly harsh practices in the past. These consequences include gender imbalance, rapid population ageing, workforce deficiencies, and symptoms of a single-children society.

The first Family Planning Law adopted in September 2002 allows provinces and municipalities to set up local regulations. It specifies that couples meeting special provisions within the law be allowed a second child. Many local governments already have laws to that effect and Anhui Province recently passed regulations allowing thirteen categories of couples to apply for permission to have a second child, while some can have a third or more. Clearly, while the one child policy remains dominant, many changes are taking place.

Close-up: Changes in the Chinese Family

The family planning policy resulted in significant population reduction in the mid to late 1990s. It has changed the Chinese family in many aspects. The photo of a typical traditional family would include a white-bearded great-grandfather surrounded by children, grand children and great grand children. The background would be a large family living room or a family courtyard garden. Such a scenario has faded into history. The Chinese Academy of Science conducted three surveys on compositions of Chinese families in 1982, 1993, and 1997. [81] The 1982 survey covered Beijing, Tianjin, Shanghai, Nanjing, and Chengdu; the 1993 survey covered Guangzhou, Lanzhou, Harbin, Beijing, Shanghai, Nanjing and Chengdu; the 1997 survey focused only on Shanghai and Chengdu. Data shows that more than half of urban families belong to the "core families" consisted of two parents and a child. Only two percent of the families support four generations under the same roof.

The survey divided families into seven types: The "single family" of one person, the "hippy family" of a well-off couple without child, the "empty nest family" of a senior couple after children have left, the "core family" with two parents and a single child, the "branch family" in which the couple lives with the parents of either the wife or the husband, the "combo family" of a couple living with parents of both sides, and the "miscellaneous family" of unclassifiable types. The report indicates that the percentage of "core families" among urban households rose from fifty-five percent in 1993 to sixty-five percent in 1997. Meanwhile, "hippy families" made up three percent of the total in 1997, six times the number in 1993. Scientists forecast that the percentage of "core families" will likely continue to rise, and so will the number of "branch families." However, "combo families" and "empty nest families" will decline in number.

Children born after the launch of the family planning policy in the late 1970s formed "core families," "hippy families," "branch families" and "empty nest families," but rarely "combo families," as the research indicates. Five factors, according to analysts, may have affected the choices: a) whether the husband or the wife used to live with his or her their parents before marriage; b) whether the couple is financially capable of supporting a family; c) whether the couple has their own housing, as housing provision varies from one "work unit" to another; d) whether their parents need care; e) whether the couple relies on parents for baby-sitting, so that they could pursue their careers.

In the past, the tradition dictates that the wedded couple lives with the husband's family. Today, newlyweds tend to form their own families away from the shadow of their parents. Among 1,600 couples surveyed in 1983, 300 lived with the husband's family, sixty with the wife's family, and about four-fifths formed their own units.

The pursuit for independence, however, is apparently inconsistent. Of those married between 1990 and 1997, three-tenths made up "branch families" living with their parents, while only two tenths did so among those who married a decade ago between 1980 and 1989. Researchers suspect that doing one's own chores and keeping the house in order may constitute a major burden in life. Hence, by living with parents, part of the burden is taken care of. This seems to be a logical outcome of the one-child policy, as researchers explains: Single children tend to lack basic skills in life.

Social Security Reform

During the pre-reform era, China had maintained a "cradle-to-grave" welfare system where SOEs were solely responsible for their employees' welfare, including life-long employment, housing, medical expenses, pension, and children's schooling. In the area of social support, the system included social relief, social welfare, social mutual help, and special care for disabled ex-servicemen and family members of revolutionary martyrs. Under fierce competition from the private sector, the traditional system is less likely to provide adequate and reliable protection.

Since the early 1980s, the government has carried out reforms in its social security system with the goal of establishing a standardized system independent of enterprises and institutions, funded from various channels, and with socialized management and services. This system was characterized mainly by basic security, wide coverage, multiple levels, and steady unification. Under the mandatory basic security provided by the state, people's basic living needs are met corresponding with the economic development level. Besides basic security, the state promotes other types of aid so as to form a multi-level social security system. Through reform and development, the government strives to build a nationally unified social security system. The government claims that a social security system that guarantees urban residents a minimum standard of living has been established across China.[82]

Since the mid 1990s, the Chinese government has undertaken reforms to the social security management system in order to bring different systems under a unified planning. This is viewed as essential to a better management and an effective supervision of the use of social security funds. The handling of social insurance affairs that used to be the responsibility of enterprises is being gradually transferred to social organizations. Beneficiaries now get their social insurance benefits from organizations in their own communities and are subjected to the latter's administration. In addition, the government has adopted a variety of measures to increase the sources of social security funds, including strengthening the collection of social security funds and raising the ratio of such funds in the overall financial expenditure. In 2001, the central finance allocated 98.2 billion Yuan to be used for social security payments, 5.18 times the figure for 1998.[83] The Chinese government has established a National Social Security Fund Executive Council specially responsible for the operation and administration of the funds acquired from reducing state shareholding, the funds put in by the central finance and social security funds collected from other channels. The National Social Security Fund comes from the central finance appropriations as well as from other channels.

Since 1998, the government has adopted a "two guarantees" policy.[84] The first is a guarantee of the basic livelihood of the laid-off personnel from SOEs. Laid-off personnel receive allowances for basic living expenses and pay social insurance premiums for them, with the required funds coming from the government budget, enterprises and other sources, mainly unemployment insurance funds. Reemployment training programs are provided to help laid-off personnel find new jobs. The second guarantee is to ensure basic livelihood for all retirees and that they receive basic pensions in full and on time. To ensure the implementation of the "two guarantees," the Chinese government has put forth three additional policies. Under these policies, laid-off workers from SOEs receive a basic living allowance from the reemployment service centers for a maximum of three years. If they still haven't found a job by the end of three years, they can receive unemployment insurance payments for a maximum of two years. If by the end of the two-year period they remain unemployed, they can apply for the minimum living allowance paid to urban residents.

According to a document released at the CPC's 16th Party Congress, during the period from 1998 to the first half of 2002, there had been twenty-six million workers laid off from SOEs, of which seventeen million had been successfully reemployed through various channels and forms. A large number of workers transferred from the secondary industry to the tertiary industry, or from SOEs to non-public economic entities. As a result of the released redundancy in the SOEs, the enterprise reform has been deepened and their competitiveness improved.[85]

Reform of the old-age insurance system was initiated throughout China in 1984. In 1997, the Chinese government adopted the Decision on Establishing a Uniform Basic Old-Age Insurance System for Enterprise Employees, in light of which improvement was made in urban areas nationwide. The basic Chinese old-age insurance system is a combination of funds from two sources: Mutual assistance programs and personal accounts. Urban employees widely participate in these programs by contributing a portion of the pay as premium into their personal accounts. Urban employers are obligated to contribute to employees' old age insurance. The majority of employer-contributed premium is used to set up a mutual assistance fund, the rest goes into employees' personal accounts. At present, about twenty percent of the enterprise wage bill and eight percent of personal wage should go to such insurance. Similarly, the basic old-age pension is in two parts: The base pension and the pension in personal accounts. The base pension is covered by the mutual assistance funds, the monthly sum amounting to twenty percent of the average social wage of the employees and the monthly pension in personal accounts come to 1/120 of the accumulated amount in personal accounts. Pensions in personal accounts can be inherited. Those who started working before and retired after the implementation of this new system are entitled to an additional pension for the transitional period.[86]

In implementing the Tenth Five-Year Plan, the government puts developing economy and maintaining social stability ahead of everything else. The government sets its main tasks as a) gradually form a market-oriented employment mechanism and control the registered rural and urban unemployment rate to within five percent; b) actively adjust labor relations and keep them harmonious and stable; c) improve the macro-regulation and control system of income distribution, and achieve an approximately five percent annual increase in both the per capita disposable income of urban residents and the net per capita income of rural residents; d) speed up the development of the urban social security system by improving its management, and establish a basic security system rural areas to help the weak groups in society to take care of their own life and work.[87]

Health Care Reform

As economic restructuring continues, health care reform has become an urgent issue. The rural/urban divide reveals significant inequality in health care coverage with rural population in a steep disadvantage. Back in the 1960s and 1970s when rural population was under the roof of the "people's communes," the "Cooperative Medical Plans" provided rudimentary health care to the areas. The system, however, collapsed after the commune system disintegrated in early 1980s, leaving most of the rural population uncovered, which stood at 63.91 percent per report of the Fifth National Census.[88] It is estimated that, while some community-based medical insurance programs exist, these programs are sporadic and cover less than ten percent of the rural population. Hospital visits remain a costly item on the bill for the rural family and constitutes a tremendous concern for the government. Many programs are being experimented, with no significant improvement available, however, in the foreseeable future.

The urban health care situation offers a different perspective: One third of the urban population is covered by one of the popular programs, the GIP (Government Insurance Program) or the LIP (Labor Insurance Program). The LIP has a long history dating back to the 1950s. It is contributed by SOE employers for their employees. The system continued as the mainstay of health care until the first part of the 1990s. The LIP is financed by the government for government employees. Reforms were necessary to the system, however, as these state and SOE-funded systems revealed inefficiency and management flaws. These reforms were conducted in four stages. From 1988 to 1994, the experiment included implementing, on the basis of LIP and GIP, systems such as cost-sharing, co-pay, using social pooling funds for the elderly health care, and catastrophic insurance in some cities. In the second stage from 1995 to 1996, a government initiated pilot system pooled LIP and GIP to form city-wide coverage systems that included cost-sharing and rationing policy based on a priority-rated service list. [89]

The pilot experiment was conducted in Zhejiang and Jiujiang cities. In the third stage, from 1996 to 2000, the State Council extended the pilot system tested in the previous stage to fifty-seven cities and regions, and subsequently to all urban areas. In the fourth phase of the reform, starting from 2000, the focus is on regulating health care providers by installing sound management procedures, such as regulating drug prescriptions, as drugs typically cost more than fifty percent of the health care expenditures versus less than ten percent in the U.S. Clearly, solving the rural/urban divide in health care provision remains an urgent and challenging issue.

Close-up: The Pharmaceutical Market

China's pharmaceutical market stood for $15 billion by 1999, two thirds of which is accounted for by foreign imports. With the WTO entry, the market is expected to top $60 billion by 2010, and become the world's largest pharmaceutical market by 2020.

The rapid growth has been fueled by demographic shifts, cultural changes in attitude, and new government policies. With respect to demographic shifts, China's urbanization is estimated to grow at around five percent annually. As urban population accounts for only thirty percent of the total population as of 1999 but eighty percent of the nation's pharmaceutical sales, urbanization constitutes the major source of market growth. As more and more disposable income is available, staying healthy becomes an important part of the metropolitan life.

Intensive work brings along with it the world's most popular urban life-related diseases, such as diabetes, high blood pressure and cardiovascular diseases. Ageing is another factor that is expected to stretch the ten percent of the sixty-and-over population to thirty percent within five decades. While people generally favor western medicine, traditional herbal medicine remains strong in the area of health maintenance. The government policy highly supports both domestic R&D and the increase of imports. Tariffs are expected to go down as foreign and domestic funds are invested in high-tech drugs such as DNA vaccines, gene therapies, and monoclonal antibodies.

The current state of healthcare, however, constitutes a significant constraint on development. Only twenty-nine percent of the population is covered by health insurance, according to the State Statistical Bureau, and most of the insured population work for SOEs. Private companies offer health insurance that is commensurate with the company's profit. Many laid-off workers are not covered by any medical insurance at all. The government pledges to limit healthcare spending to below five percent of the GDP, and drug spending between eleven percent to thirteen percent of the healthcare cost by 2010.

Market entry for foreign pharmaceutical companies remains difficult. Licensing approval may take up to three years. Moreover, the government gives priorities to imports that China cannot produce. Despite the complex approval system, foreign pharmaceutical products account for one third of the market. Companies such as Janssen Pharmaceutica, Inc., SmithKline Beecham, and Pfizer Inc. are manufacturing and selling products in China. Another problem that foreign companies are faced with is the lack of intellectual property protection. In addition, much effort is needed to get the drug into the "State Reimbursement List."

Despite difficulties, most Western companies consider China's pharmaceutical market as having a great potential. In fact, foreign pharmaceutical companies investing in China have been making money during the past two decades.

(Source of data: Qi Bao. "Pharmaceuticals: Paying the Price for Medicines," *China Business Review* 5, vol. 27, 8-11.)

Welfare and Housing Reforms

The government established the social welfare system in the 1950s to provide funds to ensure the livelihood of senior citizens, orphans and the handicapped persons who live under hardship conditions. The NPC issued the "Law of the People's Republic of China Guaranteeing the Rights and Interests of Senior Citizens," "Law of the People's Republic of China on Protection of the Handicapped," and "Regulations Concerning Work on Providing *Five Guarantees* in the Rural Areas." The laws stipulate that in urban regions elderly widows and widowers who are childless, helpless, and living alone, eligible handicapped persons, and orphans receive special concentrated dwelling spaces, while a combination of concentrated and scattered forms of dwellings are allocated to those in the rural areas. Concentrated establishments include social welfare homes, old-age homes, sanatoriums, and children's welfare homes. For handicapped persons, government aid includes the formulation of preferential policies for establishing social welfare enterprises of diverse types to help create job opportunities for those who are able to work.

In a country with 1.29 billion people, housing provision has always been a challenge. During the pre-reform era, the SOEs provided apartments to married employees and dorms to unmarried employees. Better housing conditions were awarded to employees commensurate with seniority, ranking, and sometimes work performance. The average urban residential space was less than five square meters or less than six square yards by the time economic reform started.

With the rise of the private sector, more disposable income was available for housing improvement. The rising demand and available cash fueled an immediate real estate boom. The state monopoly is in a process of gradually phasing out. Starting from 1979, the government allows new houses to be sold at cost prices in Xian, Liuzhou, Wuzhou and Nanning on experimental basis. The successful trial resulted in the same policy being extended to sixty cities of over twenty provinces in 1981. Due to decades of communist control and the impact of the Land Reform Movement, there was a general lack of confidence in housing ownership, which constituted a barrier to the housing market. To open up the housing market, a one third sharing system was adopted during this period with the individual, the work unit and the state each contributing one third of the cost. The system was eventually discontinued due to lack of state funds.[90]

In the latter half of the 1980s, the State Council adopted the policy of raising rents and meanwhile putting more new housing units on the market, encouraging people to purchase houses instead of relying on state-subsidized vouchers for residential rents. The new policy was backed by the amended Land Law that provided better protection for real estate development through permission of flexible and longer-term leasing. The real estate boom took off after Deng Xiaoping inspected the economic development of southern coastal cities in 1992 and reiterated the policy of continuing with the reform despite the Tiananmen crackdown. Reassured with the economic direction, consumers finally poured money into the housing market. Investment reached seventy-three billion Yuan the same year of Deng's inspection or seventeen percent higher than the level of 1991. By the end of the 1990s, the government decided to phase out state-subsidies and encouraged mortgage financing as well as the rental market. In 1986, consumers purchased less than fourteen percent of the new houses, while in 1999 eighty percent of new houses were sold. Despite the fact that the Asian financial crisis and a complicated taxing system put a damper on the overheated housing market, residential houses have finally become a marketable commodity. Government taxes and various community management fees,[91] however, may cause hindrance to further development.

Foreign Trade and Investment

The "Open Door" policy has led to rapid foreign trade and investment. The total value of import and export in 2002 reached 620.8 billion US dollars, including 325.6 billion US dollars in export and 295.2 billion US dollars in import, up 21.8 percent over the previous year. In 2002, China's export to the United States was seventy billion US dollars, representing an increase of 28.9 percent over the previous year. The exchange rate of the Chinese currency Ren Min Bi (RMB) was stable, standing at one US dollar for 8.2773 RMB Yuan at the end of the year.[92] Foreign trade accounted for only 9.6 percent of GDP at the start of the reform in 1978. Now, its weight in national economy had reached fifty percent of the GDP in 2002, accounting for five percent of the world trade. According to World Bank's estimate, China's share in world trade could well double in the next twenty-five years.[93]

In addition to the favorable economic policies, China's foreign trade structure represented a favorable predisposition for the ensuing trade boom. Product processing accounts for more than half of the trade volume. Most of the Foreign Direct Investments (FDI) and Foreign Invested Enterprises (FIE) are export-oriented businesses. Therefore, both imported and exported products mostly originate from foreign firms and primarily in the sectors such as machinery and electronics. This is a tremendous change from the foreign trade in the past when the products were primarily homemade handicraft. In 1978, for example, sixty-three percent of China's exports were primary products, the share of which was reduced to only ten percent in 2001.[94] On the other hand, however, because the main body of the trade is value-added processing, the profit margin is typically small. China's foreign trade is therefore appropriately characterized as inter-industry type instead of intra-industry type.[95]

The inflow of better than fifty-two billion dollars of foreign investment in 2002 made China the largest host country of foreign investment. The boom in the inflow of foreign funds is even more impressive considering the weak legal context and the one-party-ruled political environment. The lack of transparency of SOEs, corruption, and trade barriers imposed by the government are often among the serious concerns. However, the unfavorable side seems to be fading away as reform deepens. China's huge market and its cheap but highly skilled labor are irresistible to foreign investors. There are speculations, however, that the cheap and skilled labor may be a short-lived transitional phenomenon. As democratization continues, labor conditions will tend to improve, which typically makes labor expensive. In this respect, Korea and Japan are best precedent examples.

The growth of foreign trade is inseparable from favorable government policies. The Chinese government has been creative in providing incentive tax packages to foreign investors, particularly multinational companies. Because these companies possess strong world distribution networks, they constitute a tremendous leading force in boosting China's foreign trade. Furthermore, with China's entry into the WTO, the unified rules and regulations tend to provide more protection and structural integration, which is welcomed by the Chinese government.

Overseas Chinese firms have also been one of the major sources of foreign funds. The traditional mindset of investing in one's homeland has constantly led overseas Chinese to seek development opportunities in China even during the most woeful moments in the history. In the past four decades, large overseas Chinese firms have made marked investments in electronics and in higher education. The medium and small firms have been the most aggressive investors. It is estimated that 60,000 Taiwan merchants[96] conduct businesses and reside in China for the long term. The Taiwan-mainland trade is expected to increase at a more rapid pace once the direct air transportation ban is lifted.

Foreign trade has taken the lead in pushing for the rule of law. Most rules and regulations are concerned mostly with two types of foreign investments: 1) FDI, the resulting companies of which are foreign-owned; and 2) FIE, the resulting companies of which are joint venture companies that are Chinese-owned. Starting in March 2003, foreign investment projects are processed by the new Ministry of Foreign Trade and Economic Cooperation (MOFCOM), the predecessors of which were the Ministry of Foreign Trade and Economic Cooperation (MOFTEC) and the State Economic and Trade Commission.

Back in 1994, the "Company Law" authorized SOEs to organize themselves as joint-stock companies and authorized these companies to receive direct foreign investment. According to the "Provisional Regulations on Utilization of Foreign Investment to Reorganize State-Owned Enterprises," promulgated by the State Economic and Trade Commission (SETC) in September 1998, if the transaction is approved and the foreign investor acquires twenty-five percent or more of the joint-stock company's equity, the company may be converted to an FIE and enjoy taxation privileges. As economic reform continues, more sectors have been opened to foreign investment, and more SOEs are up for sale. The question eventually arises: Can any Chinese company be bought by foreign business entities?

The answer to the question is "generally yes." Legal procedures permit foreign investors to buy shares or assets of an FIE, a non-FIE domestic enterprise, a company limited by shares (CLS), or an SOE. If the target company is listed on the Shenzhen or Shanghai stock exchange, the investor may either buy its unlisted shares or listed "B" shares which are not sold to Chinese citizens. If the target company is an SOE, then the deal will likely need additional approvals from the Ministry of Finance, the National Development and Reform Commission (NDRC), and the State Asset Supervision and Administration Commission (SASAC).

Some sectors, however, remain completely forbidden or partially open to foreign investment. The *Catalogue Guiding Foreign Investment in Industry* (Catalogue) provides information on regulations concerning such categories. The latest Catalogue that took effect in April 2002, shortly after China's World Trade Organization entry, opened up key sectors, such as telecommunications, gas, and water, to foreign investment.

In terms of levels of ownership, the rule of thumb is, there is no maximum limit in general, unless specified in the Catalogue. However, companies in such areas as telecommunications, financial services, and transportation tend to be majority-owned by the Chinese government. Since the early 1980s, in order to attract foreign investment, the government had granted general tax privileges to FIE companies regardless of the size of foreign stake. Starting from 2003, however, FIEs with less than twenty-five percent of foreign investment may still register as FIE, but may not enjoy special tax status.[97]

The following is a selected list of laws recently promulgated or amended in the area of foreign trade:

1. *Several Provisions on Changes in Equity Interest of Investors in FIEs*, Ministry of Foreign Trade and Economic Cooperation (MOFTEC) and State Administration for Industry and Commerce, 1997. Coverage: Contractual joint ventures, equity joint ventures, wholly foreign owned enterprises, and foreign invested company by shares.
2. *Provisional Regulations on Utilization of Foreign Investment to Reorganize State-Owned Enterprises*, the State Economic and Trade Commission (SETC), September 1998. Coverage: FIE registration and taxation regulations.
3. *Provisions on Merger and Division of FIEs*, MOFTEC and State Administration for Industry and Commerce, 1999. Coverage: Contractual joint ventures, equity joint ventures, wholly foreign

owned enterprises, foreign invested company by shares, and domestic enterprises.

4. *Interim Provisions on Domestic Investment by FIEs*, MOFTEC and State Administration for Industry and Commerce, 2000. Coverage: Limited liability company and company by limited shares.

5. *Notice on Relevant Issues Regarding the Transfer of State-owned Shares and Legal Person Shares of Listed Companies to Foreign Investors*, the Ministry of Finance, China Securities Regulatory Commission, and State Economic and Trade Commission, 2002. Coverage: Non-listed shares of companies that are listed on the stock exchange boards.

6. *Interim Provisions on the Administration of Securities Investment in China by Qualified Foreign Institutional Investors*, China Securities Regulatory Commission and People's Bank of China, 2002. Coverage: Listed companies.

7. *Interim Provisions on the Utilization of Foreign Investment to Restructure State-owned Enterprises*, the Ministry of Finance, State Administration for Foreign Exchange, 2003. Coverage: SOEs.

8. *Interim Provisions on the Acquisition of Domestic Enterprises for Foreign Investors*, MOFTEC, State Administration of Taxation, and State Administration for Foreign Exchange, 2003. Coverage: Primarily domestic enterprises.

Close-up: Coca-Cola in China

Arrived in 1979 when Deng Xiaoping launched the "Open Door" policy, Coca-Cola was the first U.S. company to open business in China. Currently, the company runs twenty-four bottling joint-ventures, mostly through Swire Beverages and Kerry Group, two Hong Kong-based companies that it partly owns. A successful FDI, Coca-Cola accounts for thirty-five percent of China's carbonated beverage market. A 2000 study conducted by Beijing University, Qinghua University, and the University of South Carolina found that the company supported 14,000 employees in addition to 400,000 hired by distributors, wholesalers and retailers. In addition, Coca-Cola has been an important contributor to SOE reform.

In the beginning of the 1980s, Coca-Cola started by importing its products sold only to foreigners at the time. Soon the company built bottling plants in Beijing, Xiamen, and Guangzhou, giving away ownership of these plants to the Chinese government in exchange for distribution rights. In 1985, the company was granted rights to sell its products to ordinary Chinese consumers. Subsequently, twenty-four bottling facilities as well as two concentrate plants were built in twenty-one cities.

Several successful strategies demonstrate the ingenuity of the management. The most impressive one is the audacious plan of working with China's bureaucracy-plagued SOEs to utilize their gigantic distribution infrastructure to promote Coca-Cola products. Some of the company's partners were large state-owned sugar, tobacco and wine enterprises with an operating history of fifty years. Others were former SOEs in the process of privatization. Moreover, Coca-Cola was able to contract with neighborhood committees that are typically formed by retirees to take charge of neighborhood crime-watch and to help the needy and elderly. The large distribution force, though inefficient in many ways, turned out to be in itself a large base of consumers of the company's products.

Another successful strategy is to advertise to the taste of the Chinese consumers. In 1984, Coca-Cola was the first foreign company to advertise on Chinese Central Television (CCTV), the government-owned TV station. Chinese viewers enjoyed the commercials for six consecutive years. The culturally appropriate, vivid and colorful commercials were aired in prime times such as national and world soccer games and Olympic games, leaving a deep impression on viewers. These commercials not only advertised the products but also showed a life style that was deemed fashionable by young people.

The third successful strategy is "thinking local and acting local." The Chinese tradition values health strengthening foods and drinks. Such drinks typically include herb or fruit-enriched liquors, tea, and countless medicinal drinks. To feed to the culture, Coca-Cola developed several local brands of which the best known is "Tian Yu Di" (Heaven and Earth), a line of non-carbonated drinks that features mango and lychee flavored drinks, oolong and jasmine teas, and bottled water. "Xingmu" (Smart) is a line of carbonated fruit drinks in green apple, watermelon, and coconut flavors introduced in 1997 and quickly became the top brand.

Faced with increasing competition from domestic brands, the company stays on track of supplying, producing and selling its products within China's borders. The company continues to creatively explore new opportunities to serve its seventh largest market and to remain in the rank of the most successful FDI in China.

(Source of data: Drake Weisert, "Coca-Cola in China: Quenching the Thirst of a Billion," *China Business Review* 28, no. 4, July-August 2001)

Towards the Rule of Law

Confucius favors the rule of virtue and ranks the rule of law as secondary. He argues that law enforcement alone would only result in more lawbreakers. Moral values are what may ultimately regulate people by implanting a sense of shame in people's mind. Apparently, the drawback of the rule of virtue lies in its lack of rigor. Moral principles are open for interpretations and virtuous rulers have been rare. The development of the market economy has led people to the awareness that playing by the rules is essential to the modern society.

Since the reform, the Chinese government has repeatedly affirmed its commitment to achieving the rule of law. In practice, however, the co-existence of the rule of the CPC and the rule of law often results in ambiguity. There is constant concern that the law actually serves the Party rather than otherwise. Nevertheless, the reform has resulted in a constant improvement of the legal environment. In practical terms, new laws constantly emerge and contribute to a safer living and business environment. Over the past two decades, China has developed an effective law enforcement system. The court has been able to make its judgment for the most part without intervention from political sources. Legal education has become an important part of school education. More importantly, the NPC has been acting more independently and responsibly in monitoring government behavior. By creating enforceable laws to protect joint ventures and foreign investments, China has been successful in attracting more foreign funds than any other country in the world.

China's entry into the WTO is seen as a binding force that leverages China to play by the rules set for all member nations. One example is the requirement of transparent accounting reports by international firms. SOEs typically have a complex internal routing system, and in a sense, revelation of the firms' financials following Western accounting standards is hardly applicable. As the SOE reform deepens, however, the transparency situation has shown improvement. As an example, the Ministry of Foreign Trade and Economic Cooperation has decided that all WTO-related laws will be translated and published before they are implemented. Consulting centers will also be set up to answer inquiries. For China, being a vast country with uneven economic development, however, how effectively the laws will be carried out remains to be monitored.

China reportedly has over 120,000 lawyers and 9,000 law firms today. In 1996, seventy-six percent of Chinese law firms were state-funded and twenty-four percent were partnerships or cooperatives. By early 2002, fifty percent were partnerships or cooperatives. Nevertheless, most private firms resemble corporate entities and lack the incentive-based, profit-sharing structures of Western partnership law firms, and lawyers have been trained primarily in such methods as rote memorization.[98]

Experience shows that any impact from a weak legal environment can be significant. For example, instead of formulating restrictions on FDIs, the government classifies FDI proposals along the categories of "prohibited," "restricted," "permitted" and "encouraged." The prohibited category includes areas of national security as well as traditional arts and techniques that China safeguards as national treasures. As such, the categorization of an incoming FDI project could lend to confusion, often making the approval process of a business plan a time-consuming and frustrating experience. Complaints regarding the cumbersome approval processes remain strong. The phenomenon is actually intrinsically a matter of lack of transparency,[99] as rules and policies are not conveniently available. Recent reports from FDI companies, however, do confirm improvement in approval processes, particularly in Shanghai and other large cities where lawyers and officials are more experienced in handling foreign investments.

Close-up: The New Patent Law

Copyright protection used to be the weakest spot of the China market. Since early 1990s, China has been praised for making notable progress in intellectual property protection following its WTO entry. The National People's Congress (NPC) passed the original *Patent Law* in 1984. The law was amended in 1992 and again in 2000 before China's WTO membership took effect in 2001. The latest amendment was made in three areas: 1) new judicial and administrative protection, 2) improved application procedures, and 3) simplified enforcement procedures. The amendment brought the law closer to the WTO agreement on *Trade-Related Aspects of Intellectual Property Rights* (TRIPs).

To prohibit unauthorized "offering for sale," Article 11 of the amended Patent Law now stresses the protection of the patent holder's control over the patented product. This remedy is particularly important in the case the infringing manufacturer is uneasy to identity. Previous amendment was not forceful enough with respect to prohibiting unauthorized sales. The latest amendment came in line with TRIPs' requirement. Article 11 states:

> After the grant of the patent right for an invention or utility model, except as otherwise provided for in the law, no entity or individual may, without the authorization of the patentee, exploit the patent, that is, make, use, offer to sell, sell or import the patented product; or use the patented process or use, offer to sell, sell or import the product directly obtained by the patented process, for production or business purposes.
>
> After the grant of the patent right for a design, no entity or individual may, without the authorization of the patentee, exploit the design, that is, make, sell or import the product incorporating its or his patented design, for production or business purposes.[100]

In addition to prohibition of infringement, the new law establishes a clear set of standards in determining damages in the case of infringement, which was unclear in the previous version of the Patent Law. Article 60 states:

> The amount of damages for infringing a patent right shall be calculated according to the losses suffered by the patentee or the

profits gained by the infringer out of the infringement. If it is too difficult to determine the damages based on such losses of the patentee or the profits of the infringer, the appropriate times of the royalties for licenses for the said patent may be applied mutatis mutandis.[101]

A common excuse for infringement is "ignorance" of the illegality of the products. In the previous version of the Law, such ignorance would have been sufficient to exempt the infringing party from being sued. The latest amendment requires that the infringing party must provide the legitimate source of the products in question in order to be excused. The burden of proof, therefore, falls on the infringing party. Article 63 states:

Any person who, for production and business purposes, uses or sells a patented product without knowing that it was made and sold without the authorization of the patentee, shall not be responsible for the damages caused so long as he proves that he obtains the product from legitimate channels of distribution. [102]

Another important aspect of the new Patent Law that did not exist in the previous version is the provision of preliminary injunction to the patent holder in the case where he/she demonstrates evidence calling for immediate actions to be taken in stopping the infringement before the court has reached a judgment. Article 61 states:

Where a patentee or any interested party who can provide any reasonable evidence that his right is being infringed or that such infringement is imminent, and any delay to stop the acts is likely to cause irreparable harm to his or its legitimate rights, he or it may, before instituting legal proceedings, request the people's court to order the suspension of related acts and to provide property preservation.[103]

When it comes to inventions, a common infringement dispute is concerned with deciding the legitimate owner(s) of multiple patent claimers. The new Patent Law requires the defendant in such cases to not only prove the unique process in making the product, but also to disprove the infringement charges. Article 57 states:

When any infringement dispute relates to a process patent for the manufacture of a new product, any entity or individual manufacturing the identical product shall furnish proof to the effect that a different process is used in the manufacture of its or his product. Where the infringement relates to a patent for utility model, the people's court or the authority for patent work may request the applicant to furnish search reports made by the patent administrative organ under the State Council.[104]

Finally, the new *Patent Law* clarifies that at the provincial level patent authorities are entitled to handling patent infringement disputes. The solution is primarily mediation in nature. In the situation where mediation is unsatisfactory, the defendant and the plaintiff may bring their case to the People's Court. Whether local authorities should be given the power to handle patent disputes used to be in itself a disputed issue, given the fact that local authorities are often ill equipped for such capacity. Nevertheless, favorable opinions seemed to have carried more weight on this issue in granting the power to the provincial level.

Business Culture, Cultural Business

The economic reform not only doubled and tripled foreign trade, but also contributed to cultural awareness. Before the door was open, neither the Chinese nor the multi-national companies were well aware of the importance of understanding one another's culture. As deals got lost and gained, both sides came to a keen awareness that "business culture" is actually "cultural business" in essence. To the old adage "location, location, location," the business community is willing to add "cultural, cultural, cultural."

The immediate cultural context is a combination of the traditional culture and its present transition. Decades of the planning economy have resulted in a weak legal environment as well as a heavy bureaucratic system. Due procedures and processes that foreign investors feel comfortable with do not reliably exist. As such, culturally appropriate approaches are often found more beneficial than fighting legal battles that could be highly costly, time consuming, and the outcomes of which could be unpredictable.

A case in time is McDonald's strategy in handling business dispute.[105]   In 1992, McDonald's opened its flagship restaurant in Beijing's prime shopping street, the Wangfujing Street, serving 20,000 customers per day and as many as 50,000 on holidays. In 1994, two years into its twenty-year land lease agreement with the city of Beijing, McDonald's was ordered to relocate. Instead of taking a tough stand by launching a war of litigations, McDonald's issued a conciliatory statement that expressed willingness to negotiate. Two years later, the Beijing Municipality agreed to pay twelve million U.S. dollars to compensate for the relocation cost, and gave the company permission to open more restaurants in Beijing. In response, McDonald's moved its restaurant 150 meters down the same street. The moral of this story is in handling disputes in a culturally appropriate way by saving the face (*mianzi*) to the Beijing municipal government.   A different approach was Leman Brother's highly publicized law suite against Chinese trading companies in 1994.   Though Lehman was able to recover $100 million debt, the company lost a tremendous amount of business.

Face-saving is often mistaken as lack of courage in confronting with the issue or with the person. In the Chinese culture, "face" usually denotes a social standing based on one's character and reputation within a given social group. "Face" is comparable to an intangible form of social currency or credit that the whole community seeks to maintain. Face-saving is reciprocal. When you cause another to lose face, you damage not only his/her reputation, but yours as well.[106]

In addition to understanding the significance of face-saving as an important relationship building strategy, one needs to penetrate into the networks of relationships, or *guanxi*.   Given the co-existence of private/state-owned business environment, *guanxi* would naturally play a crucial role in the market. Western attitudes toward *guanxi* are generally unfavorable. *Guanxi* is often taken as synonymous to corruption, bribery, or back scratching. Such misunderstanding is not only wrong but also may well derail business relationships. *Guanxi* serves as a security system that shields a company from eventualities that arise from either a weak legal environment or wrongful implementations of the law.[107] As the amount of trust is unequally distributed, gaining access into Chinese businesses would require efforts in cultivating, expanding, and nourishing the network for the most part.

It must be indicated that as industrialization and democratization continue, the reliance on *guanxi* will minimize. Completely phasing out a traditional behavioral pattern such as *guanxi* is impossible. The fact that developed countries such as Japan and Korea embrace similar cultural patterns serves as a proof. The following accounts of business experience are a case in time, illustrating the importance of networking:

> When our first container came through we had to go to the Shanghai docks and talk to the authorities there. Until they got to know us, we didn't exist. Their attitude towards regulations is, 'I won't provide any assistance because it gets me into trouble.' Until we understood that, we struggled. Whereas if you go to the docks at home, the people there will give you some suggestions. We were newcomers trying to find one container. The Shanghai container storage is enormous. Our problem was that we didn't know the system. I don't think they are being vindictive; it is just our lack of knowledge of how they work.
>
> In dealing with the bureaucracy you cannot expect a Western response. A Western response might be a five-minute response to give you the answer you want. In China you get frustrated after the third week, and you eventually find you could have done it three weeks ago. When we first went to Suzhou [Jiangsu Province] it took us seven weeks to open a bank account. We were being frustrated that things were going wrong. It took us only two weeks in Tianjin. The reason was we knew the ropes. We thought they were being difficult, but we didn't have all the permits and all the regulations in place.
>
> People go there with the wrong attitude, they don't acknowledge that it is a different system and they have to know and understand the system. They start applying Western standards, and when they don't achieve what they want, they can get very dogmatic.[108]

Negotiation is another area where cultural understanding is preponderant. Due to decades of the planning economy, the top-down processing pattern in decision making has become the norm. Negotiators are often employees who do not have the right to decision-making at all. Their responsibility is to report to the higher level. Furthermore, unwilling to take any responsibility, for fear of jeopardizing the next promotion, or simply due to lack of motivation, their bureaucratic attitude could well make negotiation sessions tedious and frustrating. Without understanding the business culture, the foreign negotiator would tend think, "This is going nowhere. We are not achieving anything. We believe we should cease now and probably go back home. There is no point in continuing with this contract, and let's walk out." However, the one who understands the cultural context would be ready for a marathon negotiation and be prepared to live with the system.

With the right attitude, one would find many creative approaches, such as building relationships with the real decision makers, and meanwhile getting acquainted with lower level officials on a golf course. Experience says that bureaucrats often possess wide discretionary powers to interpreting rules and regulations and finding ways to move the project. Things that look infinitely complicated may actually be straight and easy. The trick is in understanding the culture.

Reform in the Diplomatic Front

The diplomacy of a country primarily reflects its economic interests. Before the reform, occupied with political campaigns, the Chinese government had little economic interests to pursue. Internationally, China's diplomacy was confrontational at best. China first joined the Soviet Camp in the 1950s, only to withdraw from it in 1960 when Nikita Khrushchev revealed his theory of "peaceful transition." Rallying support from the "third world countries," China stood up against both superpowers, the USSR and the U.S.

To defy the Soviet pressure, China skillfully took advantage of conflicts between the two superpowers by leaning toward the American side, known as the "strategic triangle."[109] The "ping-pong diplomacy" of 1971 was a brilliant diplomatic maneuver when China unexpectedly invited the U.S. ping-pong team. In the following year, President Richard Nixon and Secretary of State Henry Kissinger arrived in Beijing for a historic week-long visit from 21 to 28 Februrary 1972.

The *Shanghai Communiqué* was signed stating that the Sino-U.S. relationship should be one based on observance of five principles that includes sovereignty and territorial integrity of both nations, non-aggression, non-interference in one another's internal affairs, equality on the basis of mutual benefit, and peaceful co-existence. The

Communiqué also states that China and the U.S. would oppose hegemony in Asia-Pacific region, a clause referring to Soviet expansion. In addition, the two sides exchanged views on some long-standing disputes of which Taiwan stood out as the major concern. The Chinese side voices its opinion as follows:

> The Taiwan question is the crucial question obstructing the normalization of relationship between China and the United States. The Government of the People's Republic of China is the sole legal government of China; Taiwan is a province of China which has long been returned to the motherland; the liberation of Taiwan is China's internal affair in which no other country has the right to interfere; and all U.S. forces and military installations must be withdrawn from Taiwan. The Chinese Government firmly opposes any activities which aim at the creation of "one China, one Taiwan," "one China, two governments," "Two Chinas," an "independent Taiwan," or advocate that "the status of Taiwan remains to be determined."[110]

The U.S. side states:

> The United States acknowledges that all Chinese on either side of the Taiwan Strait maintain there is but one China and that Taiwan is a part of China. The United States Government does not challenge that position. It reaffirms its interest in a peaceful settlement of the Taiwan question by the Chinese themselves. With this prospect in mind, it affirms the ultimate objective of the withdrawal of all U.S. forces and military installations from Taiwan. In the meantime, it will progressively reduce its forces and military installations on Taiwan as the tension in the area diminishes.[111]

President Nixon's visit brought about a dramatic change in the relationship between the two countries. The Sino-U.S. relationship was normalized only in 1979, after the Carter Administration abandoned the U.S.-Taiwan defense treaty and removed all U.S. military troops from Taiwan.

With its military forces and intermittent weapons purchases from the U.S., Taiwan is, by any objective measure, defending its sovereignty. During the 1990s, Taiwan went through a series of democratic reforms that transformed the Nationalist Party's (KMT) single-party rule to a multiparty system. Economically, Taiwan emerged as one of the "Asian tigers" in the region. For the Chinese government, however, Taiwan is an inseparable part of the territory and is bound to return. Any nation that wishes to establish normal relationships with China must first cease such relationships with Taiwan. During the past decade or so China has been aggressively engaging in Taiwan's "home returning" process. In 1996, for example, in an attempt to influence the outcomes of Taiwan's presidential election, China resorted to military threats including missile tests within a close range of the island's coastline, which provoked immediate response by the United States.[112]   As the U.S. shifts its priority to the war on terror in recent years, presumably the Bush Administration may make more concessions to China in order to form a broad anti-terrorist alliance. What this could mean to Taiwan's destiny remains to be seen.

As a matter of the general tendency, since the reform of 1978 the Chinese government has obviously been keeping a low profile in world confrontations, concentrating on economic development and on maintaining domestic stability. Deng Xiaoping had reiterated time and again that without a strong economy, China would have no say in world affairs. Thus, in the diplomatic arena, China maintains equal distance between Russia and the United States, which is better known as the "independence diplomacy." By 1989 when Gorbachev visited Beijing, the Sino-Russian relationships had been significantly improved. For example, Russian troops were reduced by 500,000 in regions bordering with China, which allowed the Chinese government to shift important resources to economic development.[113]

An important change in the tradition of diplomacy management is in the significant reduction of the leaders' personal influence. With the focus set on developing the economy, China's diplomacy has been consistent in the past two decades. The independence diplomacy had been carried through by Jiang Zemin since he was elected President in 1993. Jiang's effort included building China's influence in the Asia-Pacific region, improving relationships with neighboring countries, and continuing to open up China to the outer world by accessing the WTO in 2001. On the issue of war on terror, China condemns the 911 terrorist attack and firmly supports the American war on Al Qaeda and other terrorist groups. China's reaction is viewed as related to the crackdown of domestic separatism in its northwest Xinjiang Uygur

Autonomous Region. On the issue of war on Iraq, China supports the effort of disarming Iraq of weapons of mass destruction (WMD), but favored the U.N. inspection against any premature use of military force. On the issue of the North Korean nuclear crisis, China is concerned about North Korea's possession of nuclear weapons, and encourages dialogues between the U.S. and North Korea.

As one of the nuclear powers and one of the major conventional weapons producers, it is no secret that China engages in weapon sales in the Asia-Pacific region. However, through such dangerous businesses China is seeking both profit and stability in the region. Given the interest of its own economic recovery, the last thing that China would expect to happen would be disruption of peace. Maintaining balance through exporting weapons has actually become a common practice internationally such that a non-proliferation treaty became necessary. In fact, in 1991, China reversed its harsh criticism toward the Nuclear Non-proliferation Treaty (NPT) and turned to support the treaty.[114] However, it is known that China engaged in missile sales to Pakistan, a country that possesses nuclear weapons. But, as some analysts pointed out, the sales of M-11 missiles were somewhat triggered by the U.S. transfer of F-16 fighter jets to Taiwan. In addition, China shares a 2,500-mile border with India which is also a nuclear power and with which China has a long-standing territorial dispute.[115] Hence, thwarting India's threat is in China's benefit. In any case, the paramount influence of China in world affairs is increasing with time.

Close-up: Timeline of U.S.-China Relations

1949	Mao Zedong declares the People's Republic of China. The KMT flees to Taiwan. The U.S. refuses to recognize the PRC.
1950	Korean War Starts. President Truman sends troops to South Korea, meanwhile protects Taiwan. China enters Korean War which ends in 1953 armistice.
1965	The U.S. bombs North Vietnam; China steps up aid to Hanoi.
1969	President Nixon suspends Seventh Fleet patrols in Taiwan Strait.
1971	China invites U.S. ping-pong team to Beijing. Henry Kissinger makes a secret visit to China to prepare for Nixon's visit.

1972	President Nixon meets Mao Zedong in Beijing and signs the Shanghai Joint Communiqué recognizing Taiwan as part of China.
1975	US President Gerald Ford visits China.
1976	Mao Zedong dies.
1979	Sino-U.S. diplomatic relationship was established. Joint communiqué states Washington will only maintain unofficial links with Taiwan. Vice Premier Deng Xiaoping visits the U.S. in January. In April, the U.S. Congress passes Taiwan Relations Act reaffirming commitment to Taiwan and pledging to maintain arms sales to the island.
1982	In a third joint communiqué, the U.S. pledges to gradually reduce arms sales to Taiwan.
1984	Premier Zhao Ziyang visits the U.S. in January. President Reagan visits China in April to meet Deng Xiaoping. Deng stresses Taiwan issue's importance in China-U.S. relations.
1985	Chinese President Li Xiannian visits the U.S.
1989	President Bush visits China in February. On 4 June, Chinese government disperses student pro-democracy demonstrations in Beijing's Tiananmen Square, resulting in sanctions by the West. The National Security Adviser Brent Scowcroft meets Chinese leaders in a secret mission in July to reaffirm relations.
1991	The U.S. announces three sanctions on China: Suspend exports of satellites and related components, restrict exports of high-speed computers, prohibit exports of missile-related products.
1992	President Bush approves the sale of 150 F-16 fighter jets to Taiwan, overturning a long-term U.S. policy.
1993	President Clinton comes into office, stresses the use of economic leverage to promote democracy in China, insists the Most Favored Nation (MFN) trading status for China be linked to specific improvements in human rights conditions. Chinese President Jiang Zemin meets Clinton at the Asia-Pacific Economic Cooperation (APEC) leadership meeting in Seattle in November.
1994	President Clinton drops policy of linking human rights reform to China's annual renewal of the MFN trading status.
1995	President Clinton authorizes private visit to New York by Taiwan's Lee Teng-hui, reversing a 15-year-old policy of denying visas to Taiwan leaders. China recalls its ambassador to Washington in protest.

1996	In March, China holds missile tests near Taiwan to intimidate voters against Lee Teng-hui running for the island's first direct presidential election. The U.S. sends two aircraft-carrier battle groups to the area in a show of support for Taiwan. Lee wins election by a landslide.
1997	Vice-President Al Gore visits China in March. China regains control of Hong Kong from the UK on 1 July. China releases prominent dissident Wei Jingsheng from prison in November who came to the U.S. Clinton and Jiang meet in Vancouver, Canada, before the APEC forum. In October, President Jiang is the first Chinese president to visit the U.S. in twelve years.
1998	June, U.S. Senate investigates China's alleged theft of sensitive missile technology and the alleged Chinese military's illegal contribution to the Democratic Party's 1996 election campaign. China denies allegations. In May, NATO warplanes in Yugoslavia air raids accidentally bomb the Chinese Embassy in Belgrade, sparking outrage from China. Bill Clinton is the first U.S. president to visit China since the 1989-Crackdown. He criticizes the violent crushing of the 1989 demonstrations and urges China to respect and preserve the basic human rights of its people. In Shanghai, Clinton reaffirms his "three no" policy: No support for Taiwan independence, no recognition of a separate Taiwanese Government, and no backing for Taiwanese membership of international organizations
1999	U.S. and China agree on terms for China's entry to the WTO.
2000	In March, pro-independence politician Chen Shui-bian wins Taiwan's presidential election. Beijing threatens to attack the island if it attempts to secede. In April, the U.S. decides to sell a new military package to Taiwan but defers a decision on some controversial weapons, including submarines and anti-submarine aircraft. In May, the U.S. House of Representatives votes to normalize trade relations with China and to set up a commission to monitor China's human rights record. In June, U.S. Secretary of State Madeleine Albright meets senior Chinese leaders in Beijing, the first high level visit since the Belgrade embassy bombing in 1999. In September, U.S. Senate passes Permanent Normal Trade Relations (PNTR) bill, guaranteeing Chinese goods the same low-tariff access to the U.S. market as products from most other nations.
2001	In March, the U.S. drops Clinton's "three no policy" on Taiwan. In April, U.S. spy plane makes emergency landing on

	southern Chinese island of Hainan after a collision with a Chinese fighter jet. China releases the twenty-four crew after President Bush states that he is "very sorry" that a Chinese pilot died in the incident. In May, the White House allows Taiwanese President Chen Shui-bian to visit the U.S., arousing Chinese condemnation. In October, George Bush and Jiang Zemin meet for the first time in Shanghai, at the Asia Pacific Economic Co-operation (APEC) summit. President Jiang backs the U.S. war on terrorism. In November, China joins the World Trade Organization (WTO).
2002	President George Bush makes his second visit to China in February, flying into Beijing on the symbolically important 30th anniversary of the summit between former leaders Richard Nixon and Mao Zedong. Mr. Hu Jintao, then Vice President, pays his first visit to the U.S. in April. In October, President Jiang Zemin visits President George Bush. They agree to work together to solve the crisis created by North Korea's admission to owning nuclear weapons.
2003	In November, the Chinese government warns Taiwan authorities led by Chen Shui-bian to immediately stop separatist advocacy for a "referendum" and urges the U.S. not to support Taiwan's separatism. Chinese Vice Minister of Commerce Ma Xiuhong summons Clark Randt, U.S. Ambassador to China, as emergency on 20 November, expressing deep regret and firm opposition to U.S. decision to impose import quota on Chinese fabric products.
2004	Chen Shuibian's winning of Taiwan's presidential election in March, apparently clouded by a mysterious assassination attempt, raised new tensions across the Strait and in Sino-U.S. relationship.

(Sources of data: "Timeline: US-China relations," *BBC News*. "Major Events of China-U.S. Ties," Embassy of the PRC)[116]

Education Reform

Opportunities to receive higher education have been dramatically improved since the 1990s. According to the Ministry of Education, universities enrolled 3,820,000 undergraduate students in 2003 or

610,000 higher than 2002. The enrollment of graduate students in 2003 was 269,000 or 6,8900 higher than the previous year. The government is expecting to inject more funding to develop education in western provinces in the coming year in response to the project of "opening the west."[117]

The following table shows new entrants and graduates in the five years period from 1998 to 2002:

Item	Unit: 10,000 Persons					
	1998	1999	2000	2001	2002	1998-2002
Entrants						
Postgraduates	7.3	9.2	12.8	16.5	20.3	66.1
General Universities	108	160	221	268	321	1078
Adult Education	100	116	156	196	222	790
Secondary Vocational Schools	520	473	411	400	470	2274
General Senior Secondary Schools	360	396	473	558	677	2464
Graduates						
Postgraduates	4.7	5.5	5.9	6.8	8.1	31.0
General Universities	83	85	95	104	134	501
Adult Education	83	89	88	93	118	471
General Senior Secondary Schools	252	263	302	341	384	1542

(Source of data: *Statistical Communiqué*, 2003)[118]

Educational System

Since 1986, the broad-based educational system of China has required a nine-year compulsory education of all children. The nine-year term includes six years of primary education starting at age seven or six and a three-year secondary education. The "six plus three" system is largely implemented in urban areas. In rural areas the "five plus four" system is widely adopted which includes five years of primary education and four years of secondary education. Pre-school education is not a requirement, although the demand is high in urban areas.

The upper-level secondary education is divided into the college-bound track and vocational track, both requiring three to four years of schooling. Secondary education is followed by four years of higher education leading to a Bachelor's degree, or an equivalent degree at a higher-level vocational institute. Those who continue with their education in post-graduate programs will be able to finish a master's degree or doctoral degree in two to three years.

In the past, the government financially supported the entire educational system. Today, educational institutions at all levels typically receive funding not only from the Ministry of Education, but also from local financial sources. The diversification in funding reflects a loosened control by the government on the curriculum that used to be routinely scrutinized during the pre-reform time. Similarly, the previous state-controlled job assignment system has disintegrated and switched to a hybrid system. Companies from the private sector competitively attract graduates with high paying opportunities or tuition incentives.

College Entrance Examination

Borrowed from the Soviet Union in the 1950s, the unified college entrance examination remains an integral part of China's state-control educational system today. The infamous component of communist theory was excluded from the college entrance examination only lately. The political test used to be a determinant factor by itself affecting the fate of candidates. In order to pass the test, candidates would have to memorize Mao's harangues. Notwithstanding such weaknesses, most students were able to access college education through competition in the 1950s to 1960s, although a sidetrack of recommendation-based policy guaranteed entrance to political vanguards who would have had no chance to get in otherwise. The entrance examination system was interrupted by the Great Cultural Revolution (1966-1976) where universities were opened only to recommended students from the ranks of "workers, peasants, and soldiers." The system was resumed in 1977 and has become the only path to college ever since.

Several important revisions have been made to the entrance examination system. Notably, Chinese, mathematics, and foreign languages were adopted in 2000 as core components for all disciplines. The system is being continuously revised to fine-tune the weight of the general requirement for candidates of liberal arts versus those of natural science disciplines. Occasionally, provinces experiment their own testing variations, particularly within the scope of provincial universities with the goal of enrolling more qualified students and allowing them to display more fully their ability.[119] In 2001, for example, out of the 5.4 million candidates, forty-eight percent were enrolled,[120] and out of the 5.27 million candidates of 2002, fifty-two percent were enrolled. This contrasts with the situation in 1981 where only 2.4 percent of the total candidates were enrolled.[121] In 2003, out of the 6.13 million applicants signed up for the college entrance examination despite the recent breakout out of the SARS epidemic, sixty-two percent were enrolled. [122] The trend suggests an enhancement in promoting college education, which represents a significant shift from the traditional elite education.

Teacher Education

With one fifth of the population engaging in learning, teacher education is of special importance. Statistics indicate that in 2001 China had 5.8 million elementary school teachers, 3.4 million middle school teachers and 840,000 high school teachers.[123] Normal education consists of three levels of institutions: The "normal university," the "teacher-training institute" and the "teacher's school." "Normal universities" offer four-year programs that lead to careers in high school teaching. "Teacher-training institutes" offer three-year programs for training the middle school teachers. "Teacher's schools" offer four-year programs for training elementary school teachers.

Normal educational institutions are highly selective, particularly at the higher education level. In addition to the regular college entrance examination, prestigious universities have recently added "entrance interview" as a standard procedure whereby candidate's knowledge, motivation, and composure are evaluated. In addition to formal training, teachers have opportunities to improve themselves through in-service training offered in multiple ways including TV-Universities, taking college courses, and so on. The *Teacher's Law* promulgated in 1993 requires secondary school teachers to possess the college degree. Similarly, normal education training is required for teaching lower levels.[124]

With the rising demand on the teaching quality, it is expected that teaching jobs will be high-paying and highly competitive in the 21st century. Incentives are already frequently provided to attract and retain good teachers. As an example, the Shanghai Municipality set up the following procedure to improve the teacher's living standard.[125]

Article 14

The average salary for teachers shall be ten percent higher than that for state civil servants of this Municipality. Primary and secondary school teachers shall be entitled to subsidies for their educational service years as well as other allowances in accordance with the provisions. The service-year subsidies shall be increased step by step.

The Teacher's Law of 1993 declared 10 September of each year to be the Teacher's Day during which students conduct various activities to pay respect to teachers.

Distance Education and Vocational Training

Distance education has been an important venue for promoting mass education since the late 1970s. The China Central Radio and TV University (CCRTVU), founded in 1979, is a state-owned institution under the Ministry of Education. Through radio and TV broadcasting, the University offers courses in Chinese, foreign languages, literature, technology, law, business, science, and so on. The courses are taught by college faculty members or professionals in various fields. In addition to continuing education, degree programs are also offered. In fact, the trend seems to be that radio and TV universities are offering more and more degree bearing programs, making distance education an important supplement to formal college education.[126] Vocational education has attracted much attention in the 1990s. The traditional opinion used to despise vocational education as the choice of those who could not enter a four-year college. Such opinion is losing ground as the market orientation is gaining momentum. Vocational education offers junior and senior levels of training during three to five years at "technical schools" and "professional high schools." Students enrolled must have received junior high education. From 1988 to 1995, vocational school enrollment rose from nineteen percent to fifty-four percent of high school students.[127] Getting into famous universities is no longer the only honorable way to success. The possession of highly needed skills, today, is valued more than the diploma from a prestigious university.

Special Education

Special education remains a weak sector in the Chinese educational landscape. Nevertheless, the economic reform has brought about many changes in this area. According to the Ministry of Education, there were 1,531 special schools throughout the country as of 2002 with 380,000 students enrolled. Approximately 266,000 special students, due to the shortage of facilities, are enrolled in regular schools and study in regular classes.[128] During the past decade, accommodative services and equipment have become more available to schools, particularly in urban area schools. For example, a dedicated special testing center was established for deaf and blind students in Zhengzhou City of Honan Province during the college entrance examination season of 2003. Testing materials were custom-designed. Test monitoring and grading were conducted by special education services.[129] Faced with the challenge of educating an estimated six to seven million disabled students, however, much more remains to be done.

Close-up: Tenure or No Tenure

Known as "China's Harvard" as well as the weather vane of China's higher education, once again, Beijing University took the lead in eliminating the deeply rooted life-long tenure system. The audacious reform proposed in May 2003 aroused heated debate in the academic world. [130]

According to the draft plan, only professors will enjoy lifelong employment. Faculty members of lower ranking are offered employment tenure contracts that are six-year renewable for the assistant professor/lecturer, and twelve-year renewable for the associate professor. Within the probationary period, faculty members will be given two opportunities to apply for promotion. Moreover, the university will outsource to fill its faculty positions instead of recruiting its own recent graduates. Within the probationary period, strict evaluation processes provide grounds for dismissal. During its transitional phase, the plan has provisions that exempt certain categories from the stringent system. For example, faculty members with twenty-five full years of employment at Beijing University will not be affected by the new plan. In addition, those who have taught for ten consecutive years and are less than ten years from the fixed age for national retirement (sixty for men, and fifty-five for women) will also be exempt from the risks of losing the teaching job.

Because higher education is state-funded for the most part, the system naturally carries the typical syndromes of SOEs. Overstaffing, under-performing, and non-performing positions cannot be eliminated. Qualified scholars are barred from their deserving positions. This is the first time for a leading Chinese university to launch such a radical reform. Reactions from faculty members are mixed. Many middle-aged faculty members blame the new plan for being potentially distractive and destructive for quality teaching. Others cheer the reform, praising it a necessary step towards a leading educational institution in the world.

The reform, however, is expected to be an uphill battle. An estimated thirty percent of lecturers and associate professors at Beijing University are expected to be most affected and may have to leave their current posts when the changes take effect. Profound changes have apparently been taking place in China's higher education since Deng Xiaoping started the reform in 1978. With

Beijing University taking the lead, tenure-reform is likely to encompass universities across the nation sooner than later.

Internet and the Society

The Internet revolution has an increasing impact on the Chinese society. The most visible result is the fast development of information technology and the popular ownership of personal computers. Never in history has communication been made so convenient. Before the start of the reform, information used to be the most sensitive area directly under the government's control. In light of Deng Xiaoping's "Open Door" policy, building electronic infrastructure has become one of the primary items on the state economic agenda. The Ministry of Information Industry[131] was established in the mid-1990s to dedicatedly direct the sector development. Meanwhile, information control constitutes an important item on the priority list of the Ministry's work. However, the most obvious daily function of this government unit is to disseminate laws and regulations, rather than law enforcement.

To improve its openness the government has set up websites at all levels from the central government[132] to municipal and provincial governments. Many web sites carry functions that facilitate people's direct input. Major official newspapers, such as the People's Daily,[133] China Daily,[134] and the Guangming Daily,[135] allow readers to openly post comments and opinions. Breaking the tradition of government secrecy and moving towards a transparent government is what is commended of the Guangzhou Municipality. "The Guangzhou Municipal Provisions on Open Government Information" promulgated on 1 January 2003, for example, stipulates that the government must not only disclose information on government affairs, but also open up for public input, making nondisclosure the exception rather than the norm. The "Provisions" aim at protecting the "right to know" on the part of individual citizens, and enforcing the "obligation of disclosure" on the part of government employees. The municipality announces major projects, particularly those that may have a deep impact on people's lives, to the public to let people provide their input before implementing such projects. Public input is forwarded by the government website. "The Open Government Affairs Leadership Small

Group" headed by a deputy mayor is in charge of supervising the implementation, which includes conducting periodic evaluations. [136]

Riding the favorable environment, the e-commerce seems to have gained momentum as well in the 1990s. The current five-year plan (2001-2005) anticipates that the e-commerce will grow from less than one billion U.S. dollars in 2001 to more than twenty billion in 2005.

While the Chinese government recognizes the need to take advantage of the e-commerce to develop the economy, information control remains the government's priority. Clearly, information freedom has not developed as fast as what the technology affords. Balancing the give-and-take has been an on-going challenge that is best reflected in the latest set of regulations *Measures for Managing Internet Information Services*[137] (the Measures) passed by the State Council and promulgated on 1 October 2000. The new regulations, for example, contain a provision in Article 15 for controlled content including the following categories:

1. Information that goes against the basic principles set in the constitution.
2. Information that endangers national security, divulges state secrets, subverts the government, or undermines national unity.
3. Information that is detrimental to the honor and interests of the state.
4. Information that instigates ethnic hatred or ethnic discrimination, or that undermines national unity.
5. Information that undermines the state's policy towards religions, or that preaches the teachings of evil cults or that promotes feudalistic and superstitious beliefs.
6. Information that disseminates rumors, disturbs social order, or undermines social stability.
7. Information that spreads pornography or other salacious materials; promotes gambling, violence, homicide, or terrorism; or instigates crimes.
8. Information that insults or slanders other people, or infringes upon other people's legitimate rights and interests.
9. Other information prohibited by the law or administrative regulations.

Items number 1 and number 3 are familiar clauses defining the conventional boundaries of allowable usage, while other items more specifically target culturally unacceptable behavior normally covered under other laws. The primary goal of the rules, apparently, is to crackdown on any attempt to use the Internet to engage in activities that are likely to derail the stability. Item number 9 is a catch-all clause common to most Chinese laws and regulations that gives the text more power. In addition, the definition of state secrets is vague at best.

Articles 16, 17 and 18 of the Measures grant the Internet Service Provider (ISP) and related administrative units the right to monitor user activities and report on violators. Monitoring the content of Internet communication appears to be serious a government effort, as Article 18 particularly stipulates:

> Departments in charge of information, the publishing business, education, public health, and pharmaceuticals; departments in charge of business administration; and departments in charge of national security, must supervise the contents of Internet information in areas under their respective jurisdictions and in accordance with the law.

While restrictions on information dissemination are stringent, there is virtually no clause restricting the reception of on-line information. This is, in fact, a progress as a result of the reform, compared with the pre-reform era when receiving foreign radio broadcast was subject to reprimand.

To enforce the law, the Measures has provisions for punishment. For example, violations may result in property and equipment being confiscated. In addition, Article 19 stipulates, "In cases where there is no illegal income, or in cases where the illegal income is less than RMB 50,000 Yuan, a fine between RMB 100,000 Yuan and RMB 1 million Yuan is assessed." At the current exchange, these figures are converted to $6,250 and $12,500 in U.S. dollars.

The following laws and regulations promulgated within the past decade or so provide more guidelines on the use of the Internet:

1. *Regulations for the Protection of Computer Software*, State Council, June 1991.

2. *Interim Provisions on the Approval and Regulations of Businesses Engaging in Opened Telecommunications Services,* Ministry of Post and Telecommunications, 1993.
3. *Measures on the Regulation of Public Computer Networks and the Internet,* Ministry of Information Industry, April 1996.
4. *Computer Information Network and Internet Security,* Ministry of Public Security Protection, and Management Regulations, December 1997.
5. *Revised Provisional Regulations Governing the Management of Chinese Computer Information Networks Connected to International Networks,* State Council, 1997.
6. *Commercial Use Encryption Management Regulations,* State Council, 1999.
7. *International Computer Information System Network,* State Bureau of Secrecy Security Regulation, 2000.
8. *Measures for Managing Internet Information Services,* State Council, 2000.

(Source of data: Ministry of Information Industry)[138]

Towards an Open Government

In March 2003, Hu Jintao and Wen Jiaobao were elected the President and the Premier of the PRC. While their short governing record does not provide for a reliable evaluation as of yet, the new leaders have nevertheless demonstrated impressive preliminary tendencies.

Political analysts have noticed that President Hu has established an image of down-to-earth populist leader, one who is more interested in gaining support from the broad masses than in forming a circle of his own protétés.[139] Hu's compassion for the poor and for the economically left-behind provinces is said attributable to his extensive experience with China's poorest regions. Before joining the central government, he had accumulated fourteen years in Gansu, three years in Guizhou, and four years in Tibet. Similarly, Premier Wen Jiabao had spent twenty-five years working in Gansu and had inspected close to 3,000 towns and counties. Already, the first economic policies have revealed a focus on improving economic conditions of inland regions by gradually shifting economic resources from the east coast to the

Great West. Eleven western provinces and the largest metropolitan center Chongqing, which holds a population of 30 million, stand to benefit from President Hu's new economic focus.

Raising China's rural income is a top priority as shown in the CPC Document Number 1 of 2004.[140] The document presents the plan of balancing the rural/urban divide by raising the prices of agricultural products. Meanwhile, encouraging motivation for raising production, employing modern technology in farming, and improving ecological conditions are viewed as important leverages to strengthening the economic growth. Moreover, the document stresses that the evaluation of a political party is based on how effectively it works to improve people's lives, but not on amazing growth numbers.

To narrow rural-urban divide, one administrative measure to be soon adopted is the complete elimination of the *hukou* or "residential status" system that has been in place since 1954. The *hukou* system's primary function is to restrict rural population from migrating to urban areas, which used to be a controlling wand of Mao's regime. On the ideological front, while President Hu has vowed to continue to carry out Jiang Zemin's theory known as the "three represents," he appears to be more concerned with the interests of the broad masses on the lower level. In practice, Hu has issued policies aiming at improving social security and welfare to better take care of farmers and laid-off workers.

What may really mark the "Hu Era" is the government reform. The reform stresses political transparency, such as revealing meeting agenda of the Party's Politbureau to the general public and giving opportunities to ordinary citizens to voice their concerns. To what level President Hu may be able to open up the government remains to be seen. His determination, however, is backed by the practical necessity that the Party must keep pace with the economy. In early 2004 the Chinese government invited public suggestions on research topics of its crucial Five-year Development Plan for the first time since 1949, signifying another landmark step towards a broad-based policy-making. In March 2003, the newly revised State Council Work Regulation states that the State Council should heed views from democratic parties, non-governmental organizations, and experts in all fields before making major decisions. Some analysts believe that since the 1990s China has entered a "decision-consultation era." [141]

Coincidentally, the strike of the "severe acute respiratory syndrome (SARS)" in March 2003 provided the much needed timing for the onset of the government reform. The SARS epidemic first broke out in November 2002 in Guangdong Province. The fast spread of the disease caught the government as well as health organizations off guard. The disease was first recognized as a type of pneumonia and did not arouse much attention. As the disease spread rapidly, the Ministry of Health and the Beijing Municipality remained in denial and covered up the outburst out of the concern for its impact on the economy. The slow interference, and particularly, the intentional cover-up, caused the epidemic to spread at an alarming speed. On April 23, the World Health Organization (WHO) put Beijing on its travel advisory list. According to WHO, as of July 2003, 5,327 Chinese contracted SARS and 384 had died. Worldwide, 8,437 people contracted SARS and 813 had died. Although Beijing was taken off the WHO advisory list on 24 June 2003, SARS monitor continues to be of high priority of the Chinese government.[142]

In controlling SARS, President Hu was determined and swift in reversing the tradition of what is known as "black box politics" by removing China's Health Minister Zhang Wenkang and Beijing mayor Meng Xuenong in April 2003. The government launched aggressive measures including broad-scaled quarantines of suspicious cases in conjunction with intensive efforts in SARS education. The government openly admitted that it learned valuable lessons from the entire event. The Xinhua News Agency summarized the experience as follows:

1. The belated, incomplete reporting resulted in the government's failure to fully carry out its duties in the initial and crucial period of the SARS outbreak.

2. Modern forms of government are characterized by transparency and openness. The Chinese government has not been accustomed to public disclosure of its activities.

3. Only by actively upholding the citizen's right to know can the government be better supervised by the public and in turn win the trust and respect of the people.

4. The current impediment to the public's views shows that the public does not have full access to a variety of information that concerns their livelihood.

5. The government needs to establish a modern crisis management mechanism.

6. In handling the epidemic, some officials were found putting people's interests after the concerns over economic losses, thus, ruining the Party's image.
7. The government should avoid taking all matters in its own hand. Instead, it should let the public know the real situation and jointly work with them to wage the war to contain the crisis.

(Source: "SARS – A Valuable Lesson for Chinese Government to Learn," *Xinhua News Agency*, 8 June 2003")

While the war on SARS revealed the populist tendency of the present leadership, a much deeper background for such a trend, in fact, goes back to the beginning of the reform. The electoral reform that has been going on in rural China since the 1980s has prepared ground for a step forward in introducing the democratic process.

The process of "universal election" in China's vast rural areas has shown a rising political zeal and high expectations of some 900 million Chinese rural population. The trial phase of the grass roots democratic election was first experimented in Fujian Province and is now being spread all over the country. China's 1982 Constitution provides for villager committees, elected by village residents, to handle public affairs and social services, mediate civil disputes, help maintain public order, and convey residents' requests and opinions to the people's government. The formal government extends from the top in Beijing down only to the township, one organizational level above the village. In 1998, the NPC Standing Committee revised and promulgated the *Organic Law of Villagers' Committees* or the *VC Law*[143]which was put into trial implementation in 1987. The 1998 VC Law strengthened the practice of "four democracies" including democratic election, democratic decision-making, democratic supervision, and democratic management. According to the Law, villagers can be directly elected into villagers' committees, whereas in the past the CPC appointed members to the committee. The VC Law incorporates multiple items ensuring that the villagers truly enjoy their democratic rights. These rights include, for example, the use of open and direct nomination by individuals rather than by any political entities or by any forms of groups. The rights also mandate that there must be multiple candidates, and that secret ballots, secret voting booths, public counting of votes, and immediate announcement of election results be adopted. The village committee is normally composed of three to seven members, including a chair, several vice chairs and ordinary members for a three-year term. The grass roots organization is accountable to the villager assembly which is a body composed of all villagers aged eighteen years and older.

The grass roots democracy is viewed as a democratic tutoring process that educates people on responsibilities and rights of a citizen, the benefits of electing accountable leaders, and above all, the rule of law. The experience is also influencing election practices and democratic governance in urban communities. In urban areas, the "neighborhood committees" have adopted similar election procedures. These committees used to be appointed by the Party to provide assistance in neighborhood conflict mediation, crime-watching, and family planning matters. In 1999 the Ministry of Civil Affairs with the approval of Party Central Committee selected twenty cities to experiment with the open election with the goal of installing urban grass roots self-governance.

A direct influence of grass roots level elections is already shown on the Party's electoral system. Local CPC secretary elections have started to follow a two-step voting procedure whereby the first step is a popular ballot on potential candidates, and the second step is a ballot within the party committee. Presumably, based on the popular input, the local party secretary is chosen from the most popular candidates. Clearly, the party's lineage, networks, and the authorities that were at the very foundation of appointments in the past are being phased out and replaced with a healthier system. It is hopeful that the future representatives of the NPC as well as those of the National Party Congresses will be elected following a system of universal election tested in the grass roots level elections, thereby achieving a broad-based democracy, rule of law, and openness.

Conclusion

Since the start of the reform, China has gone through a dramatic transition. From a state-planned economy on the verge of collapse, China has transformed into a prosperous quasi-market economy in a relatively short period of time. The CPC has gone through a tremendous transition as well. From a party that led the nation to assiduously engage in the proletarian dictatorship, the CPC is in the process of transforming itself into a populist political force. Its membership now draws from various social strata, including entrepreneurs, or plainly put, the modern-day capitalists. These trends seem to represent a rapid reversal of the deeply rooted conservatism and totalitarianism. Interestingly, much of the guidance has been derived from the past failures. But China has certainly made the right turn finally after centuries of struggle. Whether China is capable of successfully carrying through the current economic and political reforms will be crucial to the world of the 21st century.

---

[1] Xiaoping Deng, *Selected Works of Deng Xiaoping (Deng Xiaoping Wenxuan)*, vol 3 (Beijing: People's Publishing Company, 1993): 174.

[2] Edgar Snow, *An Autobiography of Mao Zedong*, translated by Wang Heng (Shandong: Qingdao Publishing Company, 2003): 43.

[3] Ibid., 37.

[4] Zedong Mao, *Quotations from Chairman Mao Tse-Tung*, ed. Stuart R. Schram (New York: Frederick A. Praeger, 1967): 51.

[5] Ibid., 5.

[6] Biao Lin, "Speech Given at the Meeting with Military Officials on 24 March 1968" in *Chairman Mao's Quotations* (Beijing: 1969): 221.

[7] Ibid., 6.

[8] Ibid., 7.

[9] Ibid., 8.

[10] Ibid., 28.

[11] Ibid., 26.

[12] Ibid., 9.

[13] Ibid., 14.

[14] Ibid.

[15] Ibid., 15.

[16] Xiaoping Deng, *Selected Works of Deng Xiaoping (Deng Xiaoping Wenxuan)*, vol 3, 199.

[17] Deng, vol 2, 266.

[18] Deng, vol 3, 224.

[19] "Statistical Communiqué 2002," National Bureau Of Statistics, 28 February 2003, <stats.gov.cn/english/newrelease/statisticalreports/1200303120088.htm> (21 November 2003).

[20] Rongji Zhu, "Government Work Report," *The 10th National People's Congress,* Beijing, 5 March 2003, <english.peopledaily.com.cn/200303/19 /eng20030319_113573.shtml> (21 November 2003).

[21] Deng, vol 3, 10.

[22] Ibid., 148-151.

[23] Deng, vol 2, 38.

[24] Deng, vol 3, 23.

[25] Ibid., 249.

[26] Ibid., 203

[27] Ibid.

[28] Deng, vol 2, 231.

[29] Deng, vol 3, 171-172.

[30] Ibid., 176-180.

[31] Ibid., 357.

[32] Ibid., 372-373.

[33] Jiang Zemin, *President Jiang Zemin's Key-note Speech on the Party's 80th Anniversary 1 July 2001* <www1.chinadaily.com.cn/highlights/docs/2001-07-01/> (16 May 2003).

[34] Ibid.

[35] Ibid.

[36] Ibid.

[37] Ibid.

[38] Ibid.

[39] Ibid.

[40] He Qifang, Our Greatest Festival, *People's Literature Journal [renmin wenxue]*, (Beijing, October 1949).

[41] Feng Hu, The Time Starts — The Ode of Joy, *People's Literature Journal [renmin wenxue]* (Beijing: November 1949).

[42] Erfu Zhou, The Morning of Shanghai, *Harvest Journal [shou huo]*, no. 2 (Beijing: Writers' Publication [Zuojiachubanshe], 1958).

[43] Qing Liu, Records of the New Cause, *The Yan River Journal [yan he]*, (The Youth Publishing Company [Qingnianchubanshe], 1960).

[44] Xinhua Lu, The Wound, *The Wenhui Newspaper* (8 November 1987).

[45] Xuan Zhang, Memories, *People's Literature Journal [renmin wenxue]*, (Beijing, March 1979).

[46] Luojin Yu, *A Chinese Winter's Tale* (The Chinese University Press, 1986).

[47] Tiesheng Shi, My Remote Qingping Bay, *Youth Literature*, no. 1, (1983).

[48] Xiaosheng Liang, There Will be a Storm Tonight, *Youth Literature*, No. 1 (1983).

[49] Xiaosheng Liang, This Is a Miracle Land, *Northern Literature [bei fang wen xue]*, no. 1 (1983).

[50] Wei Zhang, The Ancient Boat, *Contemporary Literature Journal [Dang Dai]*, no. 5 (1986).

[51] Xiaosheng Gao, Li Shunda Building His House, *Rain and Flower Journal [yu hua]* (July 1979).

[52] Zilong Jiang, The Story of Factory Manager Qiao, *People's Literature Journal [ren min wen xue]* (July 1979).

[53] Guowen Li, Garden Street Number Five, *October [shi yue]*, no. 4 (1983).

[54] Yi Zheng, The Old Well, *Contemporary Literature Journal [Dang Dai]*, no. 2 (1985).

[55] Swedish Academy Nobel Prize Press Release, 19 October 2000.

[56] Yuan Ma, *Up and Down the Road Is Flat and Wide* (China: Beiyue Arts and Literature Publication, 2001).

[57] Xingjian Gao, *The Other Shore — Plays by Gao Xingjian,* translated by Gilbert C.F. Fong (Hong Kong: Chinese University Press, 1999).

[58] Xingjian Gao, *The Other Shore*, 41.

[59] Yuan Ma, *Up and Down the Road Is Plain and Smooth*, 3.

[60] *China Statistical Yearbook*, National Bureau of Statistics (Beijing: China Statistical Press, 2002). See also: Nicholoas R Lardy, *Integrating China into the Global Economy* (Washington, DC: The Brookings Institution, 2002).

[61] Township and Village Enterprises (TVEs), 31 May 2000, <www.chinaonline.com/refer/ministry_profiles/moa-tve.asp> (27 June 2003).

[62] Hongyi Chen, *The Institutional Transition of China's Township and Village Enterprises: Market Liberalization, Contractual Form Innovation and Privatizaion* (Ashgate Press, 2000).

[63] See various issues of *China Statistical Yearbook* 2001 - 2003, National Bureau of Statistics (Beijing: China Statistical Press). A good summary of POE growth can be found in Aimin Chen "The Structure of Chinese Industry and Impact from China's WTO Entry," *Comparative Economic Studies* (Spring 2002): 72-98.

[64] *White Paper on Labor and Social Security in China*, China State Council Information Office (2002).

[65] *Job Prospects Grow Better* (CPC Congressional Document), 12 November 2002, <www.16congress.org.cn/english/features/48511.htm> (2 July 2003).

[66] Jing Luo, "China: Cities vs. the Countryside," *The World and I* (October 2001): 20-25.

[67] Aimin Chen and Edward Coulson, "Determinants of Urban Migration: Evidence from Chinese Cities," *Urban Studies,* Vol. 39, no. 12 (2002): 2189-2198.

[68] Jing Luo, "China: Cities vs. the Countryside" *The World and I* (October 2001): 20-25

[69] "The Qinghai-Tibet Railroad Project," *The People's Daily Network*, <www.chinapage.com/road/qinghai-tibet-railroad/tibet-rail.html > (28 January 2004).

[70] "New Year Means a New Car in Tibet," *The People's Daily*, 25 January 2004, <english.peopledaily.com.cn/200401/25 /eng20040125_133274.shtml> (28 January 2004).

[71] "Dramatic Transformation of Lhasa Planned; New Railway Station Announced," *TIN*, 13 June 2001, <tibetinfo.net/news-updates/nu130601.htm > (28 January 2004).

[72] Jing Luo, "China: Cities vs. the Countryside."

[73] Joe Young, "Hukou Reform Targets Urban-Rural Divide," *The China Business Review* 3, vol. 29 (May-June 2002): 32.

[74] Ye Zhang, "Hope for China's Migrant Women Workers," *The China Business Review* 3, vol. 29 (May-June 2002): 31.

[75] Constitution of the PRC, 1982.

[76] National Population and Family Planning Commission of the PRC, <sfpc.gov.cn/en/family.htm> (29 July 2003).

[77] "Fifth National Census Communiqué No. 1," 15 May 2001, <www.stats.gov.cn/tjgb/rkpcgb/qgrkpcgb/200203310083.htm> (2 July 2003).

[78] Leslie Chiang, "China Tries Easing Once-Brutal Approach to Family Planning," *The Wall Street Journal* (Friday, 2 February 2001, A1, p.1).

[79] "Two Child" Law Does Not Mean Change of Birth Control Policy in China," *The People's* Daily, 20 June 2000, <fpeng.peopledaily.com.cn /200006/20/eng20000620_43481.html> (29 January 2004).

[80] Ibid.

[81] National Population and Family Planning Commission of the PRC, <www.sfpc.gov.cn/en/family.htm> (29 July 2003).

[82]*China Social Security Reform: White Paper,* China State Council (Beijing: 29 April 2002).

[83] Ibid.

[84] "Major Phased Achievements Gained in 'Two Guarantees,'" *The People's Daily (on-line edition)*, 1 November 1999, <fpeng.peopledaily.com.cn/199901 /11/enc_990111001003_HomeNews.html > (30 November 2003).

[85] "Labor and Social Security Profile," CPC Document of the 16th National Congress (12 November 2002), <www.china.org.cn/english/features /48647.htm> (30 November 2003).

[86] "Labor and Social Security in China," *Chinese Government White Paper,* 29 April 2002, <www.china-embassy.org/eng/zt/zfbps/t36545.htm> (30 November 2003).

[87] Ibid.

[88] "Fifth National Census Communiqué No. 1." (15 May 2001).

[89] GG. Liu, P. Yuen, T. Hu et al., "Urban Health Care Reform: What Can We Learn from the Pilot Experiments?" in Chen A., Liu GG., Zhang K., eds., *Urbanization and Social Welfare in China* (Aldershot, UK: Ashgate Publishing Limited, 2003).

[90] Shunfeng Song, "Policy Issues Involving Housing Commercialization in the People's Republic of China," *Socio-Economic Planning Science* 3, no. 26 (1992): 213-222.

[91] Shunfeng Song, George S-F Chu, and Rongqing Cao, "Real Estate Tax in Urban China," *Contemporary Economic Policy,* 4, no. 17 (1999): 540-551.

[92] "Statistical Communiqué 2002," China National Bureau of Statistics, 28 February 2003, <www.stats.gov.cn/english/newrelease/statisticalreports /1200303120088.htm> (3 July 2003).

[93] "China:Foreign Trade Reform," *World Bank* (Washington DC, 1994).

[94] *China Statistical Yearbook 1992-2002,* China National Bureau of Statistics, (Beijing: China Statistics Press).

[95] Nicholas R Lardy, "Chinese foreign trade," *The China Quarterly,* 131 (1992): 691-720. See also, Barry Naughton, "China's emergence and prospects as a trading nation," *Brookings Papers on Economic Activity,* 2 (1996): 273-344.

[96] Jing Luo, "Notes of a Visit to Taiwan," *Laiyin Forum,* no. 5 (München, Germany: October 2003): 38-41.

[97] Emma Davis, "A Road Map for China's Mergers and Acquisitions," *China Business Review* 30, no 4 (July-August 2003): 12-17.

[98] Stanley B Lubman, *Bird in a Cage: Legal Reform in China After Mao* (California: Stanford University Press, 2001).

[99] Kenneth Davies, "Toward a Rules-Based FDI Policy Framework," *China Business Review* 30, no 4 (July-August 2003): 57.

[100] *Patent Law of the People's Republic of China,* August 25,2000, <www. trademarkpatent.com.cn/EN/default/laws/laws_list_patent.asp> (13 July 2003).

[101] Ibid.

[102] Ibid.

[103] Ibid.

[104] Ibid.

[105] "McDonald's Amicable on Dispute over Beijing Site," *South China Morning Post,* (10 December 1994). See also: Mingjer Chen, *Inside Chinese Business, A Guide for Managers World Wide* (Boston: Harvard Business Press, 2001): 146-147.

[106] Ming-Jer Chen, *Inside Chinese Business,* 72.

[107] Ibid., 71.

[108] Carolyn Blackman, "Local Government and Foreign Business," *China Business Review* 3, vol. 28 (May-June 2001): 31.

[109] Brian Ripley, "China: Defining Its Role in the Global Community," in *Foreign Policy in Comparative Perspectives — Domestic and International Influences on State Behavior,* eds. Ryan K. Beasley et al. (Washington D.C.: CQ Press, 2002): 125.

[110] "Quarterly Documentation," *China Quarterly* 50 (April 1972): 402.

[111] Ibid.

[112] Robert S Ross, "The 1995-1996 Taiwan Strait Confrontation: Coercion, Credibility, and the Use of Force," *International Security* 25, no.2 (2000): 87-123.

[113] Andrew J Nathan and Robert Ross, *The Great Wall and the Empty Fortress: China's Search for Security* (New York: Norton, 1997).

[114] Weixing Hu, "Nuclear Nonproliferation," in ed. Yong Deng and Feiling Wang, *The Eyes of the Dragon: China Views the World* (Lanhan, Md: Rowman and Littlefield, 1999).

[115] Brian Ripley, "China: Defining Its Role in the Global Community," 134.

[116] "Timeline: US-China relations," *BBC News*, <news.bbc.co.uk/1/hi/world /1258054.stm> (30 November 2003); and, "Major Events of China-U.S. Ties," Embassy of the PRC <www.china-embassy.org/eng/zmgx/t35075.htm> (30 November 2003).

[117] Ji Zhou, "Education Reform 2003-2004, Review and Forward Looking," 6 January 2004, <www.edu.cn/20040106/3096913.shtml> (1 February 2004).

[118] "Statistical Communiqué of The People's Republic of China on the 2002 National Economic and Social Development," National Bureau of Statistics, 28 February 2003, <www.stats.gov.cn> (29 July 2003).

[119] "Beijing to Try New College Entrance Exam Plan," 11 December 2001, <test.china.org.cn/english/MATERIAL/23402.htm> (20 June 2003).

[120] "2.6 million college students enrolled this year," *The People's Daily*, 28 November 2001, <english.peopledaily.com.cn/200111/28 /eng20011128_85550.shtml> (20 June 2003).

[121] "More Chinese Qualify for Higher Education," Xinhua News Agency, 8 July 2002, <service.china.org.cn/link/wcm/Show_Text?info_id =36353&p_qry=college%20and%20entrance%20and%20exam> (20 June 2003).

[122] "China's National College Entrance Exams Proceed Smoothly," *The People's Daily*, 8 June 2003, <english.peopledaily.com.cn/200306/08 /eng20030608_117853.shtml> (20 June 2003).

[123] *Education in China* (Beijing: Ministry of Education, 2002).

[124] *The Teacher's Law*, 31 October 1993, <www.spe-edu.net/info/2801.htm > (20 June 2003).

[125] *Procedures of Shanghai Municipality for the Implementation of Teacher's Law of the People's Republic of China*, 21 October 1997, <www.efesco.com /eng/wf/lp/lp_Labor_12.htm> (20 June 2003).

[126] China Central Radio and Television University, <www.crtvu.edu.cn/> (18 June 2003).

[127] China's Vocational Education, <www.edu.cn/20010827/208328.shtml> (18 June 2003)

[128] "Ministry of Education: Statistics of Special Education," 25 June 2002, <www.spe-edu.net/info/426.htm > (20 June 2003).

[129] "Honan Establishes Dedicated Special Testing Center," *People's Daily Network*, 12 June 2003, <www.spe-edu.net/info/3006.htm > (20 June 2003).

[130] "Tenure on tightrope at Beijing University," 11 July 2003, *China.org.cn* <test.china.org.cn/english/culture/69491.htm > (July 20 2003).

[131] Ministry of Information Industry, <www.mii.gov.cn/mii/index.html> (7 December 2003).

[132] www.gov.cn, <www.gov.cn/frontmanger/centralGov.jsp> (7 December 2003).

[133] *The People's Daily*, <english.peopledaily.com.cn/home.shtml > (7 December 2003).

[134] *China Daily*, <www.chinadaily.com.cn/en/home/> (7 December 2003).

[135] *Guangming Daily* <www.gmw.com.cn/gmw/default.htm>.

[136] *Guangzhou Municipal Website*, <www.gz.gov.cn/> (15 July 2003).

[137] "Measures for Managing Internet Information Services," (1 October 2000), <www.usembassy-china.org.cn/sandt/netreg2000.html > (24 July 2003).

[138] Ministry of Information Industry <www.mii.gov.cn/mii/zcfg.html>(28 February 2004)

[139] Cheng Li, "China's Next Phase: Hu's New Deal?" *China Business Review* 3, vol. 30 (May-June 2003): 48.

[140] *CPC Document Number 1 of 2004* (CCTV, 8 February 2004).

[141] "Expert:Policy-making opens to public," 1 January 2004, <chinadaily. com.cn/en/doc/2004-01/02/content_295402.htm> (3 January 2004).

[142] WHO <www.who.int/ csr/sars/country/en/> (27 July 2003).

[143] The Organic Law on the Village Committee of the People's Republic of China (Provisional) <cartercenter.org/viewdoc.asp?docID=469&submenu =news > (7 December 2003).

Index

About the Author

Jing Luo received his BA and MA degrees from Beijing University, and his Ph.D. from the Pennsylvania State University. He is currently Associate Professor of French and Chinese studies at Bloomsburg University of Pennsylvania.